FULL
THROTTLE
AND TORQUE
MY ALIEN ROADTRIP

A **thrivival** guide for brilliant,
sensitive, slightly quirky humans finding
their voice and their way

GRY STENE

Copyright © Gry Stene, 2025

All rights reserved. No part of this publication may be reproduced, distributed, or transmitted in any form or by any means, including photocopying, recording, or other electronic or mechanical methods, without the prior written permission of the publisher, except in the case of brief quotations embodied in critical reviews and certain other noncommercial uses permitted by copyright law. For permission requests, write to the publisher, addressed "Attention: Permissions Coordinator," at the address below.

Gry Stene
grystene.rocks
Walyalup-Fremantle
WESTERN AUSTRALIA

Ordering Information:
Quantity sales. Special discounts are available on quantity purchases by corporations, associations, and others. For details, contact the publisher at the address above.

Printed in Australia by Ingram Spark

Designed by Nathan Maddigan www.nathanmaddigan.com
Edited by Gry Stene, Nathan Maddigan, Gia (Generous Intelligent Assistant)
With thanks to Liv Braseth Stene, Romney Jones, Joanne Cooper, and Ingvild Stene for their insight, clarity and encouragement.

 A catalogue record for this work is available from the National Library of Australia.

National Library of Australia Cataloguing-in-Publication data:
Creator: Stene, Gry.
Title: Full Throttle and Torque - My Alien Roadtrip / Gry Stene.
ISBN: 978-0-6454857-5-2
Subjects: Business / Inclusive Innovation.
            Self Help / Personal Development.
            Neurospicy Magic.

First Edition

Disclaimer:
The material in this publication is of the nature of general comment only, and does not represent professional advice. It is not intended to provide specific guidance for particular circumstances and it should not be relied on as the basis for any decision to take action or not take action on any matter which it covers. Readers should obtain professional advice where appropriate, before making any such decisions. To the maximum extent permitted by law, the author and publisher disclaim all responsibility and liability to any person, arising directly or indirectly from any person taking or not taking action based on the information in this publication.

For my grandmothers, who passed down strength in quiet, steady ways - through food, through stories, through knowing when to speak and when to simply hold space.

For the women in my family - my mother, my aunts, my cousins, and my sister, the wild, wise women who embody strength disguised as laughter and love.

To my entire family, the brilliant, oddball crew I had the lucky draw to be born into. Thank you for making curiosity normal and difference a gift.

To Dave, who continues to show me that love isn't earned through doing, but received through being. You pick up on my state of mind before I do, and remind me that soft can be strong, too.

And for all the beautifully wired, quirky, sensitive, shape-shifting, extraordinary souls who've ever felt like they didn't quite fit in: this roadtrip is yours, too. You are not alone. You were never too much. You were always just right.

* A gentle note to the reader

This book includes personal stories that touch on difficult themes - including childhood trauma, domestic violence or non-consensual encounters, and challenges around food and body image.

These moments are not shared for shock or sorrow. They're here because healing doesn't happen in a straight line - and because naming the truth has power.

If any chapter feels heavy, it's okay to pause. It's okay to skip. It's okay to return when you feel ready - or not at all.

Your nervous system knows what you need. Trust it. You matter most.

FOREWORD

I wasn't surprised when Gry told me she was going to write a book about her life. Gry is a modern *it girl* in every sense of the word - stylish, charismatic, trendsetting, an influencer. She's someone who truly has something to share with the world. But beyond being an engaging leader with a strong presence and natural ease with people, Gry is also a little quirky - an outsider, a loner.

We bonded over that - appearing to fit in and command the room, while quietly feeling intimidated or out of place inside. We worked together in a male, technical environment where we were often devalued and overlooked.

I was in Vancouver and Gry was in Perth; we couldn't have been farther apart if we tried geographically, yet we were completely aligned in spirit. We connected over the barriers we faced - not just in our work, but in our shared determination to pursue what we wanted, rather than what we were given - a quality celebrated in men, but often criticized in women.

What could have been discouraging became fertile ground for creativity and purpose. The adversity inspired us to create change within our communities. Gry's ideas about equity, community engagement, and technology blossomed into *STEAM Engine Global*, *IT Girls Rock*, and *rAIse IT Right* - initiatives that reflect both her vision and her courage.

I've had the joy of riding alongside Gry on her wild journey, thanks to Zoom and other technologies that made the vast distance between us almost invisible throughout nearly 20 years of friendship. Her accomplishments during that time have been numerous and inspiring.

She's helped women, young people, and unconventional thinkers find their voice, their visibility, and their value. She's worked with companies to unleash the hidden talent that often goes unseen, and founded organisations that extend her reach and amplify her impact.

Technology, for Gry, is never the destination - it's the bridge that connects people to purpose, confidence, and each other. Together, we created *The DREAM Compass*, a framework that encourages people to dream big, make plans, and align their actions to live a rewarding and purposeful life. I've also had the privilege of being Gry's "wing-woman" in many workshops, an amazing opportunity to learn from her passion, creativity, and energy.

It's funny how much insight you gain about someone once you learn about their family. Though I'd heard stories about Gry's loved ones over the years, reading the details of her childhood, siblings, and parents deepened my understanding of her - and, unexpectedly, of myself. It's a reminder of how our early experiences continue to shape who we become.

Parts of her book felt like pouring my own heart onto the page; so many of her stories resonated deeply, especially her reflections on feeling like an outsider, an "alien" in the world. I think that's something we all feel at times - and it's comforting to be reminded that we're in good company.

What you're holding isn't just Gry's story. It's a rallying cry for anyone who's ever felt like they didn't quite fit in. Her words will challenge you to question old rules, laugh at your own missteps, and embrace the quirks you've been told to hide. This isn't theory - it's lived wisdom, forged on real roads and in real rooms where belonging didn't come easy.

Read it with an open heart, and you'll find more than inspiration - you'll find permission. Permission to ride full throttle into your own story, torque and all.

Joanne Cooper

AI-informed project manager, life coach, and community builder dedicated to enabling purpose, connection, and impact.

Table of Contents

PRE-START CHECK 001
Preparing for the Ride
Prologue: Riding into Uncharted Territory — 001
Checking the Engine: My Story, Your Map — 003
Prelude: Charting the Course — 005

FIRST GEAR 019
Kickstand Down - Fuelled by Fire, Driven by Love
STAGE ONE: Growing Up to Stand Out — 021
STAGE TWO: Family Contrasts — 037
STAGE THREE: Lessons from Adversity — 051
STAGE FOUR: Itchy Feet - Belonging in Motion — 063

SECOND GEAR 071
Ignition - Understanding My Alien World
STAGE FIVE: Owning Your Inner Alien — 073
STAGE SIX: The Cultural Chameleon — 089
STAGE SEVEN: Navigating Life's Intersectional Highways — 101
STAGE EIGHT: The Misfit Chronicles — 113

THIRD GEAR 121
Shifting Gears - Unleashing Your Full Potential
STAGE NINE: Lessons from the Edge — 123
STAGE TEN: Trailblazing Through Barriers — 133
STAGE ELEVEN: Harnessing the Power of Vulnerability — 145

FOURTH GEAR 155
Love on the Open Road - Navigating Relationships & Belonging
STAGE TWELVE: Human Being, Not Human Doing — 157
STAGE THIRTEEN: The Good Girl Curse — 167
STAGE FOURTEEN: Lessons in Love and Loss — 179

201 FIFTH GEAR
Full Throttle - Celebrating Uniqueness and Advocacy
- 203 STAGE FIFTEEN: Amplifying Voices
- 215 STAGE SIXTEEN: The Power of Connection Across Differences
- 233 STAGE SEVENTEEN: Owning Your Spotlight

245 SIXTH GEAR
The Road Less Traveled - Embracing Change and Adventure
- 247 STAGE EIGHTEEN: The Allure of the Unknown
- 259 STAGE NINETEEN: Pivotal Journeys
- 271 STAGE TWENTY: The Art of Reinvention

285 SEVENTH GEAR
Cruising in Torque - Crafting Your Legacy & Impact
- 287 STAGE TWENTY-ONE: Revving Up for Change
- 297 STAGE TWENTY-TWO: Embracing the Open Road

309 THE OPEN ROAD AHEAD
Live Your DREAM - Full Throttle & Torque
- 310 The Road So Far: A Legacy of Purpose
- 311 The DREAM Compass: A Vision Born from Shared Experience
- 312 Mapping Your DREAM
- 313 A New Chapter: Building the Future
- 313 Reflection for the Reader
- 314 rAIse IT right: Technology with Soul, Leadership with Purpose
- 315 Reflective Pause: Before You Go

317 ABOUT THE AUTHOR
- 319 **Keep Riding With Gry**
- 327 What People Say About Gry
- 329 Books and Stories that Fuelled My Journey

PRE-START CHECK

Preparing for the Ride

*Courage doesn't come from knowing the way -
it comes from moving anyway.*

Gry Stene

Prologue: Riding into Uncharted Territory

It's August 1997. I'm riding my Harley Davidson, throttling full blast toward a destination unknown. And I am loving it - the freedom, the adventure, the paradoxical peace that comes with the torque of the engine beneath me.

Just a couple of days earlier, I hit a watershed moment. I had accepted redundancy from a job I genuinely loved - but a workplace I could no longer tolerate. The unchallenged patriarchy there had become too loud to ignore. It was stifling me. No salary was worth that compromise.

The very next day, serendipity struck. A friend of a friend invited me to her brother's 40th birthday, some 600km north of Sydney. I didn't hesitate. I needed space. I needed movement. I packed a few things, got on my bike, and set off on my first-ever solo road trip.

The open road has a way of stripping everything back to its essence. There's nowhere to hide when it's just you, your thoughts, and the rumble of the ride. Every twist, every turn, every long, straight stretch became a mirror. A reflection of the terrain I was navigating inside myself.

Part of me was fleeing something. I can see that now. The slow erosion of my voice, the compromises I'd made without realising it. Years of being the good girl, the peacemaker, the one who didn't rock the boat too much. It's funny - how much of ourselves we bury, unnoticed, until the road gives us perspective.

But I wasn't just running - I was heading toward something. I just didn't know what it was yet.

As the landscape blurred by, each kilometre helped distil something inside me. The rhythmic pulse of the ride, the crisp air against my face, the hum of the engine in my bones - it was all I needed to begin remembering who I was. That ride became more than a roadtrip. It was a turning point. The first glimmer of my inner compass, a way of navigating imagination, truth, and possibility. I didn't know that at the time. I just knew I was beginning to feel more *me*.

Riding boldly into the unknown is terrifying, no question. But it's also exhilarating. Each turn of the throttle reminded me that momentum matters more than certainty. And courage doesn't come from knowing the way - it comes from moving anyway.

That ride was a reclamation. A shedding. A quiet homecoming to the woman I'd started forgetting under the weight of roles and expectations. It was a new beginning. A whisper of the freedom I'd always craved but hadn't quite claimed.

I'll circle back to some of the more intriguing parts of that journey later. But for now, just know: this ride was the ignition point. The start of the roadtrip I'm inviting you on - a story of freedom, transformation, and the kind of adventure that changes you from the inside out.

Checking the Engine:
My Story, Your Map

*I am not afraid of storms,
for I am learning how to sail my ship.*

Louisa May Alcott

My name is Gry Reidarsdotter Stene. At 60 years young, inspired by wild rides like the one you've just read about, I finally sat my butt down and started writing this book. I told myself I'd have the first draft finished by my 61st birthday - March 22, 2024. Wildly optimistic I know.

Spoiler alert: I didn't quite make it.

In the past, I would've spiraled into self-criticism - another missed deadline, another 'why can't I just finish things like normal people?' moment..

But not this time. Not anymore.

Now, I see it differently. This isn't failure. This is me being kind to myself. I'm understanding how my beautifully wired, delightfully chaotic, neurospicy brain works - and writing anyway.

This book, though a little late, is living proof that self-acceptance doesn't mean giving up. It means knowing your rhythm and riding it full throttle.

This is my story - but it's also an invitation. If you've ever felt like you don't quite fit in… if you've felt too much or not enough, too sensitive or too blunt, too loud or too invisible… this book is for you. You're in the right place.

And just so we're clear: I'm not here to whitewash or sugar-coat anything. I write things as I see them. This is *my* experience, not a judgment on anyone else. It's messy, it's nuanced, and it's mine. It's probably neurospicy and unfiltered.

I'm a migrant. A *wise woman* in tech. Menopaused. Neurospicy. Loud, soft, funny, fierce. Often a little too much for certain rooms - and just right for others. I care deeply. I speak up when something's not fair. I'm driven by inclusion, integrity, and instinct - and I no longer apologise for that.

 Pre-Start Check: Preparing for the Ride

Only in recent years did I start to realise that my lifelong pattern of reading the room, adjusting my tone, overthinking the smallest interactions... wasn't just personality. It was part of a deeper wiring. A way of adapting early - especially when people's words and body language didn't match. It made me confused, so I learned to make myself smaller. To manage the energy. To become the easy one.

I now know it for what it is: a kind of shape-shifting. Not performance. Not fakery. Instinctive protection.

It took a while, but I've learned to embrace that awareness. It helps me see my blind spots. It helps me own my power.

So, why share all of this now?

Because I know I'm not the only one. I know there are so many of us - misfits, feelers, rebels, oddballs, quiet revolutionaries - who've spent years trying to fit into boxes we were never built for. And I also know this: when we stop contorting ourselves, and start trusting ourselves, things change. Big time.

This book is part memoir, part map. Not a one-size-fits-all blueprint - but a travel companion for your own adventure. A gentle nudge to explore your inner terrain. A reminder that the quirks you've tried to hide might actually be your greatest strengths - your superpowers.

Your very own "Hitchhikers Guide to the Galaxy" - only this one is for navigating your inner universe.

I've been sitting on these stories for years - decades, really. And they've finally started knocking louder. It's time to tell them.

Let's pack up, strap in, and head out. Not to find a new self - but to come home to the one that's always been there.

A Breath Before the Ride Begins

What's your story engine?
What part of you keeps going, even when you're unsure of the path?
What parts of yourself are asking to be seen more clearly, more kindly, more fully?

Prelude:
Charting the Course

*You'll never understand the road ahead
until you learn to love the path that got you here.*

Unknown

Every roadtrip has a moment before the engine turns over - a quiet pause, a glance at the map, a deep breath. This is that moment.

Before we jump into the fast-moving curves and wide-open spaces of this story, I want to take a beat. To tell you a little about how I got here - and what I've learned about riding through life as someone who has never quite fit the mold.

This part of the journey is about unpacking the early signals: the things that shaped my wiring, my worldview, and my weird and wonderful relationship with identity, justice, belonging, and boldness.

It's also where you'll first hear about something I later came to call my DREAM Compass. Back then I had no idea I was building it, but the early signs were already there. Years later, through powerful conversations and creative work, it took full shape. For now, just know it's a tool that grew from my quirks and questions - and that it turned difference into direction.

What's in a Name: Writing Your Own Story

My name, Gry, isn't just a weird collection of letters. It's a beacon of my heritage. A relatively modern Norwegian name, rooted in Old Norse, it means *sunrise* - a symbol of new beginnings, a fresh start.

As the firstborn, the first spark of my parents' union, my name carried hope, a new dawn. There's beauty in that. But as a child, I didn't always see it that way.

I didn't meet anyone else called Gry until I was in my teens. For a long time, I wished for something more ordinary. A name people recognised, a name that didn't need explaining, one that didn't make me feel like I was arriving in a room five seconds before I actually entered it.

Pre-Start Check: Preparing for the Ride

In Norway, we roll our R's, and pronounce my name quickly, almost like there's no vowel at the end. To explain, the Y sounds more like the Y in *Gary* than in *try*. My friends in Botswana had no problems saying it, and in England's multicultural mix, I never had to explain it.

It was only when I moved to Australia that pronunciation became an issue. To combat the many creative ways people tried to say it, I adapted. "My name is Gree," I'd say, spelling it out - "like *green* without the n."

At the time, it didn't feel like a big deal. But looking back, I can see it was one of the many quiet ways I learned to adjust myself to make things easier for others, to better fit wherever life took me.

My middle name, Reidarsdotter, connects me directly to my roots. It means "Reidar's daughter". Like many cultures use "son of", mine says exactly where I came from - and from whom.

It evokes the Viking era, and that side of my family story: tradition, bonds, family, lineage. Unlike names like Johnson or Petersson, mine doesn't blend in easily. It stands out. And that, too, has been both a gift and weight.

I've always had mixed feelings about patronymic naming. My brother's middle name, Livsson, honours our mother, Liv - "Liv's son". A matronymic twist that wasn't traditional in Viking times, but one that feels like a small gesture toward balance. It always made me think: what stories do our names carry when we *choose* what to preserve?

My connection to my father is complicated. He loved us deeply, but his struggles with addiction made it hard for him to give us the security we deserved. My parents separated when I was five. I knew it was the right decision, but back then it left a mix of confusion and longing in its wake.

So while my name connected me to him, it also carried a kind of ache. A question. A gap.

As a little girl, I wanted to be like everyone else. To disappear into the crowd, not stand out with an odd name. I didn't want to explain myself - I just wanted to *belong*.

But names have a funny way of finding their essence. And eventually, so did I.

The same qualities that made my name feel like a burden as a child are what make it - and me - stand out now. My name taught me that individuality carries its own quiet power, even if it takes years to fully own it.

It's taken time, but I've come to embrace the richness of the story my name carries. And I've realised that blending in was never the point. I wasn't meant to dim my light - I was meant to shine.

This part of my story isn't really about pronunciation or lineage - it's about belonging, adaptation, and the journey from self-editing to self-honouring. It's about understanding that the things that set us apart are often the very things that anchor us when the world feels unsteady.

Name Your Story:

What does your name say about you?

What story does it carry - and what story do you want it to tell?

What's in a Title: Full Throttle, Torque, Alien Roadtrip

"Full Throttle & Torque: My Alien Roadtrip" is how I've lived, how I've learned, and how I want you to feel as you turn these pages: bold, curious, in motion, and unapologetically *you*.

Let's start with the alien bit.

I've lived in multiple countries, worked in more industries than I can count, and spent most of my life moving through worlds where I never quite fit in, but observed and absorbed everything with curiosity and longing. Always searching for a way in. Whether it was my cultural backdrop, my neurospicy wiring (a term I now love and claim), or just the way my brain works, I often felt like I was beaming in from somewhere else. Familiar enough to pass. Different enough to always notice the gaps.

That feeling crystallised more than a decade ago, when I was preparing a keynote for the Women in Mining Summit in Western Australia in 2012. I was reflecting on what it felt like to build a career and a life across so many landscapes - none of which were quite built for someone like me.

That's when the title came to me: "My Life as an Alien".

I didn't flinch from the label. Alien didn't mean "wrong". It meant observant. Adaptive. Honest. Awake. My alien roadtrip is my story and has been the ride of a lifetime.

Full Throttle & Torque is how I ride - on my Harley, yes, but also in life. I don't do things halfway. Whether I'm chasing down new ideas, confronting

Pre-Start Check: Preparing for the Ride

injustice, or navigating unfamiliar territory, I move forward with momentum and meaning.

Riding has always been a symbol for me. It's freedom, it's control, it's clarity. When I'm on the road, wind in my face and engine thrumming under me, I remember who I am. There's no pretending. Just movement. Just me.

A tiny disclosure: my Harley is currently sitting in my shed, waiting for a lot of TLC before it can roar back to life. Writing this book has reminded me how much I miss the ride, and it's inspired me to get her back on the road.

This book is a thrivival guide, an open invitation for you to ride full throttle, and claim *Your Voice, Your Space, and Your Life - On Your Terms*. It's your permission slip to stop waiting, stop shrinking, and start riding as your whole damn self.

If you've ever felt unseen, underestimated, told you were too much, or felt like you were not enough, this is your roadmap. It's a mirror for the rebels, the feelers, the fixers, and the misfits. It's a reminder that the things that make us different are exactly what the world needs more of.

So whether you're neurospicy, globally minded, wildly sensitive, or just over trying to "find your people" anywhere that costs you too much - you're welcome here.

You don't have to tame your spark to be worthy. Just fire it up and follow what feels true.

Fuel for the Ride

You won't have all the answers yet, and that's okay.
You just need enough courage to turn the key.
And be open to riding together in solidarity.

Seeing the World Differently: Navigating Identity

Understanding and embracing my own unique differences has been a long and often surprising journey. I've always believed that diversity of thought and individual uniqueness are essential for creating a better, more sustainable world. But believing that in principle is one thing. Living it - when how I'm perceived doesn't always match how I feel inside - is something else entirely.

From the outside, I come across as confident. Outspoken. Unafraid to tackle tricky conversations or stand up when something's not right. And that's all true - especially when I'm fired up about injustice. My sense of fairness runs deep. In fact, a relatively new friend recently called me a Justice Warrior, and I've decided to wear that badge with pride.

But what people don't always see is what's going on behind the scenes.

Inside, I'm constantly scanning - reading people, reading the air, reading between the lines. My nervous system is on high alert for anything that might signal disapproval or rejection, even if it's only in a glance or the way someone closes an email. I've since learned this is known as rejection sensitivity, and it explains a lot. Like why, after speaking up in a meeting and watching my input fall flat, I could spend hours spiraling - rewinding, replaying, wondering if I'd said too much or simply did not belong in the room at all.

It's exhausting.

For a long time, I didn't understand why this happened - why well-meant actions were sometimes misread, or why I would walk away from interactions feeling like I needed to "fix" something that hadn't been broken. As a natural problem-solver, I prided myself on being adaptable and resilient. But that same adaptability often came at the cost of my own wellbeing. I told myself, *"The final outcome is what counts"*, even when I was the one absorbing the cost.

Then, during a particularly frustrating chapter at work, I found myself venting to a trusted friend:

Me: "A direct report, one of my team leads, is consistently disrespecting me and undermining my authority".
Her: "You don't have to take things personally".
Me: "It's definitely personal. He is very clear in his intention".
Her: "Even if it feels personal, you don't have to take it that way".

That landed. Not because it erased the sting - but because it gave me a new way to process it. I started realising that even when something *feels* personal, it doesn't have to become part of my story. That awareness gave me breathing room. It let me stay present - even when emotions ran high - and choose a different response.

And that's when things started to shift.

Pre-Start Check: Preparing for the Ride

Recognising Neurodivergence

In recent years, conversations around neurodivergence - things like ADHD, autism spectrum, sensory processing challenges, and the lesser-known *justice* and *rejection* sensitivity - have become more common. The pandemic amplified this sense of alienation for many people because we were so isolated. Suddenly, more people were recognising themselves in these traits, and the language to describe them became more accessible.

For women like me, the overlap between age, hormones, culture, background and brain adds an extra layer for differences. I've seen it in others and in myself - women who've "held it all together" for decades, only to feel like things start unravelling at menopause. Turns out, it's not unraveling - it's revealing. The systems we built to cope no longer hold, and the truth of our wiring comes into view.

I've chosen not to pursue a formal diagnosis, and not because I don't relate. On the contrary - I see myself in so many neurodivergent traits. But I also deeply appreciate how my brain works. I love the creativity, the energy, the hyper-focus, the intensity. I know it's not always easy to live with. But I wouldn't trade it.

There are challenges, of course. I still walk into rooms and scan for disapproval. My radar is tuned a little too finely sometimes. But now that I understand what's happening, I can take a breath. I can pause. I don't have to spin out - or at least not every time.

Finding the right language to describe my brain and behaviour was a huge shift for me. I was having a conversation with a younger woman who was looking for a mentor. She casually used the term "neurospicy", and I lit up. *That.* That was it. That word held both the fire and the flair of how my brain works. It made me smile. And more importantly, it reframed everything. I wasn't broken. I was boldly, beautifully wired.

I also want to be clear: when I use the word neurospicy, I'm describing my own experience, not labelling anyone else's. Neurospicy means different things to different people, and I know that many with neurodivergent brains have faced struggles far greater than mine. For me, it's a word that helps me hold both the fire and the flair of how I'm wired, with a touch of humour and lightness. It's how I choose to name my difference.

The language gave me permission - not just to be me, but to celebrate my differences unapologetically.

The Bigger Picture

This isn't actually a book about neurodivergence. It's more a celebration of what makes each of us unique.

We are all part of the beautiful chaos of human variety - whether it's our brain wiring, gender, race, age, ability, or identity, we must recognise that differences are not something to manage, but to value.

I want to live in a world where we honour what makes us distinct. Where we stop asking people to "fit in" and start asking how we can expand the space. Where difference becomes the source of connection.

When we stop hiding the things that make us different, we don't just free ourselves - we give other people permission to do the same.

If Not Now Then When: Finding my Moment

If not now, then when? If not me, then who?
Hillel the Elder

I'm in my 60s, and while I feel proud and full in many ways, I also feel something calling me forward.

There's more I want to do. More I *need* to do. I have the chance to uplift people who've been left out or left behind. To help others see the beauty in their own wiring, their own differences. To hold up a mirror that says, "*You're not too much. You're exactly right*".

There's a particular kind of joy in watching someone realise they're finally being heard. Valued. Seen.

As a speaker, author, coach and leader, I guide people home to themselves. Help them embrace the quirks they once tried to hide. It's become my calling, even when the work doesn't always come with a juicy paycheck.

I've made peace with that. I know I'm exactly where I'm supposed to be - building community, encouraging boldness, fighting for fairness, helping people get back in the seat of their own lives.

This book started as a personal project - a way to gather my stories. But it's become a call to action, for anyone who's ever felt like they were living life just a little sideways.

 Pre-Start Check: Preparing for the Ride

The world needs voices like ours. Voices that ask better questions. That challenge old stories. That hold the door open for someone else.

If you've ever wondered if your story matters - this is your sign. It does. You do.

Your Moment, Your Move

What's calling you right now?
What are you no longer willing to hide or hold back?
And how can you use your voice to light the way for others?

Roots and Wings

Growing up, family gatherings were loud, joyful, and beautifully chaotic. Between both sides of my family - my parents, grandparents, aunts, uncles, cousins - there was a deep and enduring emphasis on individuality. You were allowed to be *you*.

On my mother's side, there were 25 grandchildren. Picture the noise, the laughter, the endless running around. It was a symphony of wild joy - cousins making mischief, uncles and aunties telling stories that made us laugh so hard we snorted, parents trying (and mostly failing) to round us all up for meals. My grandparents' home was the beating heart of it all - a place where you were always welcome, always fed, and never left without at least one good story.

Summers with my father's side were just as vibrant. My brothers and I joined our 10 cousins for games that turned into epics - imaginative adventures that stretched into those long, light Scandinavian nights. We made kingdoms out of sandpits and battles out of berry picking. That unstructured freedom taught me so much about collaboration, creativity, and finding joy in shared experience.

The generosity and openness of my grandparents created a foundation of belonging that still anchors me to this day - one of true kinship. Their stories, their steadiness, their belief in family - those things transcend time and distance. They gave me roots. And a sense of being held.

Family of Contrasts

Within my immediate family, the dynamics were more complex. My parents believed in raising independent thinkers. We were encouraged to be ourselves, speak our minds, and ask big questions. And we did.

But at the same time, there was the unwritten rule of janteloven, the cultural code in Norway that quietly insists you shouldn't think you're better than anyone else. So even while we were raised to speak up, there was always a boundary - stand out, but not too much. Shine, but don't outshine. That paradox shaped me early.

But it was also a household where contradiction lived alongside care.

My father, despite his deep love for us, struggled with alcohol addiction. He wanted to give us safety, but couldn't always provide it. When my parents separated - I was five - it brought more stability - but it also left a tender scar. My relationship with him remained loving but complicated, and it planted the early trust issues that I've carried all my life - especially with men.

One day my father brought a bird, a young magpie I think, into the house for us kids. It was alive, panicked, flapping wildly around the living room, knocking things over and terrifying all of us.

My mother and our baby-sitter - both scared - came to the rescue. They opened the windows, ushered the poor bird out, and calmed the chaos. That was my mother: afraid but steady, strong without a show. A fiercely loving, practical woman who carried us through difficult times with grit and grace.

Still, it wasn't easy. Living with someone in active addiction leaves its mark. My mum was resilient, but at times, the stress and fear came out as abruptness or shouting. My response? Stay small. Keep my brothers quiet. Don't make waves. Be a good girl - because being good was the safest way to be loved.

I also learned to hide in plain sight. I'd sit quietly among the adults, still as a mouse, while conversations swirled around me. They rarely noticed I was there, but I noticed everything - the whispers, the secrets, the tension beneath the words. It was another way of staying safe, but it also became one of my sharpest tools: listening, observing, picking up what others missed.

When my stepdad entered the picture a couple of years later, things shifted. He brought with him a calming presence that changed many things. He did more than support the ethos of individuality - he *embodied* it. With quiet consistency, he showed us what steady love looks like. No big declarations. Just the kind and gentle, grounding support. The kind that teaches you how to show up for yourself and others.

I was the eldest of three for a long time - my two brothers came twenty months and nearly four years after me. And then, when I was ten, our little sister arrived and brought a whole new joy into the family.

 Pre-Start Check: Preparing for the Ride

As the big sister, I felt responsible. I was the peacemaker, the rule-checker, the fairness police, the protector, and the conductor of everything we did. If someone was being picked on, I'd step in. If my sister was crying over a brother who kept hitting piano keys mid-practice just to wind her up (true story), I'd intervene. Later I would declare to my parents - tears shooting out from my eyes - sometimes with righteous fury: "*I'm never, ever going to be nice to my brother again!*"

Siblings have their way of getting under your skin - but also becoming your people. Now, as adults, we've found our rhythm and a shared sense of humour about it all.

Despite the age gap, my sister and I have always been especially close. We share a drive for creativity, invention, and a slightly offbeat way of seeing the world. Possibly the most entrepreneurial of the bunch, we often find ourselves dreaming up big, weird, wonderful ideas - and actually acting on them. With varying degrees of success.

These contrasts - between the expansive, loving extended family, the steadiness of my stepdad, the turbulence of my father's struggles, and the ever-shifting dynamics of our little unit at home - shaped how I understand belonging, identity, and what it means to be truly seen.

It's no coincidence that I've spent much of my adult life helping people feel welcome in spaces that don't always know how to hold differences. That I fight for inclusion, advocate for the vulnerable, and instinctively create room for people to show up as themselves. These instincts were born from watching people I loved either fall through the cracks or rise, against the odds.

Celebrating Individuality

The ethos was always clear: being unique and different was accepted, and expected.

Around our dinner table, debates were loud and frequent. We were taught to question things. To make our case. To stand our ground - even if we didn't agree. Summers were spent outdoors, wild and free, encouraged to explore and imagine and just *be* without judgement.

Imagine my grandparent's house surrounded by a big, sprawling garden with berry bushes, a coastline full of fish, and more friends and family than you could count. It was paradise and it was home. It was where I learned what it felt like to belong.

Of course, it wasn't always easy. Like the time two cousins both wanted me on their side during a disagreement - when all I wanted was to make sure everyone still liked me. That was my shape-shifter in action. Long before I had language for it, I was already tuning myself to the emotional tone of the room. Already managing energy.

Or when we moved from northern to southern Norway and I spoke a different dialect. You've never seen anyone adapt so fast. I changed the way I spoke, the words I used, the rhythm of my voice - so I could belong. So I wouldn't be teased. So I wouldn't stick out quite so much.

At home I didn't have to shift. I didn't have to explain. My quirks were accepted and met with love and curiosity. The message was: *you'll figure it out in your own time.* That safety net gave me the courage to explore, express, and eventually embrace who I really was.

Although I must admit that sometimes this freedom felt like a burden, like I could not ask for help and guidance because I didn't want to bother anyone with things. I'd figure it out.

The Duality of Belonging

My family gave me my first sense of home. A place where love was loud, voices were many, and difference was celebrated.

It also prepared me for the more complicated truth. Not every space will welcome your whole self. That sometimes, acceptance has to be built from scratch. That fitting in and being accepted are not the same thing.

What I learned is this: true belonging doesn't require you to shape-shift. It asks you to show up as you are, and to hold space for others to do the same.

And when that space doesn't exist yet? We create it.

Roots Before the Ride

How has your family or upbringing shaped your sense of identity?

What lessons - positive or challenging - have helped you embrace your unique self?

Before We Shift Into Gear

This ride is a journey of visibility, voice, and velocity. Of curiosity, courage and community.

It's structured around seven Gears - each one reflecting a new level of motion, clarity, and power. Sometimes it's slow and intentional. Sometimes fast and fierce. But each Gear holds a truth that had to be remembered, claimed, or fought for.

You don't have to move through them in order. You might downshift, coast, or take a scenic detour. That's how real change works.

If you've ever felt stuck between the brake and the throttle… this roadmap was built for you.

A Note Before We Begin: Finding the Words

When I first read *Strong Female Character* by Fern Brady, something shifted in me.

Fern, a Scottish comedian and writer born in 1986 - the same year I first encountered artificial intelligence - lays bare her experience of being autistic in a neurotypical world with a rawness that left me both rattled and seen. Her story is not mine - her path is louder, messier, more intense in parts - but it cracked open something I hadn't fully acknowledged: that many of the experiences I'd attributed to culture, upbringing, or personality might have had a deeper wiring.

Where Fern's journey blazed with fire and friction, mine was quieter. I masked well. I absorbed the rules. I shaped myself to fit in. But underneath, I recognised the confusion, the over-analysis, the emotional intensity, the unfiltered reactions, the longing to connect - and the regular misfires in doing so.

Reading her words, I was struck by how much I had managed to "pass" - and how much that passing had cost me.

This book is not a diagnosis or a manifesto. It's a journey - across continents, careers, and countless selves - towards understanding, integration, and eventually, joy. Fern's voice helped me see things I had quietly carried for decades. While her journey is hers and mine is mine, I want to honour the resonance.

We come from different generations. We've lived wildly different lives. And still, there is a shared undercurrent that speaks to what this book is really about: the long, sometimes clumsy, always courageous path to living as your full self.

And the more I encounter stories like Fern's - fierce, funny, unfiltered - the more I see myself reflected. Not in the specifics, but in the threads that run beneath. I've come to feel increasingly aligned with life on the autism spectrum - not in a way that takes space from others, but in a way that reclaims space for myself. There are things I simply tucked away as a child because there *was* no space for them. For me. I just got on with it.

Recently, I had the opportunity to meet Alison Shamir, author of *Conquer Your Imposter*. That conversation changed something for me. She explained that what we often call "imposter syndrome" is more accurately described as the imposter phenomenon. And just like Fern's story helped me name something I'd always felt but never articulated, Alison gave me language for something I thought was just a personal flaw.

The imposter phenomenon affects up to 70% of people at some point - men and women almost equally. What differs is how it shows up - and how it's judged. Men might brush it off or see it as part of the growth journey. For women, those same thoughts are more often scrutinised, internalised, or seen as weakness.

What I took most from Alison's work is this: overcoming imposter phenomenon doesn't start with confidence. It starts with self-worth. With rewriting the story we tell ourselves about ourselves.

And now, looking back with fresh language and a wider lens, I'm ready to explore those tucked-away spaces - and finally, to own them.

So what happens when you face both external silence and internal self-doubt? You shrink. You shape-shift. You watch, instead of speak.

FIRST GEAR

Kickstand Down - Fuelled by Fire, Driven by Love

*Without leaps of imagination or dreaming,
we lose the excitment of possibilites.*
Gloria Steinem

Childhood memories are curious things.

They blur the line between fact and feeling. What we remember isn't always what happened - it's how it landed. A smell. A look. A moment that settled somewhere deep and stayed there.

My earliest years were a messy, beautiful mix of adventure and adaptation. We moved often, guided by my parents' shared wanderlust and, at times, detoured by my father's struggles. Between them, they created a world bursting with life, layered with contradictions - and grounded in love.

We started our journey on a windswept island perched at the very top of Norway, closer to Russia than anywhere most people have heard of. The cold was relentless. The wind was unforgiving. Extra blankets were a must.

But even there, in the bleakness, I remember warmth. Not just from the blankets. From the people.

Despite the weight my father carried, he was magnetic. Loud, funny, and endlessly curious. My mother - practical, grounded, and no less spirited - was right alongside him. Wherever they went, interesting people followed. Smokers, thinkers, drinkers, dreamers. Our home was often full, and somehow, even as a toddler, I sat in the centre of it all.

I don't remember the words. But I remember the feeling. That deep, cellular kind of knowing.

I was loved.

Even then, I understood the value of staying out of the way. Life moved fast. Emotions shifted quickly. Rooms filled and emptied with energy, and I learned to sense it all. I stayed quiet. I watched. I learned how to read people before they spoke.

My big personality was there - but I tucked it away, waiting for when it felt safe to let it show.

Those early years were a kind of training ground. A small, personal map of what was to come: joy and movement. Love and loss. Big energy. Deep feelings. And an unshakable sense of wonder about the world and my place in it.

This is where the story really starts. It's where the fuel first sparked into fire.

As you read these early chapters, I invite you to tune in to your own beginnings. The way you were wired. The messages your body understood before your mind had language. The ones still shaping your ride today.

The things that rooted you.
And the wings that began to form.

STAGE ONE
Growing Up to Stand Out

*Our journeys start with roots that anchor us and
wings that lift us toward new horizons.*

Adapted from Goethe

What shapes us in childhood often lingers well into adulthood - sometimes as anchors, sometimes as fuel, and sometimes as questions we spend decades trying to answer.

For me, growing up was about learning how to stand out without standing *too* far apart.

To be bold… but not too much.
Curious… but not disruptive.
Different… but still safe.

I often felt a little off-centre - too intense, too excitable, too "something" for the neat boxes around me. But those early years also gave me deep roots: in love, in fairness, and in imagination. They taught me how to find my place - without shrinking to fit it.

Let's go back to those beginnings - the messy, awkward, sometimes magical moments that shaped who I was becoming. As you read, I invite you to think about your own first experiences. What early moments planted the foundation of who you are now?

The Soundtrack of Childhood

Patter, patter, patter - screams of glee.

Tiny feet thudded across the creaking floors of my grandparents' eight-bedroom house. My cousin shouted, "Karolina is coming!" and the air filled with delighted panic. We scattered like wild things - ducking behind doors, under beds, into closets.

Karolina wasn't real. She was our family ghost, and everyone knew she lived in the loft. I imagined her with grey hair, a hunched back, and a broom that threatened naughty children. Every cousin had their own version of her, and *each one was terrifying and thrilling.*

That chaos - of giggles, whispers, thudding feet, and creaking stairs - was the soundtrack of my childhood summers. A symphony of silliness. Our own collective folklore.

My grandparents' home - part residence, part local police station taking up half of the downstairs area. My grandfather was the head of police on the island, and I remember being allowed to visit that part of the house occasionally. We marvelled at the stories the police officers shared, and I think they secretly loved having us around.

The entire house was a sanctuary of noise and love. It came alive each summer with 25 grandchildren, their parents, and enough energy to power up the entire island.

We didn't live there full time, but whenever we returned, it felt like coming home.

It smelled like coffee and stories.
It sounded like clinking plates and belly laughs.
It pulsed with adventure.

A Blend of Mischief and Connection

I was one of the younger ones in that first wave of cousins, and my older girl cousins were *everything*. Surrogate sisters. Fashion icons. Worldly sages. Chaos-makers. They shared their clothes, ideas, and secret plans with me, and I followed along wide-eyed and eager.

For a girl who spent much of her time looking out for her younger brothers, these moments of *being swept along* felt like freedom. It was where I first tasted the kind of feeling part of things that didn't require me to lead or organise - just *to be.*

And sometimes, instead of joining in, I'd sit quietly right in the midst of the grown-ups, hiding in plain sight and collecting secrets they didn't realise they were spilling. It felt delicious, like being let in on a mystery only I knew.

It was mischief and connection. It was family as a force field.

Whether racing from Karolina or sitting cross-legged for a story from my grandfather, I felt like I belonged to something larger than myself.

These were the roots.
This was the hum.
This was where the wings began to form.

A Symphony of Joy and Belonging

The house was never quiet. The hum of conversation, the clatter of plates, the giggles of children - it all wove together like a symphony. Each voice, each laugh, each creak of the floorboards added to the melody of kinship that echoed through every room.

In this house, everyone had a place. It didn't matter if you were family, friend, or a stranger who'd wandered in - you were welcomed, fed, and included. My grandmother's kitchen was the heart of it all, a place where love and flour dust mingled in the air. My grandmother's love and warmth were the strings that tied us together, filling every quiet moment with laughter or intrigue.

The Heart of the Home: The Kitchen

The kitchen was a stage, and my grandmother was the conductor. With practiced precision, she orchestrated meals that seemed to appear effortlessly, as though the pots and pans danced to her tune.

No one left her kitchen hungry - or untouched by her quiet demeanour and steady care.

Bread dough rising in the corner. The hiss of something frying on the stove. These were the sounds of care - of love baked into every meal. My grandmother nourished us with food, warmth and quiet wisdom.

I remember watching her at the old wooden cooker. I don't think she ever got used to the modern electric stove. She did things her way. She was my hero. Still is.

The Echo of Laughter: Storytelling and Shared Memories

Every gathering had its stories - some repeated until they were as familiar as nursery rhymes, others new and surprising. My grandfather, with his cheeky manner and actor's flair, could turn the smallest anecdote into a legend. As children, we already knew that most of his stories were made up - but we never knew which parts were true and which weren't.

His stories were lessons wrapped in humour and suspense, and we became part of them, interrupting with questions, laughing in unison, or groaning when we'd heard the punchline too many times. It wasn't about the ending; it was about the ritual of sharing.

Cousins and Chaos: The Joy of Being Swept Along

My older cousins were my heroes: daring, clever, and endlessly inventive. For me, they were a glimpse of who I might become. We spent our days inventing games, acting out plays, and creating worlds within the walls of our grandparents' house.

Each one had their own magic, and each became a model for what I wanted to be. The eldest of six mirrored back my "little ma" tendencies. The second was effortlessly stylish, always with the best clothes (which I gratefully inherited). And my closest cousin felt like a big sister - full of wisdom and, occasionally, some wildly off-script detours.

We're still great friends today despite how far we live apart. Thank goodness for the internet. We may not speak for months, or even years, but when we meet, we don't drop a beat.

One summer, I became a roving reporter. Someone - maybe all of us - decided we'd start a family newspaper. I was given the "breaking news" section, and I remember racing around collecting stories - mostly from the adults, who humoured me with tall tales and cheeky winks. To me it felt real. And important.

Those moments made me feel seen.
They made me feel *included*.
And that feeling stayed with me long after the games ended.

Two Sides of the Family: Where Belonging Took Root

The joy of my mother's side of the family was balanced by the quieter, more spacious rhythms of time with my father's side. We didn't see those cousins as often, and maybe that's what made those visits feel almost dreamlike - slower, softer, full of their own kind of magic.

Summers with my paternal cousins were threaded with tree climbing, secret missions, and whispered conversations under the stars. The energy was different - less neurospicy, more grounded - but just as rich in possibility.

I still remember the dark water and the pull of the lake we cycled to together. I'm fairly sure we cycled - but some of the details blur. What remains clear is the feeling of curiosity, freedom, and quiet connection.

Each side of the family shaped me in its own way, giving me an appreciation for both exuberance and stillness. For being loud and being held.

The Magic of Being Different

In a family as loud, opinionated, and vibrant as mine, it was hard to stand out - and yet, I often felt like I stood apart.

I knew my mind was fast, like everyone in my family. Ideas came in bursts - quick flashes that sometimes left others behind. My feelings were just as big, but I subdued them. I felt everything deeply - joy, sadness, excitement, disappointment. But I never made a scene. I was the quiet one. The good girl. The one who stayed out of the way.

At home, that was okay. My family was full of debate and imagination. There was space to be different, and different was often celebrated. But outside those walls, we were kept in check by the unwritten Jante's Law, akin to Tall Poppy Syndrome in Australia and New Zealand.

A Family That Embraced Debate

At home, our conversations weren't small. They were sprawling and spirited. Full of energy and strong opinions. Around the dinner table, it was normal to argue, defend your ideas, and be expected to listen when someone pushed back.

This is where I first learned that disagreement didn't have to mean disconnection. That curiosity was a bridge. A compass. That it was possible to be different and still belong.

Those loud dinners planted seeds I didn't know I'd need later - seeds of resilience, clarity, and the ability to see multiple sides at once.

When Being Different Became a Superpower

At home, being different was just part of the mix.

My siblings ran with my ideas (most of the time), even when they were a bit out there. My grandparents answered my questions with stories - often long ones that led to even more questions. No one told me I was too much. They just made space for me to be who I was.

It took me a while to realise how rare that was.

In other places, I felt the need to measure my energy, to gauge how much of myself I could show. But at home I started to understand that the things that made me stand out didn't have to be liabilities. They could be real assets.

That understanding came quietly, in bits and pieces. No dramatic moment, but a growing awareness that I wasn't wrong - I was just wired differently. My curiosity, my emotional depth, the way I noticed what others didn't - all of it could be useful. Maybe even powerful.

I didn't feel different at home because I am convinced that every person in my family has some level of neurodiversity. We are all same, same and different.

Finding Confidence in Curiosity

One summer, I became completely fascinated by the stars and planets. Why were they there? What were they made of? Did they move? Could I ever get close enough to see them properly?

I asked my grandmother question after question, expecting her to grow tired of me. Instead, she handed me a notebook and said, "Write it all down. Keep track".

So I did. I filled the pages with thoughts, questions, theories, and wild ideas. I was given permission to explore what lit me up.

That notebook gave me more than enough space to write. It gave me confidence. It told me that curiosity was something to value. That even when I didn't have the answers, the questions mattered.

That moment stayed with me - it wasn't dramatic, but it was quiet and real, and it reminded me that the way I see the world is something to hold onto.

It was more than learning - it was permission to wonder.

Before You Ride On

Think back for a moment. When was the first time you knew you were different? Not in a dramatic way - but in that quiet, inner sense of "I don't quite see the world the way others do".

Was it something you proudly owned? Or something you tucked away?

As you keep reading, bring that version of you along. The curious one. The deep-feeling one. She still has a lot to teach you.

Adventures in Adaptation

For most kids, home is a place of permanence - a fixed point in their lives. For me, it was a concept that shifted with every move.

My parents (mum, biological father, and stepdad) treated change like an open invitation. So, we packed up, adapted, and started again. To me, change meant rediscovering community, rebuilding friendships, and figuring out - again - how to belong. I grew to love it.

The Many Faces of Home

I have already shared glimpses of these experiences, but here I've laid them out in order, so you can see how the timeline unfolds.

Vardø: The Northernmost Beginning - Before I turned two

Despite being under the age of two, my earliest memory is from Vardø, the remote island near Norway's northeastern tip. The cold was so biting my parents layered extra blankets over our covers at night.

Yet under all that frost, I remember warmth. It came from togetherness.

I was only a baby, but I remember my parents' friends from all walks of life, gathered at our place, discussing the world, education and politics. Not always agreeing, but always with humour.

Midsund: A Time of Sun and Shadows - Aged two to five

When I was about three, we moved to Midsund, a village on a larger island between Ålesund and Molde in the northwestern part of Norway. We lived in a quadriplex - four connected homes - many of our neighbours were fellow teachers.

Midsund was filled with salt air and summer joy. But also shadows.

My father's illness became harder to ignore. I couldn't articulate it, but I knew something was uneasy. I remember running with neighbourhood kids by day - and watching my father with quiet worry. When was he going to flip again?

I knew from a very early age that he could be extremely unpredictable. I could tell by his gait, but I didn't know what caused it. He would be jolly, but his eyes didn't quite connect.

At five, our lives shifted again. My mum made the hardest choice - to leave my father.

Søvik: A New Chapter - Finding my feet again before I turned six

After a short stint at her parents' house, she took a teaching job at a finishing school in Søvik, on a neighbouring island. We moved into a one-bedroom apartment inside the school building.

One bunk bed, a toddlers bed, and my mum's single bed. My youngest brother was so little and clung to Mum so tightly that she often had to sleep with her arm hanging down from the bed so he could hold her hand. Søvik became our reset button. A sanctuary. The beginning of something steadier.

It's also when my stepdad entered our lives - quiet, solid, and kind. They met in the summer of sixty-nine, around the time of the moon landing. They are still going strong.

It started out with the occasional visit. I remember running down to the main road to meet him on the main road. The disappointment when he was not on the bus. This strapping, military man had walked from the airport and taken a shortcut. I think he came down to the main road to find us. I felt shy and embarrassed that we had missed him, but ecstatic to see him.

I adored my stepdad. He was the steady replacement for the father I had lost so many times. Creative and handy, he was always building or fixing something, and I loved tagging along. Being near him gave me a sense of safety I hadn't known before - and it stayed with me, wherever we lived. That steadiness would follow me across continents.

At some point it became more permanent. He was a steadying presence in a still-spinning world. He got a job and we were going to settle in the north when a call came.

Vikane: A House with History - I had just turned eight

My stepdad was called back home to Vikane to care for his grandmother. My mother was only too happy to move to the milder climate, so we all packed up.

The house we moved into was nearly 100 years old. Creaky. Full of strange corners and ghost stories. I swear it was haunted. At night, walking to my bedroom through the pitch-dark upstairs hallway made my heart race.

But even with its quirks, the house was alive with love. We made it ours.

One year, my brothers and I decided to set up a haunted ride that we planned to charge money for. We converted one of the outhouses in the forest behind the house with creativity and flair. It was a bit dark. It was a bit muggy. And it was definitely scary.

Turns out nobody had money to pay, but we had had a lot of fun setting it up, and managed to overcome our fear of the dark in the process.

Manstad: A Home Built with Purpose - Early teens

Later, we built a new house in Manstad, about a 20 minutes drive from Vikane. My stepdad was a carpenter and with a little help from friends and family, our new home became reality. We were part of it too, sanding and painting, our little hands part of every wall.

It wasn't far from our last house in distance, but miles apart in culture. At least that is how my siblings and I experienced it.

It was a home built for a family our size - solid, warm, with underfloor heating, and close enough to walk to school. We were excited about settling into this new place, surrounded by kids our own age. I looked forward to starting secondary school and making new friends, even though I already missed my old crew.

Just as life in Manstad began to feel settled, the biggest curveball came: our parents sat us down and told us we were moving to Botswana. They had joined NORAD (the Norwegian Agency for International Development) as teachers - for two whole years.

The first four months in our new house were filled with adjustments: new schools, new friends, parents often away for courses, and endless trips to the health clinic for every vaccination under the sun.

It was 1976, and Africa was a massive unknown from where we stood. Not everything went smoothly. I remember my 11-year-old brother and me being given double adult doses of vaccines - in the buttocks, sitting upright instead of lying down. I can still feel the ache of it that lasted for days.

The months passed quickly and Manstad turned from home to home base. A place to return to. A new foundation.

Botswana: Learning New Languages of Belonging - Mid teens

We left freezing Norway on November 4, 1976, and landed in Lusaka, Zambia, on our way to Botswana. I will never forget the first impressions. The palm trees. The smells. The heat.

Gaborone, our first stop, was nothing like the icy fjords of Norway. The air was thick with heat, alive with sound - crickets at night, birds at dawn.

We stayed at the President Hotel in the centre of Gaborone while my parents did their local training and onboarding. The shaded verandah stretched under jacaranda trees that dropped purple blossoms like confetti. Beautiful, but not much for kids to do. It felt like another world, far from everything I had known - and yet something in me expanded.

My siblings and I were invited to spend time with other Norwegian families while my parents were attending courses. Picture a bunch of chalk-white Norwegian bodies after a day in turquoise pools. Most of us were burned to a crisp. It was the seventies. Nobody knew about ozone layers or sunscreen, and somewhere there's still a photo of my youngest brother, purple-red against the white sheets. You live and learn.

At thirteen, going on thirty, I was allowed to stay up with the adults after my siblings went to bed. An eclectic mix of idealistic foreign aiders aged between twenty-five and forty. The stories I heard were exciting and made me want to live an adventurous life like them.

After a couple of weeks, we moved to Mochudi, which became our home for the next two years. It felt like hours from the capital, and my siblings and I were the only European children at the local schools.

Even the wood was different. Back in Norway, I was used to soft pine that split easily under an axe. In Botswana, the hardwood was dense and unyielding. One afternoon, my blunt little axe slipped and sliced my shin instead. It was only a shallow cut, but enough to leave a scar - and to give my stepdad the shock of his life. For me, it became a metaphor for everything in Africa: harder, sharper, less forgiving, but also richer, stronger, and deeply grounding. Through it all, my stepdad was there to steady me when I faltered.

Botswana taught me that "home" wasn't about geography. It was about connection. About learning the language of acceptance and love in whatever form it came. And the courage to show up, again and again.

Looking back, it seems wild that I had only just started learning schoolbook English in Norway. Stepping into a totally new world with a totally different language took courage and tenacity. But when you're addicted to human connection, you find a way.

Manstad and Fredrikstad: Reclaiming my land and stepping into adulthood

Returning from Africa was a very different experience to what I had expected, but in truth, it shouldn't have been a surprise. We had only lived in this house for a few months before we disappeared into Botswana, and when we came back, we carried experiences no one at home could imagine.

I had one semester left of secondary school before moving on to high school in Fredrikstad. I wanted to believe I could make new friends, but as a "country girl" I felt I had to prove my worth.

More about that coming up.

The Art of Starting Over

That's the thing about change: you never fully arrive. You just learn to keep moving. Each time, the rhythm was the same: say goodbye, start again. New faces. New rules. New possibilities. It was exciting, but it was also exhausting.

Still, those shifts taught me something powerful. Starting over doesn't mean losing who you were. You carry her with you, and layer by layer, version by version, you build her up. Or at least, so I thought. I always doubted I belonged, but I think the others included me.

Finding Adventure in the Unknown

While some might have resented the constant motion, I craved the adventure. Every new place felt like a fresh page - stories waiting to be written, people waiting to be met.

Even as a kid, I knew that *home wasn't a place - it was something you created.* A mosaic of people, memories, feelings, and routines. Connections and belonging.

Reflection for the Road:

When have you had to start over?
What did you carry forward - and what did you leave behind?

Knocking on New Doors

Being the big sis came with its own quiet weight. I was a guide, a scout, a bridge to the unknown. Every time we arrived somewhere new, I'd enthusiastically steel myself to be the first to knock. To break the silence. To say, "*Hi, I'm Gry*".

I loved the unfamiliar. I've always been an eternal optimist. It never occurred to me that this might not be the done thing, or that people might not welcome it. Where I came from in the North, dropping in on people was normal.

In Vikane, it meant finding the courage to walk up to unfamiliar doors and start conversations that would shape the rhythm of our time there.

My nerves buzzed with excitement like static under my skin, but I knew I had to do it - for me, for my brothers, for the family we were still figuring out how to be.

Friendship and Fortresses

One of the first friends I made was the boy next door. He wasn't exactly warm and welcoming - not at first. A little guarded. Possibly shy. Maybe thrown by my Northern accent. But over time, curiosity won him over, and we became thick as thieves for years to come.

Together, we turned the neighbourhood into a world of wonder. Our fortresses and cities were legendary - huge, intricate structures that housed entire crews of kids through long winter afternoons. We ran battle drills and defended imaginary kingdoms, our laughter echoing down frozen streets.

Those forts weren't just about play - they were our initiation into imagination, leadership, and loyalty.

They taught me that unfamiliar places could become home. That shared adventures build a sense of familiarity.

Building Bridges Across Differences

Every house move meant new codes to crack. Unspoken rules. Strange accents. Different expectations. But as the eldest - and as someone naturally tuned into emotion - I became a kind of translator.

If my brothers felt left out or unsure, I'd bridge the gap. I didn't always have the right words, but I had instinct. I could read a room before I even entered it. I could sense the shift in a smile, the pause in a conversation. These little cues became my compass.

And bit by bit, I realised I wasn't just good at adapting - I was good at connecting. At helping others feel like they could exhale. Whether in the playground or later in boardrooms, I often found myself making the first move. Setting the tone. Creating the space.

When was the last time you knocked on a door - literal or metaphorical - and took the first step to build a connection?
What helped you overcome the hesitation?

Lessons That Last

Moving houses often meant learning to hold on and let go in equal measure. I discovered that roots aren't just something you grow into the ground - they're something you carry with you.

Those early years were my scaffolding. My blueprint for how I move through the world.

I grew up in a family that celebrated differences, that taught us to speak up and lean in, to ask questions and build community. And from that, I learned:

Resilience is staying strong and at the same time being in movement.
Belonging may feel like blending in, but it comes from having a safe space and community where you can be brave enough to show up, quirks and all.
And joy and hardship? They can sit at the same table and share dessert.

I didn't find my safe space in one place, in one house. I found it in every moment - playful, painful, honest - where I was fully myself.

Tuning Up: The Power of Belonging and Individuality

You are perfect. To think anything less is as pointless as a river thinking that it's got too many curves.
Jen Sincero, *You Are a Badass*

When I first read those words, I laughed out loud - partly because they sounded too bold, partly because they felt like the truth I'd been avoiding.

For so long, I'd believed that standing out was dangerous, that blending in was the way to stay safe and liked.

Sincero's reminder hit like a revving engine: you can't drive your life from the back seat and call it freedom.

Confidence isn't about being louder or tougher. It's about deciding that who you already are is enough fuel to start the ride. Every curve, every quirk, every "too much" is the shape of your unique road.

When you stop waiting for permission to belong, you begin to build a life that fits. You become the driver - not the passenger in someone else's story. That's what "badass" really means: not ego, but ownership. The courage to show up, fully, even when the world hands you a smaller map.

So before we go any further, take this as your green light.
You don't have to fix yourself to deserve the ride.
You just have to start it - full throttle, curves and all.

Reflective Pause: What You Carry With You

Before the loud declarations of adulthood, there were quiet agreements. Unspoken rules. Sideways glances that told you what was "too much" or "not enough."

In order to stand out, you have to know what you've been standing under.

This is your moment to look back, not to judge, but to understand.

What did "being good" look like in your early world?

What parts of you did you edit to earn approval or avoid conflict?

Can you trace the roles you played - peacemaker, achiever, observer - to their origins?

What might happen if those early versions of you were seen again - not as masks, but as messages?

You're not starting from scratch.
You're starting from knowing.
From choice.

And remember - you don't have to ride this stretch alone. Find your people, mentors, or guides who see your potential and help you bring it fully to life.

STAGE TWO
Family Contrasts

*Families are the compass that guides us.
They are the inspiration to reach great heights, and our comfort when we occasionally falter.*

Brad Henry

How do the contradictions within your family shape who you become?

Families are full of texture - equal parts comfort and chaos, celebration and sorrow. Mine was no exception. I was born into a constellation of characters, each one vibrant, flawed, unforgettable. Some offered shelter, others stirred storms.

But all of them, in their own way, shaped the person I became.

Looking back, I see that those contrasts weren't flaws in the system. They were the system. Joy and tension. Safety and unpredictability. It was never either/or, it was always both. And that's what shaped me - the push and pull of love in all its messy forms.

As you read, I invite you to think about your own family tapestry. The threads that strengthened you. The ones that tangled. And the parts you're still learning to weave into your story.

Both of my parents were teachers - idealistic, curious, determined to make life meaningful. My father was the spark: charismatic, creative, the energy in the room. But my mother had her own light - warm, vibrant, with a laugh that could fill a space and a gift for making people feel seen. She matched his charisma with her own kind of charm, and when things wobbled, she steadied the ship.

They were, in many ways, two of a kind - both creative, both alive with spark - but it was my mother who could carry both joy and responsibility at once. Together, they were the dual currents that set the foundations for who I grew up to be.

My Father - The Light and Shadow

My father was an exquisite storyteller and entertainer. When he was sober or had only had his first round of drinks, his stories could weave worlds that pulled you in and made you feel like you were living in the heart of the tale. He had so much life and enthusiasm that between him and my mother, our home ran on an endless current of energy. They were fun, charismatic, and magnetic. People were drawn to their energy; our house became a hub of life, laughter, and connection.

I remember my first journey by myself to visit him after the separation. And being allowed to come with him to school. To me, it was a massive treat - I felt so grown up stepping into his world. His students adored him, and I felt proud that he was mine. He was larger than life with his big beard and booming laugh. But, in my childlike curiosity, I had played with his lighter, and during a break his whole beard went up in flames. It was over in moments, but I was mortified.

To me, being loved and accepted was everything, and for a split second I thought I'd ruined it. He laughed it off, but I carried the weight of guilt. Even in joy, I sensed how fragile love could feel.

When my first brother was born, a mere 20 months after me, my father became my adult. My mother had enough on her plate nursing my brother and keeping the household together while preparing to return to work, so my father became my guide, my entertainer, and my greatest source of joy. He saw me completely, and I soaked up that love like sunshine. Still, behind his sparkle, I could feel something shifting - something less certain.

Alcohol was the shadow. It slowly stole the man I trusted. At first, it made him more amiable. Over time, it took more than his joy; it took away his reliability, his essence.

A Rift and a Lesson in Forgiveness

As much as I loved him, life with my father wasn't easy. In my thirties, after an incident where I felt he had wronged one of my brothers, I made the difficult decision to distance myself. When I moved to Australia, the physical distance made it easier to maintain the emotional boundaries I needed. For the last 7-8 years of his life, we were estranged.

I felt justified at the time - protecting my brother was more important than accepting my father for who he was. But when I received news of my father's passing at 64, it rattled me. I hadn't known he was unwell. His death was sudden, and it forced me to confront the unresolved feelings I'd buried.

I don't regret the choice itself, but I do regret clinging to it for so long. I see now that my refusal to reconnect was less about him, and more about me trying to carry the grief of loving someone who couldn't love himself enough to stay steady.

A New Perspective

My father's second wife, the mother of my three half-sisters, had a different approach. She gave him space when he needed it - a room of his own where he could retreat when the weight became too much. He could "drown his sorrows" without the guilt of disrupting the household, and when he was ready, he'd emerge.

In some ways, I believe she saved him, not by fixing him, but by loving him in the way he needed. Together they built a life centered around music, creativity, and sustainability. In their imperfect way, they created something beautiful.

The Complexity of Legacy

Looking back now, with more awareness of ADHD and neurodivergence, I wonder if part of his struggle came from a restless, racing mind that couldn't always be contained by conventional life. He brimmed with creativity, music, and vision, but he couldn't find calm without external comforts like alcohol. I see echoes of those traits in myself - the fire, the energy, the endless ideas - but I also see how awareness and understanding can shape outcomes differently.

His ideas, his warmth, his laughter - they could fill a room. But his light flickered, and sometimes the shadows lingered longer than I wanted to admit.

I carry the parts of him that shine: his imagination, his spark. And I've made peace with the parts that ached. They're his, not mine to carry.

My Mother - The Lively, Steady Flame

What goes on in a three-year-old's head is not something anyone can fully see. But even at that age, I was observing, absorbing, and trying to make sense of the emotional climate around me. I watched my mother closely - her movements, her moods, her resilience. I could sense her energy shift before she spoke a word. My small body may have been busy playing, but my radar was always on.

I became a mini-me of my mother. Copying her moves, words and manners.

A Force of Love, a Field of Strength

At the time, she had three children under four, a full-time teaching job, and a partner who couldn't be counted on. That's a load most people would buckle under. But she moved through it with a kind of forward momentum I've come to recognise as drive - the kind that doesn't come with drama or declarations, but with showing up, day after day.

She anchored us, but she was also our guide. Her warmth and humour drew people in. Her laugh could fill a room, and she had this way of making everyone feel seen. I recall travelling on the same bus as her going to high school. She would be at the front chatting away loudly with everyone and anyone. I would be hiding in the back with my peers, embarrassed about her loud voice and distinct accent. But there was also a sense of pride that snuck in. My mum was pretty amazing. There was a sparkle in her eyes and an openness that made our home feel safe, even when things around us weren't.

But like all humans, she had limits that could lead to hasty interventions. When the shouting and tension became too much, I learned to shrink. I became the "good girl" out of necessity - quiet, well-behaved, safe. I knew when to disappear and when it was okay to shine again.

She could still be fiery. She wasn't always easy with feedback, especially when it didn't align with her truth. There was a streak of insecurity at times when she felt uncertain in certain situations - sharp, unexpected. But her love never wavered. I always knew I was loved, even if it wasn't always spoken. She believed in our potential, held fast to her passions, and kept the wheels turning at home while building her career.

The Power of Maternal Influence

It's hard to name all the ways she shaped me. Through her actions and her blind spots, her gifts and her grit, she taught me what it means to lead with empathy. She showed me that being strong and independent doesn't mean you never crack - it means you still choose to show up, even when you're not sure how.

And she's still that way now. In her late 80's, she's sharp as ever - totally there in her brain even as her body is fading - and we still have lively video call conversations about everything from politics to family gossip. Her spark hasn't dimmed; it's simply taken on new forms.

She was lively and steady, fierce and tender, flawed and luminous. In her own way, she carried both spark and ballast - and that paradox shaped me just as much as my father's light and shadow.

My Siblings - Bonds that Shaped Us

Being the eldest child is a unique role - part leader, part guinea pig, and often, part protector. My siblings were my first friends, my partners in crime, and the people who tested my patience like no one else could. Our bond was shaped by love, resilience, and the unshakeable ties of growing up side by side.

I was the first child, but also the first big sister - an early leader, emotional translator, and occasional referee. They were my forever tribe, the ones who knew how to push every button - even the ones I didn't know I had.

Skule - My First Brother

Skule arrived just 20 months after me, born on our maternal grandmother's (mormor) birthday to great fanfare. Farfar, our paternal grandfather, was thrilled - the first male heir in his line. I think I still held the favourite grandchild spot, though. Some of my earliest memories are of sitting with farfar in his study, eating tiny licorice bullets (my absolute favourite), soaking in the feeling of being special.

Growing up, Skule and I often felt like two halves of the same rhythm - curious, idealistic, intense. We looked alike, moved alike, and understood the world in overlapping patterns. His creativity always ran through people and loyalty. He gave everything to the people and places that needed him, often putting others first.

That made him the kind of person you always want in your corner - steady, committed, generous - but it also meant he could run himself dry.

He hit the wall hard. Not just fatigue, but a full collapse of energy and identity. Eventually, at 57, he was diagnosed with ADHD. That late-in-life clarity reframed decades of overextension, quiet overwhelm, and misdiagnosis. Suddenly, the years of running on empty had a name.

Skule has always been a deep thinker, bursting with sharp insights and unusual ideas. Fiercely honest, sometimes to a fault, his words can land before the gentle soul behind them has time to show. But that honesty is also what makes him a visionary in his own right - not because he chased big titles or recognition, but because he lived his truth, even when it didn't fit the mold.

School was tough for him, as was life at times. His sensitivity made him a target, bullied not just by classmates but, heartbreakingly, even by teachers. Yet through all of it, he's remained one of the most thoughtful, loyal humans I know - creative, caring, and unwilling to give up on the people he loves.

Skule is the dedicated father of six and he always made sure he was there for them - until his burnout - but now he is back.

Grim - My Second Brother

Grim brought a different kind of spark into our world. A whirlwind of mischief, music, and ideas, he arrived with boundless energy and a twinkle in his eye that rarely dimmed. He teased, he pushed limits, and he kept us laughing - sometimes at ourselves, sometimes at him.

But Grim has always been more than the family jester. He's a brilliant creative soul, with near-perfect pitch and an instinct for bringing people together. Music became his language early on - sparked during our years in Botswana - and he's carried it with him ever since. Whether through community events or spontaneous jam sessions, Grim knows how to create belonging wherever he goes.

He followed his passion fearlessly, choosing the creative road even when it didn't promise security. For decades, he poured himself into music, storytelling, and connection - always leading with heart. And then, in his 50s, he made a different kind of brave decision: to return to study. He realised that if he wanted to secure more stable work, he needed a formal qualification. So he went back to school - years after most people would even consider it. Now, he's nearly finished his degree, and I am so proud of him. Not just for the study itself, but for the courage it took to choose a new path, and walk it with grace.

As kids, the three of us were thick as thieves. Sure, we fought (who doesn't?), but the love was always just beneath the surface. And as we've grown older, that thread has only become stronger and more resilient. The chaos of childhood has softened into deep appreciation - for each other's quirks, for the shared journey, and for the ways we've each carved our own path.

Ingvild - My Baby Sister

Ten years after me, my sister arrived. I adored her from the moment she was born. She was my safety blanket in social settings - the sweet, curly-haired buffer who made my extroverted-yet-shy heart feel more at ease.

I brought her everywhere, and because she was so cute, she became the perfect icebreaker. Everyone wanted to say hi and touch her hair, making it easier for me to connect and have conversations.

Her childhood was different from mine. When we moved to Botswana, she was only three. While my brothers and I were old enough to navigate the new culture, she was too young to remember much of our life in Norway. And when we returned, the Norway she came home to wasn't the one we'd left. Our new district was more cliquey, more rigid, and she was only just about to start school. She was different - foreign because we had lived and because of her brain - and because of that, often excluded.

But like me, she's a survivor. Ingvild has spent most of her adult life in leadership - often the only woman in the room, and often carrying more than her fair share. That uphill battle took its toll. After years of pushing through, juggling work and raising four children, her burnout finally forced a reckoning. Her diagnosis of ADHD and other neurodivergent traits were not a label, but a lens that helped make sense of the overwhelm she had carried silently for so long.

And still, she rises.

She's building a life that works for her - with support, self-awareness, and a fierce kind of grace. Despite her own health challenges, she runs her own health and wellness studio and is carving out space as an entrepreneur. Her home is currently filled with two of her nearly-grown children, two adult dogs, and, right now, eleven puppies. It's chaotic. It's beautiful. It's entirely her. And I couldn't be prouder.

And as for me? I realise I never grew out of needing a safety blanket. These days, it's my dog. At conferences or events, I'll look for someone who seems even more uncomfortable than I am, take them under my wing, and introduce them around. It takes the focus off me, while helping someone else feel at ease.

A trick I learned with my sister, carried forward into every room I walk into.

The Others We Didn't Know

It's funny how life unfolds. I feel closer to some cousins than to my father's other children. Still, even without growing up together, there's a quiet connection I feel with a few of them - threads of shared story tugging at the edges.

In my late twenties, I learned my father had two children before he met my mother - a boy born in 1959 and a girl in 1960. My mother had known of one, but such things weren't spoken about then. I'm not sure she would've married him if she'd known there were two - but I'm glad she did.

For me, it didn't change much. I already had my two brothers and baby sister. But when our older half-brother reached out, it felt... weird. As if we were bound by something I didn't fully share.

I didn't have the same bond I had with the siblings I grew up with.

Both were born 'out of wedlock' and placed in foster or adoptive homes. My half-sister stayed connected to her birth mother, but my half-brother's path was heavier. He often spoke of his "amazing adoptive mother," yet the wound of rejection lingered. He struggled with addiction, and passed away at 62. He deserved more peace.

I already knew about three younger half-sisters to my fathers second wife - born in '92, '93, and '97. They carry a different version of our father, one shaped by time, healing, and the quieter rhythms of his later life. And at some stage I found out about one half-brother born in 1974, whom I've never met.

Life is fragile, and families are rarely tidy. The bonds we grow up with shape us - but so do the ones that arrive later. Chosen, unchosen, unexpected. All of them teach us something about love, loss, and the search for belonging.

The Hammer Curse

Not all family legacies arrive neatly packaged. Some are whispered, half-hidden, and heavy.

One of them came to me through a message from my niece - my older half-brother's daughter. We'd never met in person, but we'd been loosely connected online. Her dad had just passed away, and she told me she had left Norway to escape what she called *the Hammer Curse*.

Hammer was our family name on my father's side. Somewhere along the line, it had come to stand for a pattern we'd seen too often: addiction, untapped potential, emotional chaos left to fester in silence. When she wrote those words, I knew what she meant.

My father carried that curse. So did her father. Two lives marked by both brilliance and self-destruction. And yet, as I sat with her words, I realised something important: it wasn't the whole family. It wasn't even half the family.

The weight of that curse had fallen on two men. Their struggles were real, and their pain undeniable. But their shadows did not have to define the rest of us.

So I told her gently: maybe it isn't a curse. Maybe it's just a story someone started telling a long time ago. And maybe it's time to write a new one. Because what I see isn't despair. I see survival. I see creativity, connection, reinvention. I see people - across generations - learning how to heal, how to grow, how to choose differently.

I see legacy, yes. But not as a weight. As a turning point.

The Women Who Raised Me

I come from a long line of strong women. Tiny in stature, maybe, but fierce in spirit. They were the ones who kept the reins of the family in their hands - sometimes lightly, sometimes with grit - carrying both the visible responsibilities and the quieter burdens I only sensed as a child. I didn't always understand their sadness, but I felt their strength.

My mormor, my mother's mother, was my rock. The bright girl denied her chance at an education, confined to raising seven children on a small island near the Arctic Circle. She had dreamed of becoming a nurse, but instead she poured her energy into making sure her own daughters got the education she never had. For me, she was living proof that even when your path is narrowed, your legacy can still be vast. She was the anchor of the family, the woman who made sure we all knew we were loved and expected to stand on our own two feet.

My farmor, my father's mother, was cut from a similar cloth. She was a fully qualified teacher, raising four boys while building her own professional life - no small feat in her time. I remember her as steady and sharp, another of those small but formidable women who kept families stitched together through sheer determination. And yet, as I grew older, I came to see the weight she carried too. Some of her boys, including my father, struggled with addiction, and I can only imagine the sadness that came with watching them wrestle demons she could not protect them from.

And then there were my mother's sisters. Eva was five years younger than my mum. They loved each other and fought just as fiercely. Their animated conversations filled rooms with laughter, sharp words, and love that always ran deeper than the disagreements. Torid, my "little auntie" - only thirteen years older than me - was different again. Close enough in age to feel more like a sister, she gave me a sense of companionship and belonging that shaped me in ways I only understand now.

These women were not flawless saints - they were fiery, complex, and sometimes overwhelming. But together they showed me what resilience looks like, what it means to hold a family, and how to keep showing up with love even when life doesn't give you everything you dreamed of.

Their voices, their laughter, their quiet sacrifices - they are stitched into who I am.

Messy Love, Lasting Lessons

The contrasts in my family weren't limited to the adults. As the eldest, I felt an unspoken responsibility to look out for my brothers - my first responsibility, my first challenge, and maybe, my first glimpse of leadership.

My two younger brothers, both born before I turned four, were mischievous, loud, and relentless in their talent for pushing every button I had. But beneath the squabbles and pranks, they were my built-in companions - partners in mischief and make-believe, my constant source of love, even when they drove me to distraction.

As adults, our bond has only deepened. Time polished the chaos into meaning, revealing the thread of love that was always there - even when it was tangled in noise and mess.

And then came my sister, ten years younger than me. She arrived when I was in a different season of life and brought with her a new kind of togetherness. Her entrepreneurial spark, creativity, and resilience often mirror my own. Our bond was forged early and has only grown stronger, despite the different paths we've each taken.

Together, we are a loud, spirited, creative bunch. And even when life gets messy, love always manages to show up in vibrant, unexpected ways.

Beyond the Shadow: Redefining Legacy

It's often said we're shaped as much by our challenges as by our joys. My family is proof of that. My father's struggles taught me about forgiveness and the tangled roots of pain. My mother's steadiness taught me resilience. And my stepdad's quiet presence showed me that love doesn't always arrive with fanfare - it can be found in the pauses, the consistency, the showing up.

But the world outside our home shaped me just as much.

I remember the first time racism felt *real* to me. Not whispered about by grown-ups or written in distant news stories, but something I could see with my own eyes.

I was fourteen. We'd gone to South Africa for a visit. Our first stop was Pretoria - the capital, just across the border from where we lived in Botswana. The city felt massive to a girl who was used to village life. Busy, polished, intimidating.

And yet, as we walked through the shopping centres, what struck me wasn't the scale but the signs. Benches marked *blankes* and *nie-blankes* - whites and non-whites. Everywhere I looked, white people shopped, ate in cafes, ran businesses. Black people were cleaning, serving, carrying, waiting. It was like someone had drawn an invisible line, and everyone knew their place on it.

I turned to my mother and asked, "Why are there only Black people cleaning? Where are all the others?" She didn't answer directly - perhaps she couldn't because she feared being heard - but I knew the truth was heavy.

Back in Botswana, my school and my friendships told a different story. I went to a local school in Mochudi, the only white student. My teachers, classmates, and friends were all people of colour. That was my everyday normal. I wasn't treated as an outsider; I didn't feel separate. The diversity of that community shaped me as deeply as my family did, and I will always be grateful for it.

And yet, Pretoria lingered.

I may not have known the academic words - *systemic oppression, structural racism* - but I felt the weight of it. And sometimes, I saw it resisted. My parents had a colleague, Imelda, an American teacher of colour, who would deliberately walk into the "whites-only" lanes in South Africa, refusing to play by apartheid's rules. More than once, she was arrested, and the American embassy had to bail her out. Watching her, I learned that even in the tightest systems of control, there were cracks - and people brave enough to push against them.

That contrast - between Pretoria's sharp divisions, Botswana's inclusiveness, and Imelda's defiance - planted something in me. A seed. A sense of responsibility I still carry. Because once you've seen injustice - really seen it - you can't unsee it. You get to choose what you do with it.

Tuning Up: Belonging Without Losing Yourself

Rarely, if ever, are any of us healed in isolation. Healing is an act of communion.
bell hooks

If Stage One explored how identity takes shape in our early environments, this one dives into the crucible of family - the place where love and struggle often blur.

bell hooks reminds us that family is not only where we inherit roles and responsibilities, but also where we first learn what love looks like, and what it does not. For many of us, family love has been messy, complicated, sometimes wounding. Yet hooks insists that love, when practiced with care, honesty, and accountability, is also the most powerful force of liberation we have.

Inside families, love can become distorted into control, silence, or sacrifice. But it can also be reclaimed as a practice: showing up, telling the truth, creating space where we can grow instead of shrink. hooks calls this a choice - to refuse inherited patterns that harm and instead build new ones that heal.

In the contrasts of family, the chaos and the care, the shadows and the light, lies an invitation. To hold on to what strengthens us, release what diminishes us, and carry forward a vision of love that frees rather than confines.

Reflective Pause: When Silence Speaks

Family shapes the way we love, lead, and belong. This pause is a gentle invitation to trace what still guides you and what no longer fits.

What family roles did you grow up holding?
Which ones still show up today, and which are ready to evolve?
Where do sameness and difference coexist in your story?
What kind of love are you choosing to practice now?

Healing begins when we name what we carry, and choose what to keep.

Find voices that help you speak yours. A mentor, advisor, or guide can help you turn quiet into clarity - and keep you steady as you practice saying what you mean.

STAGE THREE
Lessons from Adversity

*I can be changed by what happens to me,
but I refuse to be reduced by it.*

Maya Angelou

Adversity doesn't wait for an invitation - it arrives unannounced, bringing challenges that test our resolve and reshape who we are.

For me, it came in many forms. Family struggles. Unspoken expectations. Unexpected twists that knocked the wind out of me and left me scrambling to find my footing. At times it felt like life only had two speeds - calm and chaos - with very little warning between the two.

Adversity wasn't just something to get through. Over time, I realised it was shaping me. Teaching me. Challenging me to push against the boundaries of my resilience and the power in my gentleness. The world didn't always make space for my sensitivity or sense of fairness - but those qualities, I've come to learn, were never flaws.

They were tools. Quiet, powerful ones.

In this stage, I'll share some of the harder lessons - what it was like to live through the messier moments, and what I came to understand about myself on the other side. From my father's struggles to my own self-doubt, these aren't stories of perfection. They're stories of persistence. Of how I kept going, even when I wasn't sure where the road was leading.

As you read, I invite you to pause and reflect.

What challenges shaped you more than you expected?

Where did you find your footing again, even when the ground felt unsteady?

The Weight of Hard Lessons

Adversity rarely shows up in neat, teachable moments. More often, it's a creeping fog or a sudden downpour - disruptive, inconvenient, and never on your terms.

My early years were laced with those kinds of moments. One minute we were laughing around the table, the next I was picking up on a tension that no one else seemed to be talking about. I learned to read the energy in a room before I learned to tie my shoelaces.

That mix of joy and unease shaped me. I learned to stay alert, to anticipate moods, to be the one who could stabilise things when they started to wobble. Especially as the eldest. Especially as the one who "just knew" when something was off.

Some of that awareness came from love. But some of it came from survival.

I developed a deep sense of fairness from a young age, primarily inspired by my mormor. Maybe it was because I saw so clearly when something wasn't fair. A raised voice that felt disproportionate. A silence that felt loaded. A promise broken, even if unintentionally. These small moments lodged themselves in me. Not as bitterness - but as fuel.

I didn't always have the power to change the situation, but I carried the weight of wanting to. That's what growing up in unpredictable environments can do. You become the fixer. The bridge-builder. The calm in someone else's storm.

But here's what I've come to realise: adversity is more teacher than thief.

It teaches you who you are when things fall apart.
It teaches you what matters when everything feels uncertain.
It teaches you how to get back up - even if you're still a bit shaky when you do.

I didn't learn these things in a moment. They came slowly, through repetition. Through heartbreak. Through watching people I loved struggle and still finding ways to show up.

Sometimes I wish I could go back and give that little girl a break. Let her rest. Let her just be a kid, instead of the one holding so much. But since I can't, I try to honour her now - by letting my careful consideration live alongside my conviction, and by reminding others that they don't have to earn their place by being the one who always holds it all together.

Too Young to Understand, Old Enough to Feel It

Bang. Bang. Bang.

"OPEN THE DOOR!"

The sound of my mother's fists on the door still echoes somewhere in me. I was four. My mother was locked outside the living room, shouting to be let in. My father - who I adored - had turned into someone else. A stranger. A version of him that didn't smile, didn't play, didn't feel safe.

He was drinking again.

I had one brother tucked under each arm. Skule was under three, and Grim wasn't even a year old. I remember holding them close, trying to be the barrier between them and whatever came next. I didn't say anything out loud - I wasn't brave enough for that yet - but I willed my mother to hear me through the door.

"Don't worry, Mamma. I've got them. I'll look after them."

My father had opened the locked bureau where he had hidden his vodka for this bender. I remember the harsh, bitter smell of whatever he poured. I remember the way the room felt - thick with tension and something I couldn't name yet. Not fear exactly, but something adjacent. Something cold. My father was there, but not really.

To me, it was just another one of those nights.

I don't remember how it ended. Maybe the janitor helped. Maybe someone else stepped in. But the part that stayed with me wasn't the ending - it was the in-between. The holding. The knowing. The becoming someone who had to keep it all together before she'd even learned to read.

Nights like these didn't break me. They shaped me. I learned to be good. Quiet. Attuned to everyone else's moods. I learned that grown-ups could disappear even when they were standing right in front of you.

When I look back now, I feel more understanding than resentment. I know now that my father was sick, not cruel. That my mother was doing the best she could with the hand she'd been dealt.

That the little girl holding her brothers wasn't scared because she didn't feel loved. She was scared because she loved too much to let go.

The Impact of My Father's Struggles

My father's presence was like a storm in the distance - dazzling, unpredictable, and powerful. I've already spoken about the tension between the warmth of his charisma and the chill that crept in when alcohol took over. That duality left a mark on me. I became adept at sensing the emotional air, to hold steady when he couldn't.

That hyper-awareness became both a shield and a skill - one that would shape much of how I moved through the world.

But I wasn't the only one shaped by it.

My middle brother, just four when we left our father, carried a different narrative. Too young to fully grasp what we'd left behind, he grew up believing our mother had done something unforgivable by leaving. He stayed in contact with our father, visiting long after I stopped. I remember how upset he was on one visit - finding him soiled, confused, unreachable. But instead of turning that pain toward our father's addiction, he blamed our mother for walking away. I never saw it that way. I blamed the alcohol. He blamed her absence.

We both felt the ache - but carried it in opposite directions.

Our youngest brother had almost no memory of the early years. He was not even two when we left. For him, our father was someone who brought presents and planned day trips. He didn't carry the same emotional weight, but he lived with its aftershocks. I often found myself watching over both of them on those visits - part older sister, part emotional translator, trying to keep things steady when I wasn't sure what "steady" looked like anymore.

Even my sister - who came later, into a calmer chapter of our family story - felt the reverberations. She wasn't there for the chaos, but she still felt the gap. Our stories became a kind of private club she couldn't fully enter. And as someone deeply sensitive, that outsider feeling left a mark, too.

Even when the stories were mostly painful, they still connected us - and that connection, by its very nature, left her on the outside.

Addiction rarely impacts just one person. Its ripple effect reshapes every relationship, every assumption, every unspoken rule. We each carried a different version of the truth. And none of them were wrong.

Unpacking Generational Patterns

They say history echoes across generations, and I've seen those echoes up close. My father's struggles didn't begin or end with him. There were threads - tangled and frayed - that seemed to pull through the stories of those who came before us. Echoes of untapped potential, emotional overwhelm, and numbing comforts when things got too loud.

The so-called "*Hammer Curse*". A phrase passed along like folklore. Whispered in conversations, half-joked about, rarely unpacked. I don't believe in curses. But I do believe in patterns.

And I've come to understand that unspoken patterns have the most power. Especially when they're wrapped in silence or that Scandinavian stoicism - where emotions hide behind polite smiles and strong coffee.

When I look back now, I don't just see my father's drinking. I see the unmet needs that might have driven it. I see a creative, passionate man who didn't have the tools - or the language - to process what was going on inside him. That emotional chaos spilled into the next generation - not just through alcohol, but through burnout, overwork, anxiety, perfectionism. Desire to be loved and accepted. Different expressions. Same roots.

To break the pattern I didn't have to cut. I just had to consciously choose which parts I wanted to carry forward. I began naming things out loud. I started tracing behaviours to their source. And, most importantly, I gave myself permission to do things differently.

That's the moment my legacy began to shift - not with blame, but with awareness. Not with shame, but with choice.

Safe Harbour in the Storm: My Mother's Resilience

If my father was the storm- wild, unpredictable, full of life - my mother was the harbour. Not quiet, not dull. But steady. Safe. She had her own spark, her own gravitational pull. People were drawn to her warmth, her laugh, her way of lighting up a room without demanding it.

One memory that sticks out is a seemingly small moment that says so much in hindsight. I was looking after my brothers, who were being rambunctious, when I planted my tiny hands on my hips and declared: *"You need to behave, or I'm going to become a nervous wreck"*.

My mother overheard me and after many years she told me how much it shook her. It was unexpected, and it mirrored the exact stress and pressure she thought she was hiding from us. She felt ashamed, guilty, and completely lost as to how to fix it.

To her credit, she didn't brush it off. She adjusted. She softened. She paid closer attention to how her stress showed up in the room. That moment helped her reimagine the version of herself she wanted to be.

She knew I was taking on a lot of responsibility for a pre-schooler and later, and she always tried to make sure I never felt it was something I *had* to do. But I was having none of that. Being "little ma" was my persona - who I wanted to be. There's plenty to be said about whether it's healthy for children to shoulder that kind of responsibility, but for me it was natural, and I wasn't going to let my mother take it away.

My mother wasn't perfect - none of us are. But her love was unquestionable. Unconditional, protective, fierce.

Today, in her late 80s, she's still got that spark. Still loved by the people around her. And with several children diagnosed as neurodivergent, she's taken it all in with grace and curiosity. *"I'm probably too old to get tested now,"* she said once, with a wry smile. Not bitter. Just aware. As if she had finally found a missing puzzle piece.

I know she found it hard to hear that we were struggling mentally. There was always a sense of guilt and a thought that she should have done more to prevent it. She was devastated when the cracks of burnout in my siblings first started opening. But when they got the right support, she realised there was no shame - and no guilt - to carry.

Her resilience has taught me more than any motivational quote ever could. But so did her joy. Her light. The way she created space for others, even when she had very little left for herself.

Shaped by Strength, Unlearning the Script

When I was growing up, strength looked like my mother, my grandmothers, my aunties.

It looked like never dropping the ball, even when you were juggling too many. It looked like greeting guests with a warm smile, even when your world felt like it was fraying at the edges.

It looked like knowing what everyone needed before they asked - and giving it, whether or not you had anything left for yourself.

Watching my mother was like watching magic and sacrifice all rolled into one. She held the centre when everything around her felt like it might tip. And in doing so, she also gave me a silent blueprint: Be capable. Be dependable. Be the one others can lean on. Don't ask too much. Don't fall apart.

And so, I followed the script.

Not out of pressure - but out of admiration. Out of love. Out of a deep desire to be accepted and loved.

I became the capable one. The responsible one. The girl who got the gold stars and kept the peace. The one who figured out what others needed and quietly delivered. I internalised the idea that to be strong was to be low-maintenance. That asking for help meant you weren't trying hard enough.

That script served me - for a long time.

But as I grew older, the cracks began to show. I was tired. I was stretched. And sometimes, I was quietly unraveling behind the scenes while still smiling to keep the vessel steady. I hadn't learned how to receive. I hadn't learned that strength could mean letting others in. Or that setting boundaries was just as powerful as showing up for others.

Unlearning that script was slow. Subtle. Often uncomfortable. But over time, I started to realise that the resilience I admired so much didn't need to come at the cost of my own wellbeing.

It's still a work in progress. Some part of me still leans toward over-functioning when things get tough. But now, I catch it. I pause. I remind myself: I don't have to hold it all alone.

And I think, in her own way, my mother eventually came to understand that too.

Finding Agency Amid Uncertainty

Adversity teaches in whispers and in roars.

Sometimes, it arrives quietly - like a new school, a new town, a fresh start with unfamiliar rules. Other times, it kicks the door down. But whether loud or quiet, each shift came with the same question: *What now?*

As we have discussed, I often felt like I had to be the one who knew the answer. The one who steadied the ship, who made introductions, who knocked on the neighbour's door first. I didn't think of it as "agency" at the time. I just knew that if something needed doing, I'd probably be the one to do it.

My innate ability to pick up on the atmosphere became my superpower. To tune into tone, body language, energy. It was a kind of emotional radar. Not just for survival - but to keep the peace, to make the ride smoother, to give my siblings a softer landing.

Those moments were my earliest lessons in leadership. Not the loud, front-of-stage kind. The quiet kind. The kind that observes before speaking. The kind that steps in when no one else will. The kind that builds bridges and gets on with it.

But for a long time, I thought self-reliance was the same as being unbreakable. That I had to be fine. That asking for help meant I was failing. I carried that belief into adulthood - not just as a badge of honour, but as a burden I didn't realise I could finally set down.

What I know now is that agency does not mean you have to do it all alone. It means it's okay not to have all the answers and still have the power to choose. To move. To speak. To ask.

It's about finding the spark of possibility in a situation that feels like it's closing in.

And it's about learning when to act, when to rest, and when to say, "I don't have to carry this by myself".

Because you can be strong, and still need support. You can be capable, and still say, "This is hard". You can be someone who *gets things done*, and still give yourself permission to pause.

That's real agency.

Navigating Uncertainty with Courage

I've already shared glimpses of what it was like to arrive in Botswana - the heat, the sounds, the strangeness of being the only white child in a small village school. But what matters here isn't just the setting. It's what those years taught me about stepping into the unknown, again and again.

At first, I shrank into myself. I knew the grammar of English, but not its rhythm. I knew how to study, but not how to belong. The silence I carried with me was equal parts survival and uncertainty.

And then Bannye appeared. More than a best friend, she became my "sister." Her presence shifted something in me. I stopped waiting to be invited and began daring to show up - asking questions, raising my hand, making mistakes, and learning that belonging wasn't about being the same. It was about being willing to connect.

Looking back, what stayed with me wasn't just the friendship, but the lesson it embodied:

You don't have to understand everything to find your way through it. You just have to be willing to step forward.

That truth followed me across borders and into adulthood. In new jobs, unfamiliar rooms, leadership moments that felt too big, I've carried the memory of that uncertain girl who slowly, bravely carved out her place to stand.

Bannye and I are still in touch, even if only occasionally. Our bond is a reminder that the courage to step forward doesn't erase the fear - it simply teaches you to move with it.

Tuning Up: What You Can Do to Address Life's Challenges

Vulnerability is not weakness; it's our greatest measure of courage.
Brené Brown

When life throws you curveballs, resilience isn't about bouncing back untouched. It's about showing up, scuffed knees and all, and choosing to keep going.

Resilience doesn't always roar. Sometimes it whispers, *let's try again.*

It might look like drawing a boundary, asking for help, or simply staying kind when life has been anything but.

Brown reminds us that courage and vulnerability are partners. Each time we name what hurts, we build emotional literacy and reclaim our power.

Resilience grows through honesty, not denial.

Here are three ways to strengthen that muscle:

Name the feeling. When you put words to emotion - anger, fear, disappointment - it becomes workable.

Take small steps. Progress doesn't have to be dramatic. One intentional action builds momentum and confidence.

Stay connected. You don't have to do it alone. Strength deepens in relationship, not isolation.

Adversity is unavoidable, but how we meet it shapes our story.

Courage isn't about never falling. It's about standing back up, again and again, with heart intact.

Reflective Pause: What Strength Looks Like Now

Resilience doesn't always announce itself. Sometimes it arrives quietly - in patience, in softness, in the small act of trying again.

When did you first learn what it meant to be strong?
Whose definition of resilience shaped your own, and what parts still fit?
What does healthy strength look like for you today?
Where could you soften, ask for help, or let go without losing yourself?

Strength isn't only about holding on.
Sometimes it's the grace to release.

You don't need to navigate that power alone. Find your crew - coaches, allies, or advisors who can help you harness it with purpose, presence, and possibility.

STAGE FOUR
Itchy Feet - Belonging in Motion

*You are only free when you realise you belong
no place - you belong every place - no place at all.*
Maya Angelou

There's a kind of tug that lives deep in your chest - a blend of curiosity and unease. A whisper that says, "what if?" even when your feet are still planted firmly in the familiar.

For me, that whisper has never gone quiet. Change has been a steady companion in my life - sometimes invited, sometimes unexpected - but always revealing. From childhood moves to crossing continents, each transition taught me something new about the world - and about myself. All my life, I've lived with that itch - itchy feet that couldn't stay in one place for too long. The horizon always seemed to be calling.

Whether it was my first solo train ride as a child, packing up for university, or adjusting to life in Botswana, each step was a lesson in courage, curiosity, and quiet recalibration - I reshaped myself and carried those new versions forward.

For me, change has always felt less like a break and more like a rhythm. A low hum I could feel in my bones. Restless. Compelling. Sometimes scary. But never silent.

I was never running away. I was chasing something unnamed but deeply felt - an urge that tugged at me every time things got too still.

Each stop along the way reflected back who I was becoming - and sometimes showed me who I was ready to grow beyond.

I think of those stretches like the open roads of my solo rides - no traffic, no turns, just me and the throttle. There's something both terrifying and freeing about that kind of space. No one ahead of you. No one behind. Just movement, and whatever thoughts ride alongside you.

Change and transformation is about the space between departure and arrival. That liminal stretch where you're no longer who you were, but not quite who you'll become.

It's about the courage it takes to step out, the curiosity that keeps you moving, and the quiet recalibration that happens when the world doesn't match your expectations - but surprises you anyway.

As you read, I invite you to reflect on your own moments of transition. What horizons have you moved toward, and what did they show you?

What did you leave behind?
What did you carry with you?
What did you discover about yourself in that in-between space?

Restless Momentum: Defining Life Through Change

In my earliest years, change was something I learned to survive - new homes, new schools, new cultures. I adapted because I had to, as the earlier stages of my story show. But somewhere along the way, what once felt like survival turned into something else.

Change became a companion. I realised early that transition wasn't only about loss or disruption, but also about possibility - a quiet invitation to rediscover who I was in a new context.

Even before I had words for it, I approached the unfamiliar with a mix of curiosity and caution. I'd scan a new place, take in the energy, and begin the slow, instinctive work of adjusting - not to disappear, but to understand how things worked.

Some people resist change. Others tolerate it. I was wired to initiate it, because of an insatiable desire to learn and connect. I wanted to see more, feel more, understand the world outside the boundaries of my upbringing.

I remember the build-up to each new chapter: the packing, the waiting, the quiet anticipation. There was always a mix of nerves and excitement, but underneath it all, a familiar buzz. A sense that something was about to shift - and that I would, too.

New schools. New homes. New friendships. Each transition asked me to try on a new version of myself. Sometimes I blended in easily. Other times, I felt like a neon sign in a black-and-white photo - visible in a way I couldn't quite control. But the contrast taught me more than comfort ever could.

When we landed in Africa, I stepped into a world that looked and sounded nothing like the one I'd known. I was a girl from the icy north, now surrounded by searing heat, vivid colours, and skies full of unfamiliar stars. And strangely, I didn't feel out of place - I felt energised.

That move planted something in me. A knowing that the world is wide and wonder-filled - and that understanding comes not from observation alone, but from participation.

As I got older, travel wasn't about ticking destinations off a list. I wasn't interested in just seeing the sights. I wanted to stay long enough to understand the story. To find the patterns beneath the surface. To learn the local greeting, eat the late-night food, hear the rhythm of a place from the people who lived there.

Whether in a Lisbon cafe or a small-town diner in the middle of nowhere in America, I was always gathering clues - tiny glimpses of what made each place pulse with life. And in doing so, I came to know myself more clearly.

Over time, I realised something: the pull toward possibility was always stronger than the discomfort of standing out. Even when change stretched me, even when I felt off-balance, I kept stepping forward.

Each move reminded me I could rebuild, expand, and evolve. Change no longer felt like something to endure - it became fuel.

And with every leap, I proved to myself that I could land.

Not always gracefully. But always stronger.

Milestones in Motion: My First Adventures in Freedom

I've always had a soft spot for solo journeys. Not the kind that starts with a dramatic goodbye at the airport, but the quiet, unassuming kind -trains and ferry rides, slow transitions from one version of life to another.

My love for movement didn't begin with motorbikes or passports. It started with a Norwegian train, a secondhand suitcase, and the quiet thrill of doing something on my own.

I was about seven when I took my first solo trip. The destination? My father's home - a place that felt both familiar and distant, like a postcard from a life I half-lived.

The train ride was an adventure in itself. I sat next to a woman and, like any neurospicy child with a story to tell, I opened up completely. No filter. No caution. Just a full download of my week, my dreams, and probably every strange habit my family had.

To me, this was connection. Storytelling. A moment to be seen.

Sometimes I wonder what that woman thought. Did she consider calling child protection? Or did she see something else - maybe a spark of independence in a girl unafraid to tell her truth to a stranger?

Either way, that trip ignited something. A desire to learn. Travel takes you places, but it also transforms you - the conversations, the shifting landscapes, the freedom to observe from a window seat all your own.

Years later, that spark grew bigger when I packed up for university at 20 after a gap year. It was my second big solo journey, and it carried more weight. I was leaving behind a whole ecosystem: my family, my responsibilities, the roles I'd long held.

With a backpack full of essentials and 40 kilograms of kitchen supplies - pots, pans, crockery, cutlery, cups, and glasses (because apparently, freedom still needs functional cookware) - I boarded a train, then a boat. Flights were too expensive, and besides, I liked the idea of moving through space slowly. Watching the land and sea change with each passing hour felt more like a rite of passage than a rushed exit.

Living in England was like stepping into a version of myself I hadn't met yet. For the first time, there were no siblings to look after, no family routines to uphold. Just me, in charge of my own rhythms and choices.

It was liberating. And, at first, a little disorienting too.

But as the weeks passed, I found joy in the details: cooking with the very pots I'd dragged across the North Sea, wandering campus corners that felt like secret pockets of possibility, learning how to live with my own company - and actually liking it.

And because I've never been one for over-planning, I left plenty of room for chance. I've always been more impulsive than methodical, preferring to see what opportunities turn up if I stay curious. Even now, I'm happiest when I stumble into the unexpected - a detour, a side street, an unplanned conversation.

And if all else fails, there's always people-watching. Whenever I land somewhere new, my first instinct is never to rush off with a guidebook. It's to find a corner table or a high step with a good view. Give me a coffee, a notebook, and a crowd to watch, and I'm content for hours, piecing together little stories from strangers' lives.

I was also quick to make new connections. It came easily - sometimes almost too easily. I could walk into a new space and find someone to talk to, laugh with, feel briefly known by. That ability was a gift, but it carried a quiet cost. For all the new friendships, I sometimes left behind the old ones. Not always on purpose - sometimes because I no longer felt connected to their rhythm or their world. Other times, because I didn't feel like I truly belonged in it.

The speed of starting again made it easy to keep moving forward, but harder to pause and hold onto what had already shaped me. And that was something I had to learn - not just how to arrive, but how to stay connected across time and distance. How to carry the people who mattered with me, even when the road kept changing.

Adventure, I realised, wasn't always about grand gestures. Sometimes it was in the quiet clicks of a life rearranging itself. Sometimes it was about making friends with unfamiliar accents. And sometimes it was simply about staying long enough to feel rooted in your own skin.

Belonging Without Borders

I've always said that "home" wasn't tied to a fixed place. By this stage, I was beginning to understand it as something even more subtle - a rhythm, a thread I could carry into each new chapter, no matter where the road led.

I learned to pick up the atmosphere without even trying - the tone, the pace, the unspoken rules. Always half-alert, worried I wouldn't fit, always looking for the subtle signs of rejection.

I was a shape-shifter before I had words for it. Adapting quickly, subtly adjusting to match the world around me - not to deceive, but to connect.

The more adaptable I became, the more I questioned who I was beneath the surface. Was I truly part of these places? Or just skilled at becoming what they needed? In retrospect, my rejection sensitivity was probably in full flow, but how was I to know?

Each new location became a kind of experiment. Could I bring all of me into unfamiliar space? Could I hold on to what felt true while absorbing what was new?

The answer wasn't clear, and the process left a mark. I started to understand that life and acceptance do not look the same for everyone. It doesn't have to be loud or permanent. Sometimes, it's a fleeting connection - a moment that tells you: you're okay here.

In Botswana, I honed in on the beauty of greeting people with intention. Of tuning into a slower rhythm of life. It was not that we were rude in Norway, but the tradition of greeting elders, strangers, was probably watered down. I wasn't used to having conversations with random people on the street, and my chatty, neurospicy brain loved it.

In England, I discovered the quiet gift of solitude. The freedom in knowing I didn't need to perform to be valid.

And in every place in between - on every bicycle ride, every walk through unfamiliar streets - I found pieces of acceptance and love in unexpected places: the kindness of a stranger, the smell of a home-cooked meal, a conversation that bridged culture through shared laughter.

Those pieces don't always fit neatly together. They're not a single story or one perfect puzzle.

They're a collage. And over time, I've come to see that's what belonging really is - a patchwork of the places and people that have made you feel seen. A home you carry, even when the road keeps moving.

Tuning Up: Embracing Life's Transitions

We travel, initially, to lose ourselves; and we travel, next, to find ourselves.
Pico Iyer

Pico Iyer's reflections on travel and belonging feel written for shape-shifters - those who've crossed borders not just geographically, but emotionally and culturally. He reminds us that travel is less about escape and more about arrival, not in place but in self.

We often treat transitions as disruptions, things to get through. But what if they're the moments where the real becoming happens? For those of us who are deeply curious, sensitive to the world's pulse, and always scanning for meaning, these in-between spaces aren't gaps in life. They are life.

Iyer speaks of "going nowhere" - the quiet, internal movement we make even while the world keeps shifting. That stillness inside the motion is where belonging often begins.

We may not always have a fixed home or one clear identity, but we can create a sense of home in motion: turning uncertainty into creativity and discomfort into depth.

The goal isn't to pin ourselves down. It's to stay awake as we move, to notice, to let change shape us without losing ourselves.

Practical takeaways:

Redefine home. Ask what anchors you when everything else shifts - a person, a practice, a ritual.

Create micro-stillness. Even in motion, carve out small pauses to listen to yourself.

Reframe the wobble. Feeling unsteady doesn't mean you're lost. It often means you're growing.

Reflective Pause: The Space Between

Transitions ask us to stretch - for our plans and our sense of self. This pause is a moment to slow down and listen to what's shifting in you and around you.

What have been some of your "in-between" moments - the spaces between who you were and who you're becoming?

Where have you felt that quiet tug that whispers, "there's more for you than this"?

When you've arrived somewhere new - in place, heart, or purpose - what felt like home?

Are there pieces of you left behind that might be worth reclaiming?

Growth often hides in the pauses between destinations.
Breathe. You're already becoming.

And remember: every traveler needs companions for the journey. Find the mentors, peers, or coaches who remind you that becoming isn't meant to be done alone.

SECOND GEAR

Ignition - Understanding My Alien World

Not all who wander are lost;
some are simply charting a course that no one else can see.
Adapted from J.R.R. Tolkien

There's a moment on every roadtrip - just after the helmet goes on, just before the engine roars - where you feel it. That quiet charge in your chest. The knowing that this stretch will ask more of you than the last one did.

That's what this part of the journey is.

"Flipping the ignition" helps you get moving. It also helps you tune into your own frequency, especially when the world around you seems to be broadcasting something entirely different. It's about recognising that your pace, your wiring, your lens on life might not match the dominant map - and deciding to ride anyway.

Let's dive beneath the surface. Into the mental backroads and emotional landscapes of what it means to feel different, to see the world differently, and to still claim space unapologetically.

We'll explore how identities intersect, how culture shapes belonging, and what it means to stop shape-shifting long enough to remember your original form.

This isn't about defining yourself by what you're not. It's about learning to name, honour, and ride with what you are.

Hold on tight. Let's turn the ignition on.

STAGE FIVE
Owning Your Inner Alien

*I was once afraid of people saying,
'Who does she think she is?' Now I have the courage to stand
and say, 'This is who I am.'*

Oprah Winfrey

There's a quiet feeling that comes with being different. Not the kind you shout about, but the kind that hums under the surface. A sense that you're tuned to a frequency the world doesn't quite recognise.

For a long time, I tried to ignore it. I tried to match the pace, the tone, the rhythm of everyone around me. I thought that if I could just blend in well enough, I'd find happiness - or at least ease. And I still do at times. I thought I was the same as everyone else. That I belonged.

But blending in is not the same as a sense of home.

Belonging starts when you stop translating yourself into something more familiar and start showing up in your original language - messy, brilliant, unapologetic.

This chapter is about what happens when you stop editing yourself to be palatable and start recognising that your "alien energy" might be the most powerful thing you have. It's not a flaw. It's your edge, your lens, your light.

Embracing the Alien Within

Feeling Different, not Alone

I didn't grow up thinking of myself as an alien.

That language came later - after I'd lived across cultures, sat in enough rooms that didn't make sense, and finally found the words to name what I'd always felt underneath.

As a kid, I felt both connected *and* apart, in a good way. I could belong in a group while still watching from the outside. I knew I was loved - but I also

knew that being easy to love meant tuning in. Reading the room. Being what people needed.

It wasn't forced. It was instinct. I wanted to help. To be good. To be kind. To make things better. But there was always a quiet layer running in the background - like a second radio station - asking: *What's expected of me here? What will make them happy?*

I remember one girl in my class who didn't quite fit the mould. She was different in ways I couldn't fully name then, but her creativity was dazzling, and I felt drawn to that spark. I suggested to the teacher that we mix the class so we weren't divided into neat rows of "good at maths" and "good at art." Instead, we worked as a patchwork of thirty children, each bringing something of our own. It was messy and lively, but it worked - and it showed me early on that difference wasn't a weakness, it was the glue that held us together. Our teacher was a very forward thinking and understanding woman.

My thoughts often arrived faster than I could explain them. My emotions ran deep, though I rarely let them show all the way. Back then, I just carried on as best I could - not realising I was already building a skillset: noticing the world closely, adjusting to it, and finding ways to fit.

Back then, though, I didn't think of myself as unusual. I assumed everyone's mind worked like mine - quick, curious, full of ideas, sometimes a little much. I thought it was normal to feel ten steps ahead, to notice the undercurrents, to want to connect dots that others didn't see.

I wasn't weird. I wasn't broken. I was me - quirky, energetic, often intense, but also kind and eager to belong. It was only decades later that I would find language to describe the difference - words that helped explain why my mind didn't quite operate like most. But in those early years, I just lived it. I smiled, I learned, I matched what was in front of me. And I wore my quirkiness like a quiet badge of honour, even if I didn't yet know what it meant.

A Starfish-Shaped Peg in a Square World

On the surface, I was the model student.

Top of the class. Eager to learn. Kind. Polite. Compassionate. My teachers adored me - not just for my performance, but for how I treated others. I was the good girl. The helper. The quiet observer who stepped in when someone needed a hand or a little protection from the group.

I looked like I fit perfectly.

But inside, I always felt slightly... off-pattern. Like my frequency was just a little out of sync with the rest of the world.

I didn't get in trouble. I didn't rebel. But I was always on alert. Reading the room. Adjusting myself to keep the peace. Clipping my own wings so I wouldn't rock the boat. I thought that's what being "good" meant.

Looking back, I realise it wasn't hiding. It wasn't fear.

It was shape-shifting.

An early, instinctive way of keeping myself - and everyone else - safe.

The Relay Race Realisation

The first time I remember feeling the sting of not being good enough was at a school sports day.

I was seven. The anchor in a relay race - last in line, all eyes on me. I was small, serious, and absolutely determined to win. I ran like my life depended on it.

And I almost did it. Almost.

I crossed the finish line just a fraction behind the other team. A second too slow. A step too late.

To anyone else, it was a close call. To me, it was devastating.

I couldn't hold back the tears. I was inconsolable - I'd lost a race, and I was *certain* I'd let everyone down. That this moment would define how they saw me. That being good, being liked, being *safe* required winning.

The teacher tried to comfort me. So did the other kids - all five of them in that tiny country school. They told me it wasn't my fault. That I'd done well. That it didn't matter. But I couldn't hear any of it over the noise in my own head.

For me, this had nothing to do with the race itself. It was about what the race meant - how much pressure I had already learned to carry, how much I craved pleasing others and feared disappointing them.

Looking back, I can see how early I started to internalise things. How deeply I felt everything. How quickly I believed that falling short - even by a fraction - meant I wasn't enough.

That race was the first time I experienced this feeling: what other kids could shrug off, could crush me.

Where I Fit Without Effort

While the relay race showed me how intense things could feel on the inside, my family showed me what it felt like to simply be.

In our big, warm, slightly chaotic extended family, I wasn't the odd one out. I was just Gry. Curious, talkative, full of questions - and totally accepted.

I was also shy. I could be intensely quiet, watching the room before stepping into it. I often needed time to warm up, to feel the rhythm of the space before joining in. But even in that stillness, I was never made to feel out of place.

No one asked me to tone it down or act like anyone else. I could be silly. I could be serious. I could run barefoot through the garden or stage a performance with my cousins and a cardboard box curtain, and nobody blinked.

They just joined in.

Family gatherings were full of mischief, laughter, and stories. If someone was a little quirky, all the better. We didn't shave off rough edges - we laughed at them, celebrated them. That kind of freedom planted something deep in me. Knowing that *somewhere*, it was possible to be fully yourself and be loved, not just tolerated.

And I found that same sense of belonging beyond family too. At Vikane and in primary school, I settled in after the first challenges with my accent and quickly became part of the group. More than that - I became part of the leadership of it. I was included in decisions, in games, in plans. It wasn't about being the loudest, but about being trusted, being relied upon. For me, it was home.

Botswana gave me a version of that too.

I stood out there - blonde hair, pale skin, European background - in a way I couldn't hide. I was the "alien" in the most literal sense. And yet, I never felt rejected.

The local kids were curious, but not cruel. I remember one lunch at school when a group of older kids crowded around me, eyes wide as I unpacked my food. One of them said, with absolute seriousness, "we heard that white people eat ugly". I am not sure what they were referring to, but guessing it was just because we were culturally different.

They weren't mocking. They were genuinely fascinated. And I was fascinated right back, but I will admit that I quickly hid the rest of my lunch in my desk. We traded jokes and shared stories, and by the end of that lunch hour, we were laughing together like old friends.

Later, when I visited some of their family homes in the villages, I was the only white person around for miles. But I was never made to feel like an outsider. I was welcomed. Seen. Included.

Botswana taught me that belonging can be about showing up with openness and being met with the same.

But as I grew older, I also learned that belonging wasn't always that simple. Sometimes it came easily, like slipping into a current already flowing - and other times, it had to be fought for, questioned, or redefined.

The Misfit Years

While Botswana taught me that I could belong even when I looked different, England showed me how connection could stretch across cultures.

University in England was a kind of beautiful melting pot - students from all over the world, all a little displaced, all trying to figure out who we were away from home. We bonded over late-night study sessions, shared meals, the common challenge of navigating life on our own for the first time, or at the pub where everyone seemed to congregate.

There was a difference, sure. But it was a shared difference. And in that, I found comfort.

Then came Australia. Friendly. Warm. Casual. Always up for a laugh. I wanted to fit in - *badly*. And the I loved the quick humour, the easy conversations, the way people "took the mickey" out of each other with what looked like effortless charm.

Botswana gave me belonging in difference. England gave me comfort in shared difference. Australia, at first, gave me something else again - the sense that I fit in.

My colleagues at Oracle were brilliant. My friends in Sydney welcomed me. On the surface, it was everything I could have hoped for: friendly, open, easy.

But underneath that warmth, I stumbled into something I had never faced before. I'd worked in Norway, the US, the UK, Sweden - across countries and cultures.

I had never seen the gap between what was said and what was actually done as sharply as I did in corporate Australia.

There were invisible rules I didn't know how to read. A pecking order that placed me - a migrant woman, outspoken, Scandinavian, clearly neurodivergent, which was not a "thing" in those days - way down the line, even when no one said it out loud.

It confused me. For someone who had learned to navigate cultures with curiosity and fairness, I suddenly had no map. What looked like friendliness often masked barriers. What sounded like equality didn't play out that way in practice.

It took me years to name what was happening. At the time, all I knew was that something didn't add up. I'd join the banter and realise too late I'd missed a cue or stepped somewhere I wasn't meant to. I was always half a beat off. Close, but not quite. It felt like everyone else had the script and I was still guessing my lines.

I'd laugh, and then worry that I'd misunderstood. I'd share, and then second-guess whether it had landed weird. I was fluent in English, but not in the cultural shorthand that made up so much of the connection.

People were lovely. Welcoming, even. But I still felt like a guest at someone else's party - one they were glad to have, but who didn't quite belong in the inner circle.

I realised that being "accepted" isn't the same as being *known*.

When I Named My Alien Energy

When we returned from Botswana, I was nearly sixteen - brimming with stories, sensations, colours, and contrasts that had changed me. I'd seen too much, felt too much, learned too much to fit neatly back into my old outlines. But back in Norway, I quickly realised most people didn't know how to meet those stories.

I'd start to share something - about the red dust, the rhythm of the days, the way the community wrapped around you like a warm shawl - and see their eyes glaze over. Not unkindly, just… blank. They had no reference point. No map for where I'd been.

It wasn't just classmates. It was adults too. People we'd known for years. Conversations slid past my stories like oil on water. I was back, but not fully returned.

That's when the alien feeling settled in - I was different, and *untranslated*. Not weird. Not wrong. Just operating on a frequency no one around me could quite tune into.

I didn't call it "alien energy" then. I just knew I felt both too much *and* invisible. Like I had a story no one could quite hear.

Years later, in 2012, I stood on stage at the WIMWA Summit in front of 400 people, delivering a keynote titled *My Life as an Alien*. I told stories of growing up across cultures, of feeling like I was always arriving, always adapting. The phrase "alien" still belonged to the external markers - moving countries, learning new codes, navigating culture shock. But something happened in that room. The words were mine, but the electricity in the air, the way they landed - that was the first time I sensed this experience might be more universal. That maybe, I wasn't just talking about place.

At the time, I still thought of it all as the product of my upbringing. My shifting identity was something I'd earned through movement and adaptation. But in hindsight, that talk marked the beginning of a deeper reckoning.

It was a business partner - someone familiar with neurodivergence through their own family - who first gently raised the possibility: *"Have you ever wondered if the way you experience things might not just be cultural?"* (Their words were a lot more direct than that).

I was in my fifties. That question landed wrong. Were they implying there was something *wrong* with me? I dismissed it, almost reflexively.

It took years before I was ready to revisit that topic. To even entertain the idea that my way of being in the world - the way I tracked micro-expressions, felt the texture of a room, noticed invisible shifts and emotional undercurrents - might not be how *everyone* experienced things.

Because for most of my life, I genuinely thought it was. I assumed other people's brains worked just like mine.

In hindsight, that keynote was the first time I gave language to something I would only fully understand much later. When I named my alien energy, I didn't feel more separate - I felt *seen*.

Because here's the beautiful contradiction: naming our difference doesn't isolate us. It invites others in. It makes us visible. And more often than not, when we show up honestly, someone else sees themselves in us.

That's the beautiful contradiction. In the late nineties, I was introduced to the term *same, same, but different* by an Asian colleague, and I loved it. I have since adopted and adapted it to read: *same, same - **and** different*.

We don't have to be the same to connect. We just have to be real.

That moment marked a shift, the early spark of something I'd come to understand more fully later: that shape-shifting wasn't just something I did to survive.

It was something I could choose - to use, to master, to direct. To *belong* on my own terms.

Same, Same - and Different

Maybe you've felt it too - that quiet sense that you're tuned to a different frequency than those around you.

I used to think that frequency came from the places I'd lived, the languages I'd learned, the borders I'd crossed. And that was part of it.

But later, I realised it wasn't just about geography - it was about wiring. The way I noticed more. Felt deeper. Processed things differently.

It might have shown up in your earliest misfit moments when you noticed more, felt deeper, processed the world in a way that didn't quite match the script.

If that's you, I want to ask:

What if being different was never the problem?
What if it was always your gift?

The quirks that made you feel out of place might just be the very things that make you belong - to yourself, to the world, in a way that's deeper than surface-level fitting in.

Who sees those parts of you and calls them treasures? And if no one does - yet - what if *you* became that person for yourself first?

We are allowed to be the same, same - and different. Connection doesn't require sameness. It just asks for honesty.

Start there.

The Early Days: Belonging Through Curiosity and Connection

From the moment I stepped into a classroom, I wasn't just another student - I was the girl with boundless positivity, endless questions that I may never have asked, and an unshakable sense of fairness. It didn't matter that I attended three different schools in year one. And beneath all that, a quiet kind of strategy: I'd find someone who seemed more shy or lost than I was, and I'd take them under my wing. That was my safety blanket. If I could help someone else feel welcome, I didn't have to think so hard about where I fit. I still do that today.

I had ideas for everything. New ways to group students. Mini-plays during recess. Class routines I thought could work better. I probably came across as a bit of a teacher's pet. But our teacher didn't play favourites - she encouraged curiosity, which gave me room to be fully myself.

I never felt like I didn't belong - I was too busy lifting others up. The bullies may have rolled their eyes, but they respected me. I respected them too. That mutual understanding created a kind of safety - for them, for others, and for me. I was just a kid.

A Different Kind of Belonging

When I was thirteen, we moved again, and this time it felt different. I was just about to start secondary school in a new school and district.

I didn't feel out of place exactly, but I couldn't quite make sense of the social dynamics. Words and body language didn't always match. People said one thing, meant another. I could feel the gaps, but I didn't know how to bridge them. So I stepped sideways.

Instead of trying to fit into a group that felt like a puzzle I couldn't solve, I made my own path. I spent time with younger kids - ones who still played honestly, spoke plainly, and welcomed me without pretense.

Looking back, I can see I was "different" in ways I hadn't named yet. But it didn't feel like a flaw. I still found ways to connect - just on my terms.

Anchored by Connection

No matter where we lived, I had a constant: my quirky, wonderful, and somewhat complex family.

They were my grounding force across continents. No matter how far I wandered, I was never really lost - I was just a call or a long letter away from being reminded of who I was.

And I was lucky. I made friends in those early years who've stuck around to this day. The kind of friendships built on shared school lunches, mischievous adventures, and stories that grew wilder every time we told them.

Those relationships became threads I could return to whenever life started to feel too disconnected.

The Power of Positivity

Looking back now, I can see it clearly: my ability to create connection was a superpower.

I didn't wait for permission or invitations - I jumped in. Whether it was writing inclusive plays for classmates or turning strangers into confidants on a train ride, I made space for others. That's how I found space for myself.

I wouldn't call that early version of me "alien". Not yet. That word hadn't landed. But even back then, I was tuned a little differently.

And I wasn't trying to fix it. I was just moving forward - with empathy, enthusiasm, and a deep-down belief that there had to be room in the world for all of us, exactly as we are.

Owning the Alien Energy: A Rude Awakening

"Gry, do you have a moment?"

My manager stood in the doorway of his office, casual but firm. I followed him in, curious, not concerned. I'd only been in Australia a few months, arriving on what I thought would be a two- or three-year adventure - long enough to contribute, learn something new, and leave my mark.

I came in ready to share ideas. I had spent years working across Europe and the USA with our Norwegian team. I'd seen what worked - and what didn't. I was ready to bring that experience into the room.

So when I settled into the chair, I expected a conversation. What I got was a command.

"I'd like you to stop mentioning things that have been done in other places during group meetings".

I blinked. "Why on earth would you ask that?"

His answer came quickly, like something he'd said a hundred times before: "You see, here in Australia, we don't like hearing that things have been done somewhere else before. It's a hangover from the British Empire".

At first, I thought it was a joke. His mouth was smiling, but his eyes told a different story.

I launched into my usual logic - how sharing successes and failures from other teams helps everyone learn. How we were part of the same company. How cross-pollination is the whole point of being global.

He let me speak. And then he cut in with a sentence that still echoes in my memory: "It would be great if you could salute me". Yup, his words.

Salute him?

The ground beneath me cracked. I came from a culture of egalitarian leadership, where ideas mattered more than ego. But now, I was being told - explicitly - that it wasn't about contribution, but compliance.

I recognise that it was said "tongue in cheek", but in my books, this was not acceptable.

The Patriarchy and Power Plays

This wasn't just a one-off moment. It was the curtain lifting on something deeper - a workplace culture built on hierarchy, power plays, and silence.

There were whispers of affairs between senior leaders and their much-younger female assistants. Whispers I didn't want to believe. But some of the women shared their stories. Quietly. Carefully.

What shocked me more than the rumours was the way people brushed them off. "That's just how it is here, Gry". "Don't rock the boat".

Even when one of my male colleagues asked our boss directly about his alleged affair with our quiet, introverted team member, the response wasn't denial. It was a smirk. A silence that said, *this conversation is over, but you're on the money.*

When I shared this with the same team member, my colleague and friend, she was mortified. It wasn't true, but she was shocked because someone in power did not shut it down.

It was overt sexism - it was control. A power structure that relied on people knowing their place. And staying there.

A Moment of Reckoning

That meeting was my first direct encounter with this new kind of hierarchy - the kind where challenging the status quo was dangerous.

My boss's words - *"Salute me"* - became a line in the sand.

I could have stayed. Kept my head down. Played the game. But that's not how I'm wired.

I didn't come to Australia to play small.

So I made the hard choice and walked away - risking my visa, my job security, and the comfort of a known path - because my values didn't fit the mould. And I wasn't going to shrink to make them fit.

That moment was a rude awakening, yes. But it was also a powerful turning point.

A moment of owning my alien energy not just in words - but in action.

From Alienation to Advocacy

The shift from feeling like an outsider to becoming an advocate is quietly unfolding, shaped by small moments of courage and unexpected connection. It began when I stopped editing myself to fit. When I refused to listen to my own voice telling me that nobody wanted me there.

I stopped trying to translate my thinking into what I thought others wanted to hear, started speaking in my own voice, and something changed.

People were approaching me after meetings or workshops - not to talk about the content, but to tell me how "seen" they felt. How something I said made them feel a little less alone.

I didn't have the perfect words, but I was honest about the messy, in-progress parts of my journey. And that honesty created safety.

I remember one woman in particular - brilliant, likely neurospicy - pulling me aside after a workshop. "I feel like I'm constantly editing myself," she said. "Like I have to water everything down to be taken seriously."

That hit hard. Not because it was new, but because it was familiar.

Rather than offering a tidy solution, I shared my own stories - the times I'd shrunk, the times I hadn't, and what those choices taught me.

Her way of thinking didn't need fixing. That was her edge.

Over the next few months, she began stepping into herself more fully. Her ideas sharpened. Her presence grew steadier. She started to shine.

That was the shift - from alienation to advocacy.

And from that point, I began building spaces where people didn't have to shrink to fit.

"Different" wasn't something to work around, but something to work with.

Creating Inclusive Spaces

One of the most rewarding projects I've led came out of that same energy.

I designed a mentorship program, pairing people from underrepresented backgrounds with senior leaders and ensuring that the mentors and mentees were supervised and supported. The goal was skill development and human connection. A key element was to equip the mentors with skills and frames so that they could support their proteges in a way that worked for all. Real conversations. Mutual learning.

And it worked.

People who had once felt invisible began to feel recognised. Some shared how their mentors didn't just help with career moves - they helped them *see themselves differently*. And the mentors often said that they felt they learnt more than their mentees.

The program wasn't perfect, but it facilitated a new way of being in the workplace. A few more doors were left open. A few more seats pulled up to the table.

Turning Pain into Purpose

There's something powerful about letting your wounds become doorways - for yourself and for others.

By speaking honestly about the messy parts - not just the wins - I built bridges. Between countries and cultures, departments and disciplines, and people who might otherwise have stayed silent.

I also became more attuned to the quiet cues. The person in the back of the room. The one whose idea got ignored until someone else repeated it louder. I started noticing - and inviting them gently to step forward safely.

When you've spent years on the outside, you develop a kind of radar. You learn to spot the people who are trying to belong without losing themselves. And you learn how to say, without saying: *You can bring all of you here.*

Because we're not meant to fit into someone else's definition of success.

We're meant to create spaces where same, same - and different isn't a contradiction at all. It's the culture.

Tuning Up: Embracing Your Difference and Rising Strong

You spend years trying to blend in, then realise the parts you hid are the best things about you.
Fern Brady, *Strong Female Character*

We can either be shiny and admired or real and loved. We must decide.
Glennon Doyle

Glennon Doyle's words are a rallying cry to drop the performance. To stop polishing our edges in the hope of being accepted. The very things we're told to tone down - our quirks, our questions, our complexity - are often where our power lives.

Fern Brady and Doyle share a fierce truth: authenticity isn't soft. It's rebellion. It's the decision to stop contorting yourself to fit into spaces that were never built for you.

For many of us, being "different" has carried the weight of loneliness or misunderstanding. But difference isn't a flaw. It's a frequency. It's how you know you're tuned to a unique purpose. The road to belonging isn't about becoming less; it's about showing up real and allowing others to do the same.

Brady's story is a reminder that what others call "too much" is often just unfiltered truth. When you stop apologising for the way your mind works, you create space for others to do the same - and that's where real connection begins.

Practical steps for embracing your inner alien:

Name your truth. Identify one part of yourself you've been hiding, softening, or apologising for. What if that part is your strength in disguise?

Trust your inner compass. When you're unsure where you belong, check in with yourself first. What feels true? What feels like compromise?

Redefine success. Ask not "Am I getting it right?" but "Am I being real?"

Every time you choose realness over approval, you rewrite the map. You remind others that belonging doesn't come from blending in - it comes from standing in truth.

Reflective Pause: Turning Up the Real You

You've seen how *difference* can be both your rebellion and your truth. This moment is your invitation to honour the parts you once tried to edit out - the ones that make your story unmistakably yours.

When you stop performing for acceptance, you make room for your truest self to breathe. This pause is your invitation to meet her again.

Where have you been trying to earn acceptance by shrinking or softening parts of yourself?
What's one "too much" or "not enough" quality that might actually be a gift?
What does real success look like when you're not chasing approval?
Where in your life could you lead by example, simply by being fully you?

You don't need permission to be yourself.
Just the courage to stop asking for it.

Your authenticity doesn't have to stand alone. Find the people who see your light, mentors or allies who help you turn your difference into strength.

STAGE SIX
The Cultural Chameleon

*Belonging is not about becoming invisible -
it's about being seen and accepted for who you are.*

Brené Brown (paraphrased)

Most of us aren't taught to shape-shift - we just do.

It's not a conscious choice. It's not even something we know how to explain at the time. It's just how we survive.

It started early, at home - sensing tension, defusing conflict, adjusting myself to keep the peace. Later, as life moved me across countries and cultures, that instinct simply repeated on a bigger stage. Without planning, I was able to pick up the vibe of spaces as soon as I entered them, matched tones, and shifted energy. What began as survival in childhood became second nature everywhere.

It wasn't people-pleasing. It felt like connection. Like coping. It felt like I was meant to be there - even if only on the surface.

But here's the trouble with shape-shifting: you get so good at it, you forget your original shape.

The world praised my adaptability. My intuition. My emotional intelligence. But what they didn't see was the exhaustion that came with always folding parts of myself away. Or the slow erosion of identity that happens when your worth is measured by how comfortable you make other people feel.

There were moments I mistook that ability for power. I thought maybe I was just multilingual in human. But underneath that, I wasn't always sure who I was when no one else was watching.

It took me years to realise that this was all about survival, not strategy. And the more I shifted, the more I disappeared.

Only now am I learning to ride differently. To let the engine hum in my own rhythm. To believe I don't have to change my colours to be worthy of the space I take up.

Living Between Worlds

Some of us live between these places.

Between languages, cultures, expectations. Between who we are at home and who we need to become to be heard in a room. Between the stories we carry and the ones people expect us to tell.

That was my normal.

When I returned to Norway from Africa, I carried the rhythm of an entirely different continent in my bones - heat, slang, laughter with layers I couldn't explain. But I had no words for how to bridge the gap. When people asked how it was, they didn't mean it. Not really. Their body language started changing somewhere between "African (black) people" and "being circled by lions in the Okavango Delta".

I stopped trying. I learned to smile, say "It was great" (if anyone ever bothered to ask) and tuck the rest into my back pocket. Not out of shame - but out of futility. Bear in mind that this was way before the internet and we only had two TV stations, so Africa was as foreign as you could get. No wonder my friends looked at me as if I was crazy.

It was here, back in our new house and community, that I felt most like an alien. Not because of how I looked or spoke - but because of how unseen I felt. The dissonance between what I'd lived and what people could hold.

There was no translation for what I wanted to say.

And years later, I learned I wasn't the only one. Quietly, in their own ways, my parents and siblings had felt it too - that same sense of disconnect. The stories are too big for casual conversation. The sense of being surrounded by familiarity, yet somehow out of sync. We hadn't talked about it at the time - we were too busy adjusting, translating, surviving. But when we finally did, it felt like finding another piece of the map.

I wanted people to see all of me, but they weren't ready.

I got good at shifting - between codes, between cultures, between masks. A cultural amphibian. At home in many waters, fluent in adaptation, but always holding my breath a little.

That's the thing about living between worlds: you become a bridge. And bridges are strong - but they're also walked on.

It also gave me something powerful. An inner stretch. A capacity to meet people where they are. To hold multiple truths without collapsing into any single one.

And that's the beautiful contradiction I've come to love: Same, same - and different.

A Whole New World: Moving to Africa

While moving from northern to southern Norway was a lesson in adaptation, moving to Africa was a full-blown transformation. At 13, I packed up my life alongside my family and stepped into what felt like a vivid dream - leaving our "friends" behind after only 5 months in our new house.

Botswana was a tapestry of bright colours, rich smells, and sun-drenched rhythms. The people were so different. Their warmth ran deeper than the weather. And even though I stood out, I never felt excluded. My school friends' curiosity was genuine. Their kindness, immediate.

Living in Botswana felt like stepping into a kaleidoscope - each day a new swirl of sensation, challenge, and discovery. I learned to trade certainty for curiosity, to meet differences with openness, and to surrender the need to have all the answers.

There were moments that reminded me how different I looked - but in the best, most light-hearted ways. One afternoon, a classmate leaned in close and squinted at my face before asking, completely serious, "What are those green spots on your nose?" I blinked, confused - until I realised they were pointing at my freckles. I'd always thought of them as brown, but against the deeper tones of my classmates' skin, they looked more like speckled moss. We burst out laughing together. That tiny moment cracked something open. My difference wasn't something to hide - it was something we could laugh about, together.

This move to Botswana changed how I thought about country and connection. Any place, no matter how unfamiliar, could feel like home if I brought along my humour, respect, and willingness to listen.

You just have to show up - with open eyes, an open heart, and sometimes, an accent that makes people laugh with you, not at you.

The Challenges of Being a Chameleon

Adapting to new environments can be a superpower. It's helped me connect with people from Botswana to Brazil, from boardrooms in Sydney to backstreets in Santiago. It's why I can walk into a room and feel the temperature before anyone says a word.

But even when you're good at it - even when it's instinctive - shape-shifting can dilute the sense of who you are.

In Botswana, I embraced the culture with everything I had. The experience has such a positive experience on me. I would not swap it for anything. I learned to understand and speak the local lingo, I joined the science club at school, and the Red Cross where we performed dances. Imagine this little blonde kid performing a traditional dance with beads around her ankles for rhythm and sound, and ululating to her heart's content in joy and happiness.

I soaked up the warmth and rhythm of daily life. But no matter how deeply I connected, I couldn't change the fact that I stood out. I was welcomed fully and gloriously as I was. And over time, I realised: you can be included without feeling like you fully belong.

That awareness was unsettling and oddly exciting. Like driving a road that looks familiar but doesn't quite feel like home.

When I lead with curiosity and trust my gut, I find flow. I don't think about adapting - I just *am*. But when I start second-guessing - wondering if I'm too much, too bold, too foreign - that's when the doubt creeps in. That's when I lose my rhythm.

The challenge is when we adapt and accidentally forget to check in with ourselves along the way. Are we shape-shifting because we're exploring and expanding? Or are we diluting ourselves to make others more comfortable? The gift of being a chameleon is the ability to connect across differences. The lesson is learning how to do it without losing your original shape.

Standing My Ground, Finding My Shape

When we returned from Botswana, I was nearly sixteen - academically ahead but socially behind. I could talk politics, write essays, and hold my own with adults. But with girls my age? I was lost.

I listened more than I spoke. I soaked in their stories about boys and parties and things I didn't quite understand. It made me an easy target.

One day after physical education, a few girls decided to knock me down a peg - or maybe just cool off the girl who hadn't yet found her place. They drenched me with ice water. I was humiliated.

But I stood up. I told them off, clear and sharp, and made it very clear what would happen if they ever tried it again.

They didn't.

Somewhere in that moment, a new version of me emerged. I didn't realise it at the time, but that's when shape-shifting started to become intentional. I had probably always done it - sensing the energy of a room, adjusting, blending in. But now it was shifting from survival to strategy.

The Workplace as a New Frontier

If childhood taught me how to adapt, the workplace taught me when not to.

By the time I entered the workforce, I'd already lived across countries and cultures. I knew how to get people to like me, how to soften my tone, how to switch gears depending on who was in front of me. But this time, the stakes were different. I wasn't trying to fit in - I wanted to be heard. To contribute. To lead.

That was easier said than done.

When I first entered the tech industry, there were actually more women in key roles than you might expect. Not everywhere, but enough to shift the tone. It gave me a glimpse of what was possible when women stepped up as leaders and refused to be the only ones adapting to be heard. It proved that leadership could sound different, look different. But even there, the deeper culture still hummed with codes I hadn't been taught.

Let's acknowledge that this may not have been what others experienced. I started my career in egalitarian, little Norway, working for large multinationals with a lot of employees and I am aware that smaller businesses struggle to find diverse talent.

Nevertheless, I found myself in workplaces filled with men where meetings were less about ideas and more about invisible rules. Especially after moving to Australia. Banter was more than banter - it was hierarchy disguised as

humour. Decisions weren't always made in the boardroom, but in the corridor, or at the pub after hours - places I wasn't always invited to, or didn't feel I belonged in.

So I did what I've always done: I observed. I noticed who got listened to, and when. And I shape-shifted - this time with intention. I tuned myself to the room. When I picked up on the subtle shifts in posture, tone, and attention, I figured out what ideas landed best, and how to package mine in a way that would be heard without losing their edge. I also began pushing back.

I started asking the questions no one else was asking. I brought in stories and lessons from other regions - lessons I knew worked, because I'd lived them. I offered new ways of connecting across cultural gaps. I suggested we try something different - partly because I wanted to be a disruptive rebel, AND because I knew we could do better.

One project in particular stands out. We were working across time zones, cultures, and languages, and the friction was real. Tensions bubbled just below the surface. So I introduced something unconventional: design thinking. Storytelling. Active listening. It wasn't flashy - but it shifted something. Suddenly, people stopped defending their corners and started leaning in. Connection happened. Collaboration followed.

And still, there were moments where I watched my ideas get ignored - only to be celebrated when someone else repeated them. Usually someone with more perceived "credibility". Usually a man.

Those moments stung. But they also sharpened my focus.

I was finally learning how to *change* the room - how to create spaces where others didn't feel the need to shrink or shift to be accepted.

That's when the real work began. The kind that goes beyond surviving or succeeding. The kind that's about making sure no one else has to go it alone.

Finding the Balance: Adaptation vs. Authenticity

I wore my adaptability like a badge of honour. I could switch lanes without effort, with barely a bump in the road. But at some point, I realised I was navigating with everyone else's map and had lost sight of my own route.

Once during a collaboration workshop, we were asked to share something we were proud of. While others spoke about awards and milestones, I told a quieter story - about mentoring a junior colleague who felt out of place.

"Helping her find her voice", I said, "meant more than any title I've ever earned".

For a second, I wondered if it was too soft, too personal. But something shifted. People came up to me afterwards, not to talk about achievements, but to share their own stories of feeling unseen or diluted. That moment reminded me: when we show up with truth, we create space for others to do the same.

But there is a nuance: authenticity doesn't mean refusing to adapt. There are times - especially across cultures and contexts - when blending in can help build trust. Sometimes the detour *is* the best way forward. But if you keep bending to fit, eventually you forget where you were going.

I've learned that if the bridge you're building doesn't connect back to *you*, it might not be a bridge worth crossing.

Standing firm in your values can come with a cost. Saying no when everyone else says yes. Choosing clarity over comfort. Speaking up when silence is the safer option. But the cost of not standing firm? That's even higher. It chips away at your sense of self until you're not sure who's holding the handlebars anymore.

That's why I developed what I now call my *inner compass*. A gut check I return to when the road forks. I ask: Is this alignment or accommodation? Am I building connections or compromising who I am?

If the answer pulls me away from myself, I recalibrate.

Because in the end, balance is about knowing when to shift gears and when to stay the course. It's about riding your road, even if it means being the only one on it for a while.

There's nothing wrong with being a shape-shifter - when it's intentional. When you can do it your way.

That's where true belonging happens when you show up with your whole, messy, multifaceted self.

When Adaptation Isn't Enough

Adaptation taught me a lot - but not about fitting in. The real lessons came from learning how to stand out with empathy.

Like a long ride through changing terrain, I learned that blending in is sometimes necessary to get through the day - but standing tall in who you are is what gets you to where you actually want to go.

One of the greatest gifts of living between worlds is curiosity. When you grow up translating cultures and emotions, you get good at asking the right questions - often before you even realise you're doing it.

And curiosity builds bridges. It's the difference between "what do you do?" and "what do you love?"

Respect Is a Two-Way Street

Respect doesn't mean shrinking yourself so others feel comfortable.

True respect - the kind that fosters real connection - means showing up as you are and offering the same openness in return. I've learned that while it's powerful to honour the cultures and communities you step into, it's just as powerful to ask for your space to be honoured, too.

That's the heart of inclusion: being invited in, having a voice, and knowing your voice will be heard and valued.

Or as prominent diversity advocates Liz Fosslien and Molly West Duffy say: Diversity is having a seat at the table, inclusion is having a voice, and belonging is having your voice heard.

Adaptation Is a Dialogue, Not a Performance

There's a moment in every room where you make a choice: perform, or participate.

I've done both. When you're used to shape-shifting, it's easy to slide into performance mode - playing the part, hitting the right notes. But the most honest, lasting connections came when I treated adaptation as a dialogue, not a disguise.

The real magic happened when I dropped the act and brought my full self to the table. That's when people leaned in. That's when conversations went from polite to powerful.

Empathy as a Superpower

Being a cultural chameleon sharpened my empathy in ways I never could've learned from a book.

As a sensitive, natural and instinctive observer, I pick up the vibe easily. I notice the quiet hand half-raised, the clenched jaw, the conversation that changed tone mid-sentence. These little cues became my GPS for deeper human understanding.

Empathy is about being *tuned in*. And when you're tuned in, you can create spaces where others feel safe to unmask, too.

The Courage to Stand Still

Sometimes, the boldest thing you can do is not to adapt but to stop.

To stop shifting. To stop second-guessing. To stop contorting yourself into what the room expects and simply *be*.

The most powerful moments in my life - the ones that changed something, even if quietly - came when I stood still. When I said, "*Actually, no. That's not okay*". When I chose values over comfort. Integrity over acceptance. My voice over silence.

Adaptation got me through the door. But standing still in my truth? That's what turned the room into a place I wanted to stay.

These are the lessons that shape how I show up in the world - not as someone trying to belong, but as someone inviting others to belong, too. Because when you ride in your own rhythm, with your own colours blazing, you create your own path - and you become a signpost for others who may be looking for one.

Tuning Up: From Fitting In to Gathering with Intention

The way we gather matters. It shapes the stories we tell and the connections we build.

Priya Parker

Priya Parker, in The Art of Gathering, invites us to rethink how we come together - and why it matters. Her work is a guide for anyone who has ever felt like an outsider learning to navigate unfamiliar rooms.

Many of us were raised to blend in. We learned to read the room, adapt, stay agreeable. But Parker challenges that reflex. She reminds us that gatherings - whether meetings, meals, or milestone moments - have the power to create genuine belonging when they're shaped with clarity and care.

The difference between showing up out of habit and showing up with purpose is intention. When we stop asking *How can I fit in?* and start asking *What am I here to create?*, the space itself changes.

Lessons from Parker on authentic connection:

Define the purpose. *Before entering a space, ask why it exists and what role you want to play. Purpose anchors presence.*

Create brave spaces. *Replace politeness with honesty. True belonging requires room for truth and care to coexist.*

Be a generous host. *Bring curiosity, attention, and respect wherever you go. The energy you bring sets the tone.*

Belonging doesn't always mean inclusion at any cost. Sometimes it means setting boundaries that protect honesty and care. You don't have to wait for someone else to create that kind of space. You can shape it, simply by how you show up.

Reflective Pause: Shifting, Shaping, Showing Up

Every room tells a story. The question is: are you following the script or rewriting it?

When was the first time you noticed yourself adapting to fit in?

Where do you still shift or translate parts of yourself to make others comfortable?

How would it feel to lead with intention instead of accommodation?

What changes when you stop blending and start shaping the space you're in?

You don't have to fit the room.
You can redesign it.

Find the people who hand you tools, not templates - mentors and allies who help you build rooms where you belong.

STAGE SEVEN
Seeing the World Differently: Navigating Life's Intersectional Highways

We are not one thing. We are a kaleidoscope of identities, perspectives, and experiences.

Laverne Cox

Life doesn't unfold in straight lines - at least, mine hasn't. It's more like a winding road trip across changing terrain. No single map can capture it all.

Each of us carries a mix of identities, experiences, and beliefs. Some are on full display. Others are tucked beneath the surface, like winding backroads only we know how to navigate. For me, those intersections - being a woman, an immigrant, neurospicy, and a cultural nomad - don't fit neatly into boxes. They don't stay in their lanes. They weave, merge, sometimes crash into one another.

And yet, in those moments of collision and crossover, I've found something solid. Belonging. Resilience. A perspective that sees the world not in binaries but in bold, brilliant mosaics. It's not always comfortable. But it's honest. And that's where the real power lives.

Understanding Intersectionality: A Kaleidoscope of Experiences

The term *intersectionality* was coined by Kimberlé Crenshaw in 1989 when she was researching the disadvantages faced by black women and how that differed from what black men or white women faced. Her theory describes how different aspects of identity - such as race, gender, and class - intersect and influence one another.

This is something I've lived for as long as I can remember - albeit from a very privileged standpoint. The experience of moving through the world with layers - some visible, some hidden - each shaping how I show up, how I'm seen, and how I connect.

For me, intersectionality has always felt like navigating a multilane highway, each lane representing a different part of who I am. Sometimes those lanes flow easily side by side. Other times, they compete for space, creating tension and the need to slow down, take stock, and figure out which direction to follow.

One of the earliest times I felt the pull of these intersecting identities was in Botswana. I was definitely "different", I was a walking intersection. My skin, my accent, my cultural references - they all marked me as a foreigner. For me, it was always about finding my way in. My curiosity, my openness, and my genuine effort to learn Setswana and take part in local traditions became powerful bridges. I still remember the pride I felt when I learnt to greet people in their own language and culturally appropriate. It was more than language - it was being seen, one word at a time.

Those intersections kept showing up throughout my life. As an adult, I found myself living and working in countries where I didn't speak the language fluently - Brazil, Chile, India, Hong Kong, the US. But connection doesn't always require perfect grammar. In Italy, I was welcomed into homes and hearts by people who didn't speak much English. We laughed, danced, and shared meals, our conversations stitched together by gestures, facial expressions, and a shared willingness to understand.

These moments have taught me that intersectionality is about far more than identity - it's about intentional connection. It's about recognising the layers we each carry and choosing to meet people where they are, with curiosity, humility, and a deep respect for difference. The road is rarely without its bumps, but it is endlessly rich.

When Vision Outruns the Room

Being able to adapt and connect across cultures can feel like a superpower - until it turns on you. There are moments when being "different" leaves you feeling unanchored, drifting between places and people but never quite landing. It can be a quiet ache - familiar yet hard to explain. For me, those moments have been more prominent while I have been in situations where I should fit in and feel safe. Like returning to Norway from Africa, or joining groups on the same mission as me. These moments, while humbling, have shaped my resilience and deepened my empathy.

I've always loved change. The unknown excites me - it energises me. I could happily sit at a bus or ferry terminal all day, watching people from every corner of the world come and go. For me, movement is life. Possibility. Even now, I get a little jolt of joy when boarding passes print or gate numbers flicker on a screen. There's something electric about change - when the engine's on, the road's open, and anything feels possible. Like when an unexpected journey turns into a meeting of aligned humans on similar journeys.

But loving change doesn't always mean I *land* it well.

Sometimes, I see what needs fixing before others even know something's broken. So I jump in - 'full throttle and torque' - ready to improve, transform, *help*. Especially when I think I'm among like-minded people - my "crew". But I've learned that vision, when it outruns the room, can feel more like a wrecking ball than a gift. In my work as a digital transformation leader, I often remind others to bring people into the process early, so they feel seen and heard. So they feel part of the journey and ready for the transformation. Turns out, that advice was just as relevant for me.

Take, for instance, the sensory chaos of busy airports - blinking lights, overlapping conversations, the clatter of heels and luggage on polished floors. For some, it's overstimulating. But not for me. I find peace in that motion. Airports feel like portals - places where the whole world passes through. I'm anonymous there, watching humanity swirl and converge in a kind of beautiful, messy harmony.

It's in offices, not terminals, where I've felt the static. In professional spaces where the rhythms are unspoken and expectations unvoiced, my neurospicy brain often struggled to sync. I'd pick up on everything - and nothing clearly. That's when the overload hit. Not from movement, but from misalignment.

But it wasn't only the physical space. It was the social static too - the moments when someone's words didn't match their body language, or when I missed the unspoken cues baked into office cultures. The incongruence or duplicity of human communication. I'd walk out of meetings wondering if I'd said too much, laughed too loudly, or completely missed the point.

One moment that stuck with me happened at a networking event. Small talk was the currency, and I was ready - keen to connect, to share ideas, to play my part. But the room was full of signals I couldn't read - the subtle pivots in conversation, the quiet nods that signalled inclusion or exclusion. It felt like I was dancing to music no one else could hear - or worse, music they'd decided didn't belong. This is why I often put my hand up to be part of the 'machinery' - the organising committee - so that I am there for a reason and don't 'have to' understand everyone.

These experiences made me want to retreat. Instead, I decided to recalibrate. It was near impossible to predict how others responded, but I could choose how I showed up. Instead of folding in on myself, I began to lean into self-

awareness. I paid attention, not just to the room but to my own rhythm. I stopped trying to match the beat and started trusting the ride.

It wasn't perfect. But it was mine.

Thinking about my airports again. They're built for movement, for in-between-ness. No one expects you to stay long. Everyone is headed somewhere. There's permission to just *be* - no mask, no performance.

Embracing Complexity: Lessons from the Road

One of the most valuable lessons I've learned is that while embracing complexity may resolve contradictions - it is also about finding possibility within them. Life doesn't happen in tidy categories. We're layered. Messy. Whole. A mosaic of who we've been, where we've come from, and who we're becoming.

Early in my career, I felt pressure to adjust myself for the comfort of others - make myself lesser. Was I the ambitious professional or the empathetic mentor? The creative problem-solver or the diligent organiser? It felt like the world wanted me to pick a lane. Life is not a series of neat lanes - it's a winding highway of experiences.

During an offsite strategy meeting, we were asked to share our defining moment. Others recounted single moments of triumph or failure. I couldn't choose just one. So I offered vignettes - my childhood in Botswana, my time navigating male-dominated industries, and my unfolding neurospicy self-awareness. Each was a lane on my highway, together painting the picture of who I was.

To my surprise, that honesty seemed to resonate. Colleagues opened up about their own complexities. I realised that authenticity is about more than being seen - it's about helping others feel safe to be seen too.

Building Bridges Across Highways

One of the gifts of embracing intersectionality is that it tunes your awareness to others' intersections too. When you own your own complexity, you become more curious about the paths others have travelled.

Some of my most meaningful connections have come not from sameness but from leaning into difference with curiosity. Like a chance meeting with a young woman of colour from Costa Rica while exploring Rio de Janeiro. We ended up travelling around the country together. We must have been the most unlikely pair - scruffy, tall, outspoken, blonde Viking woman alongside an immaculately dressed, young, very dark, petite Costa Rican. We got so many weird looks and had so much fun telling people we were sisters or cousins. We found shared ground in our love of fairness and humour.

Connection and inclusion, I've learned, is making space for and celebrating differences.

Sometimes, it's the simple acts that open the door: asking someone to share their perspective, pronouncing their name properly, genuinely wanting to know their story. These small bridges cross big distances.

Real connection can be built on similarity in a variety of dimensions. And it's fuelled by respect.

The Superpower of Seeing the World Differently

When you've spent your life navigating intersections, you develop a kind of superpower. You start to see connections where others see walls, ask questions others might not think to ask, and approach challenges from angles many wouldn't consider.

For me, this superpower wasn't something that emerged over time. From being the only European girl at a school in Botswana to being the only woman in the room at work, every experience sharpened my ability to adapt and connect across divides.

Sharing your complexity can be a gift. It can be the bridge someone else needs to cross from isolation to connection.

Seeing the world differently opens you up to connect deeply - even when language and culture don't align. I've found that curiosity is the closest thing we have to a universal language.

In Brazil, where I was still trying to get my head around a language that sounded nothing like the Portuguese I had picked up in Portugal, I shared meals and stories with people who didn't speak English. Through gestures, laughter, and a willingness to understand, we connected with surprising ease.

And then there was the cab ride in Sardinia, Italy. The driver was older, deeply rooted in his language and traditions. I spoke barely any Italian; he spoke no English. But we both wanted to connect. So we tried. Bit by bit, sentence

by broken sentence, we shared stories about our families, our countries, our journeys. That ride stayed with me - we could barely communicate, but the effort, the warmth, and the mutual respect in the trying, made me feel warm and fuzzy.

That's what complexity feels like to me - travelling the world and meeting new people. A hundred languages in the air, a thousand stories passing by. And I love it. Airports, train stations, bus and ferry terminals may seem chaotic, but to me they're choreography. I can people-watch for hours from a cafe in a busy tourist town, calm and anonymous, just watching the world come together and scatter again. It's like witnessing life in motion: hellos, goodbyes and reunions, nerves and excitement, all swirling together in one giant heartbeat.

Or it's the pulse of a South Asian street at dusk - horns blaring, chai brewing, conversations crisscrossing like wires. It might look like chaos, but there's a rhythm in it. A rhythm I feel at home in.

These experiences remind me that while intersections can feel like barriers, they're also doors - if we're willing to step through them.

The Gift of Perspective

When you don't fit neatly into one box, you start seeing what others might miss. You notice the small dynamics - the unspoken rules, the micro-shifts in tone, the stories beneath the surface.

It's a gift that's helped me build deep friendships, and one that's been invaluable professionally - especially when advocating for inclusion or challenging assumptions that go unchecked.

Being different isn't always easy, but it gives you a kind of X-ray vision. You see both the beauty and the blind spots in systems, conversations, and cultures. And when you use that vision with intention - to build shared purpose instead of just observing - it becomes a catalyst for change.

Finding Connection Across Highways

One of the most powerful lessons I've learned from navigating life's intersectional highways is this: when you acknowledge your own complexity, you become better at recognising it in others. Intersectionality is about celebrating differences and at the same time exploring the ways we can connect more deeply, when we choose to meet each other with curiosity and care.

I've seen this play out in both personal and professional spaces. As a mentor and coach, I've worked with people standing at the crossroads of race, gender, culture, and ambition. Many of them felt pulled in opposing directions - torn between who they truly were and who they thought they had to be to succeed. I knew that feeling intimately.

So instead of offering polished advice on how to "fit in", I asked them different questions:

"What if you could lead in your own way?"
"What if your strengths - not others' expectations - shaped your path?"

Those conversations were about coming home to themselves. They were about helping them feel whole, seen, and capable of leading without erasing any part of who they are.

That's what connection across highways looks like. Recognising the bumps or differences as part of a richer, more layered map - and then saying, "Let's walk this together".

Friendships Forged Through Shared Complexity

Some of my most meaningful friendships began in "misfit moments" - those instances of quiet recognition when you realise someone else is dancing to a similar off-beat rhythm.

I met one such friend during my first formal leadership role in the tech industry. We were both navigating the same maze of unspoken rules and invisible hierarchies. We connected over frustrations, yes - but also over our shared belief that our differences weren't disadvantages. They were our leverage.

That friendship became a lifeline. It turned a difficult workplace into one of growth, shared wins, and the kind of camaraderie that keeps you grounded.

Respecting Differences Without Needing Sameness

Connection does not require us to erase what makes us different - it's about respecting it.

You don't have to share the same intersections to walk alongside someone. In fact, you will struggle to find two people with the same intersectionality. You just need curiosity, empathy, and the willingness to stay open.

As a leader, I've tried to build environments where people don't have to shrink to be seen. Where accents, quirks, and layered stories are not just welcomed, but valued.

Because when we meet each other fully - without needing to mirror one another - we build something deeper. We turn the journey from a solo ride into a shared roadtrip.

Finding Your Crew: When the Vibe Just Clicks

Not all friendships are built slowly over time. Some arrive like lightning - instant recognition, a shared laugh, and the unshakable feeling of having found your people.

Just before I moved to Australia, I was invited to a party at a motorbike club in Oslo. I wasn't expecting anything beyond a fun evening, but what I found was a group of people who felt like home. We connected quickly, and someone put words to the magic - we shared the "same reference background". It wasn't a formal phrase, but it stuck. A shorthand for shared values, similar outlooks, an unspoken alignment that made being together feel easy and real.

Years later, I found that same connection again in a motorbike club in Sydney, founded by a woman who believed women should ride, not just pillion. She may also have secretly thought that having a motorcycling club could be a great way to meet great guys, or maybe that's just me. At the time, women made up at least 40% of the riders - a beautiful inversion of the usual stats. Many of us joined not just for the love of the ride, but because the men in the club respected us, welcomed us, and shared our values. That, to me, was everything.

It's not just about motorcycles, though. I've had that same feeling with people from wildly different walks of life. There's a kind of resonance you can't always explain - it's values-based, not surface-level.

When I left Norway for what I thought would be a max three-year adventure in Australia, I had a huge circle of friends. My farewell party - held at the bike club - was packed with people I loved. Bands played, glasses clinked, stories flowed. And then, a send-off at the airport from a wild mix of friends and family.

I remember wearing my orange top and purple jeans so the people picking me up would recognise me - only to land and find I was on my own. I have no idea how they got a message out. No mobile phones in 1996. Just me and a taxi driver trying to find the Oracle office. Imagine the bemusement at my eclectic attire when I reported in at the office at a time where there was only one "mufti day" (casual wear day) per month.

But even in this new world, I found my people again. At Oracle, I bonded with an international crowd. Mostly single, definitely child-free, making good money - and ready to make the most of it. It was party time and possibility.

Years later, what started as a plan to buy an investment property in Perth, became a full-blown life pivot. I called a former manager and friend - someone I respected deeply - for advice on where to buy a property in Perth. Without missing a beat, he suggested it might be time to move and help him build his tech team. Within days, he flew me over, lent me his car, and showed me around. By day four, I had bought a house, accepted the job, and committed to a whole new chapter.

So I packed up my Harley, my worldly possessions, and my two Bullmastiffs, and flew across the country to my little cottage in sunny Walyalup (Fremantle), south of Boorloo (Perth). But as sun-soaked as it was, Western Australia had a very different rhythm. I didn't know anyone. Social circles felt impenetrable. And thanks to a motorbike injury that left me with migraines, even a light beer to take the edge off wasn't an option. The shyness crept in - and for the first two and a half months, I felt deeply alone. No crew. No cues. Just me, my dogs, and the unsettling hum of "what have I done?"

Until January 17, 2005.

I was introduced to a group who'd just returned from South Africa. And boom. There it was again. That shared reference background. That knowing. That instant sense of fitting together. Within days, I had a tribe of 50. Not by blood or birth, but by resonance.

And just this past year, I've found it again - a group of women with entrepreneurial spirits, big hearts, and even bigger dreams. We are radically honest, wildly supportive, and deeply relieved to have each other. Our own little pod. A safe space on the journey.

It's not about sameness. It's about resonance. It's about that inner click that says, "*You see me.*" And really, what more could any of us ask for?

Your Intersections Are Your Superpowers

For years, I wanted to blend in. But I've come to realise: true inclusion happens when you show up with your whole, messy, multifaceted self.

Your intersections - cultural background, neurospicy mind, immigrant story - are your core strengths. They allow you to build bridges, challenge the status quo, and shape spaces where we invite complexity - and celebrate it.

So if you've ever felt like you don't fit into one category, take heart. The world doesn't need more sameness. It needs more people who see things differently. Your intersections are the key to your impact. Your legacy.

That's what complexity feels like to me - like the chaos and calm of an international terminal. A hundred languages in the air, a thousand stories passing by. And I love it. I don't need everything to make sense. I just need the freedom to move through it with curiosity. To chart my own flight path.

Towards a more connected world where we celebrate differences and everyone feels welcome, valued and inspired when they show up as themselves - full throttle and torque.

Tuning Up: Understanding Intersectionality and the Power of Multiple Identities

When facts do not fit our understandings, we have a choice: we can discard the facts, or we can discard the understandings.
Kimberlé Crenshaw

Intersectionality helps us see how different parts of identity combine to shape experience. It does not flatten people into categories. It clarifies why two people can stand in the same place and face very different barriers and possibilities.

Crenshaw's insight is practical. If someone is hit at a crossroads, you need to know which directions the traffic came from to respond with care. The same is true in life. Gender, race, class, sexuality, ability, age, culture, and migration can intersect to amplify harm or reduce access. When we ignore the angles, we miss what is actually happening.

For many of us who have felt like outsiders, this lens offers relief. It validates complexity. It explains why some rooms feel heavier to enter and why the same behaviour is judged differently depending on who you are and where you stand.

Using an intersectional view means you ask better questions and design better responses.

Practical applications:

Name the crossroads. *Notice which parts of identity are active for you or others in a given space.*

Check the default. *Whose needs does this policy, process, or tradition assume as standard. Who is left out.*

Design for edges. *Build practices that work for those at the margins first. Everyone benefits when the edges are considered.*

Honouring the full story is not about perfection. It is about precision and care. When we see the angles, we see each other more fully.

Reflective Pause: Riding in Your Own Rhythm

Complexity is not a burden. It is a map.

Which intersections shape how you move through the world right now?

Where have you been asked to simplify your story to be accepted?

What shifts when you honour your differences and invite others to do the same?

How might treating your complexity as a strength change one decision this week?

Your rhythm is not a glitch. It is guidance.

And sometimes, the right company helps you keep the beat - mentors, allies, or guides who remind you that your complexity is your composition.

STAGE EIGHT
The Misfit Chronicles

Why fit in when you were born to stand out?

Dr. Seuss

Some people spend their whole lives trying to fit into the molds society hands them. But for those of us who've always felt a little "otherly", fitting in can feel like riding someone else's bike - awkward, constricting, not made for your frame.

I've always known I wasn't designed to be small or quiet. I was born to take up space, ask questions, and challenge the status quo. But knowing that and embracing it are two very different things.

This stage is about the moments that taught me to stop trimming my edges to fit in - and to lean into my differences instead. It's about how being a misfit turned from something I thought I had to fix into something I've come to see as a superpower.

The Art of Masking

Many of us learn to mask early - an invisible shield we use to blend in when standing out feels too risky. For me, it started in childhood as a way to navigate social expectations that never quite fit the shape of who I was.

I learned to dial down my excitement, even when my head was bursting with ideas. I trained myself to follow the unspoken scripts, to hold back the endless questions, and to stifle the laughter that sometimes came at all the "wrong" moments. I became hyper-aware of how I was perceived, constantly adjusting to avoid judgment or rejection.

At some point, I started believing my ideas weren't good enough. But now I know they didn't lack merit - I was often too far ahead. I was trying to solve problems before others even saw there was one. My speed became noise in rooms that weren't tuned for it. So I slowed myself down to match a tempo that wasn't mine.

But the cost of masking was steep. The more I toned down my quirks and energy, the more disconnected I became - from others, from joy, and from the most honest version of myself. If I didn't feel accepted, I felt invisible.

Much later I started to understand the toll it had taken. Every moment of pretending chipped away at my sense of belonging - I knew I was welcome, but I felt that I was leaving parts of myself outside the room.

A Lesson in Unmasking

In an earlier chapter, I share a moment when I first unleashed my differentness. After a lot of deliberation and holding back, I decided to share: "I've spent much of my life feeling like I'm from another planet", I said. "My mind works differently, and I see connections that others miss. It's both a gift and a challenge".

I braced for awkward silence - but instead, heads nodded. Someone even said, "I've always felt that way too". That moment reminded me that unmasking doesn't always lead to rejection. Sometimes, it creates the very connection we were craving all along.

Why We Mask

Masking can feel like the only way to stay safe, especially when you're neurospicy, culturally different, or wired to see the world through a different lens. But the truth is, unmasking - showing up fully - isn't just liberating for us. It's a quiet invitation to others. It says: You're allowed to be real here.

Taking off the mask can shift a space. It creates a ripple of authenticity that gives others permission to stop performing and start being. And that's where true connection begins.

Misfit Moments That Shaped Me

Misfit moments have a way of leaving imprints on our lives, like skid marks on the road. For me, they were lessons in resilience, self-discovery, and learning to belong on my own terms.

My first week at a new school after yet another family move. I was determined to fit in. But I quickly learned that my accent and mannerisms marked me as *different*. I mimicked the local dialect and social cues, trying to blend in. On the surface, I succeeded. But inside, I felt like an imposter - disconnected from my true self for a while.

When I moved back to Norway from Botswana, the cultural shift hit hard. My stories, my rhythms, even the way I *saw* the world felt too foreign. I'd been changed by an experience most people around me couldn't understand.

Later, in high school, I remember being teased about my rural accent. Just harmless banter, the way teenagers do. But I hated it. I didn't want to be the odd one out. I started sanding down the edges, trying not to sound *too* country, too different.

And at university, surrounded by more affluent peers, I self-selected out of certain circles. Everyone was kind and welcoming, but I'd convinced myself I didn't belong.

Ironically, years later, a friend laughed and said, "It's funny how important it is for you to be *different*" - referring to the time I changed my lunch order just because she picked the same thing. We both cracked up, but she wasn't wrong.

The same girl who once tried so hard to blend in was now fiercely protective of her uniqueness.

Misfit moments like these taught me something essential: acceptance often begins with self-acceptance. You don't need to erase what makes you different - you need to own it, so others feel safe to do the same.

The Gift of Perspective

Being a misfit sharpens your ability to see things others might miss. When you don't quite fit into the expected mold, you learn to navigate the unspoken rules, notice the dynamics, and read between the lines.

This perspective has been a subtle kind of superpower in my personal and professional life. As a leader, it's helped me advocate for those who felt sidelined. As a friend, it's made me a better listener and more empathetic. And as someone who's often ventured beyond the marked roads, it's given me the courage to create spaces where others feel they belong.

The gift of being a misfit is the ability to bridge gaps - to see where people are disconnected and build connections where none seemed possible. Instead of seeing differences as barriers, I've learned to see them as opportunities to expand and enrich the conversation.

Turning Misfit Moments into Opportunities

I thought the goal was to stop feeling like a misfit - to finally belong somewhere. But I've learned that being a misfit is kinda cool - it's something to embrace.

Misfit moments can become opportunities for growth and connection when we reframe them. Here are a few lessons I've carried with me:

Celebrate Your Quirks
What makes you different is also what makes you valuable. Instead of hiding your quirks, find ways to use them as your fuel.

Build Your Tribe
Not everyone will get you, and that's okay. Focus on finding the people who do - the kindred spirits who see your value and cheer you on.

Redefine Belonging
Belonging means finding or creating spaces where you can be fully yourself.

Learn From Misfit Moments
Every time you feel out of place, ask yourself: What can I learn from this? How can I use this experience to grow or help others?

Advocate for Others
Use your experiences to support those who feel sidelined. Speak up, challenge exclusionary norms, and make room for others to shine.

When we own our misfit moments, they stop being sources of discomfort and become catalysts for transformation.

Finding Connection in Misfit Moments

Some of my most meaningful relationships have come from shared experiences of feeling out of place. There's something profoundly comforting about meeting someone who knows - without explanation - what it feels like to be a misfit.

One such connection happened during the early days of my career. I bonded with a colleague who also felt like they didn't quite fit the mould of what a "successful professional" should look like. We shared stories of awkward meetings, misunderstood humour, and moments when our ideas seemed to land sideways. But instead of shrinking from these experiences, we found confidence in each other's support.

It reminded me of a teenage friendship - one that cracked open a whole new understanding for me. She was the popular one, the golden girl, the one I thought had it all together. But one night, she shared what her family had been through, and I remember feeling like the ground shifted. That moment was the beginning of me realising that things that look "perfect" on the outside often carry invisible scars on the inside. It was the first time I truly understood that everyone has a story, and connection begins when we dare to listen for it.

Together, we turned our differences into assets, creating a friendship culture where individuality was celebrated. We were surviving the roadtrip - and we were thriving. We were finding joy in what made us unique, and using that as a foundation for change.

Being a misfit can feel lonely at times. But when you find connection in those moments, it's like discovering a lighthouse in the fog - proof that you're not navigating the world alone. It's about finding your crew. And daring to be fully, audaciously, unapologetically you.

The Strength of Standing Out

Standing out has never been the easy path - but it has always been worth it. For every moment of discomfort or misunderstanding, there's been a moment of profound growth, self-discovery, and unexpected connection.

Being a misfit gave me resilience - the kind that anchors you when others question your choices. It gave me the courage to challenge outdated norms and carve out new paths. And perhaps most importantly, it reminded me that what might look like chasing attention - may be about staying true to yourself, even when the world wants to edit out your differences.

I've come to see that there's real strength in being unapologetically different. It means bringing a unique voice to the table - one that adds depth, insight, and innovation. It also means creating strong spaces where others feel safe enough to stand out too.

The journey of being a misfit isn't about arriving somewhere you finally "belong". It's about finding peace in who you are - and knowing that the right people, the ones who truly see and value you, will find their way into your world.

But here's the truth I don't always say out loud: I still live in a place where I don't feel like I fully belong. I've been part of communities where showing up as my unfiltered self - the one who speaks up, sees solutions early, and jumps

in to make things better - hasn't always been welcome. Sometimes that felt like rejection. And sometimes, I now understand, it was my own sensitivity - my radar tuned so finely to potential rejection, I couldn't see the nuance.

That's why I'm sharing this. Because I know I'm not the only one. And because maybe, just maybe, naming it creates a little more space. A little more safety. A little more sense of home.

Tuning Up: The Power of Difference

It is not our differences that divide us. It is our inability to recognize, accept, and celebrate those differences.
Audre Lorde

Audre Lorde's words remind us that difference itself isn't the problem. The harm lies in what we do with it - in the ways fear, habit, or hierarchy teach us to mistrust what doesn't mirror us.

Lorde framed authenticity as activism. To show up as your whole self in a world wired for sameness is not indulgence; it is courage.

When we honour what sets us apart, we do more than liberate ourselves - we invite others to expand too.

The power of difference is relational. Each time we choose curiosity over judgment, or celebration over comparison, we strengthen the collective fabric. Communities thrive not through uniformity but through honesty.

Practical ways to lean into difference:

Challenge the script. *When you feel pressure to conform, pause and ask if it serves truth or just comfort.*

Celebrate daily wins. *Notice the small moments when you choose authenticity over fitting in.*

Amplify others. *When someone else steps forward in their truth, acknowledge it. A small gesture can be a lifeline.*

Standing out is not rebellion for its own sake. It is an act of service - a reminder that courage is contagious and inclusion starts with visibility.

Reflective Pause: Daring to Be Seen

Difference can feel risky, yet it is often where freedom begins.

Where in your life have you toned yourself down to be accepted?
When did you first learn that being different meant being "too much"?
What would it look like to treat those traits as power, not excess?
How might your openness make it safer for others to be real too?

You are not here to fit the frame.
You are here to expand it.

Surround yourself with those who see what you're building - mentors, collaborators, and allies who remind you that being seen isn't vanity. It's leadership.

THIRD GEAR

Shifting Gears - Unleashing Your Full Potential

*You may encounter many defeats, but you must not be defeated.
In fact, it may be necessary to encounter the defeats,
so you can know who you are, what you can rise from,
how you can still come out of it.*

Maya Angelou

As the engine roars and the road stretches ahead with unexpected turns, life shifts into higher gears. That's when the challenges show up - the kind that test your resolve, push your limits, and make you confront your fears head-on.

This part of the journey is your invitation to lean into your voice. To stop seeing struggle as a dead end, and instead as the spark that lights your resilience and self-discovery. Because sometimes it takes the rough terrain to teach you what you're really made of.

We'll explore the thresholds that shape us - the moments where comfort zones end and growth kicks in. Like turning a blind corner in the rain, unsure what's waiting ahead. These chapters unpack the lessons tucked into setbacks, the barriers we've ridden through, and the quiet superpower found in letting yourself be seen.

Whether it's in your relationships, your work, or the stories you tell yourself, this stretch of road is about harnessing your full potential by getting comfortable with discomfort, rewriting the scripts that no longer serve you, and riding your unique path with clarity and courage.

So, take a deep breath, check your mirrors, and settle into the saddle. This is where we rediscover our strength, remember what matters, and keep rolling forward - towards the next horizon.

STAGE NINE
Lessons from the Edge

You can't grow if you're comfortable.
Susan David

The edge is where we meet the truest version of ourselves - the unfiltered, unguarded self that emerges when comfort is stripped away. It's where the terrain gets rough, the weather turns, and the trail demands more from us than we thought we could give. It's where fear and courage collide.

For me, these edges came in many forms: navigating cultural shifts, fumbling through professional setbacks, and stepping into advocacy when silence felt safer. Each moment pushed me further than I thought I could go - and shaped who I became.

This stretch maps those edges. Like hairpin turns on a mountain road, they weren't always visible until I was right on top of them. But once I leaned in, I discovered something powerful: those sharp bends, those moments of unease, were where real growth happened.

Let's ride that edge together.

The Early Edges: Childhood and Survival

Life doesn't ask for permission before pushing you to the edge. Some of my first thresholds came long before I could define fear or resilience.

That moment that surfaces every time I have hypnosis or timeline theory. That time that I can do nothing about and still it rears it ugly head in everything I do.

Like that time when my mother stood outside the locked living room door, pounding to get in, while I held onto my younger brothers. Inside, my father was helping himself to the bottle stashed inside the bureau. I knew from an early age what was coming and braced myself.

Stay quiet.
Don't stir the waters.

My heart dropped to my gut.

I didn't want to upset him - because that could've spiraled into something catastrophic. But in that chaos, something steadier rose up in me. A calmness. Focused. Fierce.

I felt deeply connected to my mother, to my small brothers, and to my own need for stillness. I held them close, even as I shook inside.

That day, I learned something that would stay with me: when the world feels out of control, you focus on what you can. You show up where you can.

I was already learning the shape of resilience without understanding what it actually meant. Not the big kind that roars, but the quiet kind that whispers: *Hold on. Stay grounded. Keep others safe.*

Those early edges taught me more than any textbook ever could:

Strength doesn't always roar - it whispers through the storm. *Even as a young child, I understood that sometimes resilience is just holding it together long enough to get through the storm.*

Chaos can be a crucible. *I couldn't afford to panic. I had to stay present and focused. Looking after my brothers gave me purpose - and maybe, in my child's mind, a shot at deserving the love I so deeply craved.*

The Edge of Belonging

The edge is not just survival. Sometimes, it's something quieter but just as profound: the edge of belonging.

I first met this edge when my family moved from northern to southern Norway. On the surface, it was just a change of address. But underneath, it was a cultural shift that felt seismic. My musical northern dialect, my openness, my enthusiasm - they all marked me as different.

It was the first time I realised that standing out could feel both empowering and isolating.

My classmates' curiosity wasn't unkind, which is more than what I can say of the adults who had no filters when it came to criticising my mother who was older than my stepdad. I felt the subtle friction of being "otherly". My humour, my way of speaking, my sense of fairness - they didn't quite fit.

Instead of shrinking, I learned to adapt, supported by the most fantastic teacher one could wish for. I leaned into my difference without erasing myself.

Still, that's when I started to notice the quiet ache I'd later recognise as rejection sensitivity. The way my body would brace for judgment. The second-guessing. The micro-adjustments.

I was worried I would be too much for the room I was in.

Years later, that same edge showed up again - this time on another continent. When we moved to Botswana, I was an outsider in every visible way. My mother was a teacher at my school, and paired with me being the only European student, there was an expectation of privilege. As the fairness warriors we are in my family, we were very conscious of this and took every measure to minimise it.

Although there was one time I recognised - and appreciated - my privilege. One of my classmates twisted my finger during a tussle over a chair (there weren't enough, and I was holding one for a friend). I was in agony and felt sick to my stomach. I even asked to go to the bathroom - something I would never normally dare to do.

When I returned, the teacher wasn't there, so I asked my friend if she thought I could go to the staff room for help. She took one look at my sheet-white (more than usual) face and nodded vigorously.

Halfway there, I saw my teacher and my mum walking toward me. I almost collapsed in relief.

My mum took me to the hospital on her pushbike. Picture this, a 40 year old blonde Norwegian woman pedalling as fast as she can with a white haired dizzy kid hanging on for dear life through the village. A bumpy 30 minute ride - and after the usual delays caused by polite conversation, it turned out my finger was fractured - and I was in shock.

I was a child among traditions and rhythms I didn't yet understand, but with a safe support system.

I never felt truly excluded.

I felt welcomed, seen, and inspired to co-create something beautiful. My curiosity became my bridge - learning to understand and communicate in the local tongue, sitting cross-legged, trading jokes and stories with my friends, showing deep respect for the culture that had opened its arms to me.

Sometimes, I stayed with my friend during school holidays while my family travelled. I got to join her family at their lands - country plots where the women and children tended the crops while the men were at the cattle posts. I have this wonderful photo of myself, sitting on the porch with all the young kids around me while the adult women work the fields. A different kind of normal, but I was fully welcomed into the song and dance.

Those days felt soft and communal - and utterly alive. I was soaking in a new kind of acceptance.

I may not be everyone's cup of tea. I might never be a perfect fit in every room. But I could always find my rhythm - through curiosity, respect, and deep listening. These became my tools.

And they still serve me now, especially in new places. There's no judgment, just a spark of interest. No shape-shifting, just presence.

And that, I've learned, is enough to belong - exactly as I am.

The Professional Edge: Learning Through Failure

Stepping into professional spaces can mean stepping off a cliff into the unknown. It's where expertise is built, mistakes are inevitable, and resilience gets forged the hard way.

Early in my career, I found myself right on that brink.

My task was to code a database generator tool for large organisations - places like the University of Oslo. The stakes were high. Expectations were steep. The path? Completely unclear. I was young, driven, intelligent... and terrified.

My colleagues were great and I felt welcome despite being the only woman programmer on my team, and terribly insecure.

For the first few weeks, I was in a fog. I second-guessed every decision, replayed every meeting in my head, and feared that one wrong move would unravel everything. I worked hard. I followed the instructions I'd written. I tested everything thoroughly.

Then came the day I was asked to train the entire IT department from the university on how to use the system - while it was still in development.

These were brilliant people. Academics. Most were my seniors. One was even the wife of my boss.

Within five minutes of the first hands-on activity, they'd crashed the system. The server went down. It took half an hour to get it running again.

The embarrassment was suffocating. I felt exposed. But to my surprise, they were gracious and kind. That moment became a masterclass in humility and grace.

And a hard lesson in how my brain processed differently. I had followed the instructions exactly. But no one had told me that users don't follow instructions. They explore. They click randomly. They test boundaries. And suddenly, I realised: the way my brain was wired - logical, rules-oriented - wasn't universal.

I also realised something else, quietly but profoundly: You should never be the only one testing your own code.

When you're the creator, your blind spots go unnoticed. That moment became an early nudge toward the power of collaboration - and the necessity of building in checks, not just effort. Resilience was not just grit. It was about allowing in feedback, allowing in other eyes.

I learned something essential that day: I couldn't expect others to approach things the way I did. It was also the first time I realised I didn't have to do it all alone.

Rather than carrying the weight myself, I started to involve my colleagues. I even involved my manager and got him on my side, many years before I learnt the importance of "managing up" - aka proactively and strategically building a positive, productive relationship with your manager to ensure mutual success for you, your manager, and the organisation.

I broke down the project into smaller, manageable steps. Each one became its own goal. I reached out for advice. I listened to feedback without defensiveness. I let myself learn through the process instead of fearing it.

And slowly, the pieces began to fit.

By the end, the system worked - and so did I. I had grown in ways I hadn't expected. What had once felt insurmountable became a living reminder that persistence, adaptability, and collaboration can turn mountains into milestones.

I also learned something deeply personal: asking for help is empowering - it's wisdom. It was one of my earliest lessons in learning to receive, not just give.

The edge of failure refined me. And that's where real leadership starts: not in getting it perfect, but in learning how to keep going.

The Edge of Advocacy: Using My Voice

Advocacy doesn't usually start with a grand speech. It starts as a quiet discomfort - a sense that something isn't right. A gentle tug on your values. A whisper that says, *This matters*.

For me, that whisper showed up early in my career, when I entered the tech industry - a space largely dominated by men. The unspoken rules of who belonged echoed through meetings, decisions, and conversations. And I knew I wasn't the typical team member.

I remember sitting in a room full of seniors, feeling the weight of expectation. I wanted to challenge the status quo - I wanted to change the conversation. Not with defiance, but with clarity and purpose.

Norway, for all its fairness and egalitarian values, wasn't immune to imbalance. I discovered I was earning 10-15% less than my peers (mostly male). Not because I wasn't performing. Not because of my education and experience. Nobody had told me that I had to self-promote in addition to doing a great job. I was furious. It wasn't just unfair - it was unacceptable. With the help of my fantastic senior colleague who took me under her wings, I challenged it. And I won.

Not only did they adjust (or level) my salary, they gave me backpay for six months. It was worth the challenge, and I hope it inspires you to stand up for yourself too.

It is worth mentioning, though, that if I had gone head on and challenged the status quo in my typical unfiltered manner, the result may not have been as successful. Even with the guidance of my very experienced mentor, I put a few executive level noses out of joint, and I dare not think about what would have happened without her gentle nudges to be "professional".

Moral of the story? Make sure you have a mentor, coach or a sponsor for everything you set about to do.

Another defining edge came when I was asked to lead a diversity and inclusion initiative much later. On paper, it was an honour. In practice, it was an uphill climb - met with eye rolls, polite resistance, and the quiet dismissal of people who thought it was just another tick-box exercise.

Progress was slow. Some days, it felt like shouting into a void. But I reminded myself: it was never about applause. It was about impact. Every small shift - a revised policy, a braver perspective, a colleague finally feeling seen - became proof that the change was working.

Advocacy taught me that real influence is rarely loud. It's steady. It's consistent. It's the choice to speak when silence would be easier. To act, even when recognition doesn't follow.

And let's be honest - advocacy is messy. Sometimes it feels like pushing a boulder uphill. It's tiring. Lonely, even. But it's also where the real work lives. Where truth replaces silence. Where discomfort sparks momentum. Where change begins.

The edge of advocacy is both heroism and heart. It's where you decide that the discomfort of staying silent is greater than the risk of being seen.

Tuning Up: Lessons in Courage and Connection

We don't even know how strong we are until we are forced to bring that hidden strength forward.
Isabel Allende

When it comes to walking the edge between fear and courage, Isabel Allende's words remind us that strength isn't forged in comfort - it's discovered in motion.

Real courage doesn't roar; it rises quietly when we choose to act, even while afraid.

True connection begins here - not in perfection, but in presence. When we allow ourselves to be real and to risk being seen, we make space for others to do the same. That's how courage ripples outward.

Strength and vulnerability are not opposites. They are twin forces that move us toward authenticity - requiring honesty, boundaries, and heart.

Practical lessons from the edge:
Lean into discomfort. *Growth doesn't happen in the safe zones. When fear whispers "not yet," take one small step anyway. Breathe. Keep moving.*

Be clear and kind. *Strength without compassion becomes armour. Speak truth with calm intent - it builds trust and deepens connection*

Normalise the fall. *Falling isn't failing. It's how we learn to steer through uncertainty and rise with a steadier hand.*

Courage isn't about endless endurance. It's about leading from wholeness - knowing when to rest, when to rise, and how to meet both with grace.

When we dare to bring strength and softness to the same table, we don't just survive the edge - we transform it.

Reflective Pause: A Moment at the Edge

Edges are invitations. They ask you to meet yourself one step further than before.

Where in your life do you feel that edge right now - the stretch between fear and growth?

What truth is asking to be spoken, even if your voice trembles?

How could honesty deepen trust in one relationship or project?

What might shift if you treated your edge not as a warning but as a welcome?

This is not the cliff.
It's the view.

And you don't have to stand there alone. Find the people who steady you at the edge - mentors, guides, and fellow travellers who remind you how far you've already climbed.

STAGE TEN
Trailblazing Through Barriers

Well-behaved women seldom make history.
Laurel Thatcher Ulrich

Breaking barriers doesn't always look like fireworks or fanfare. Sometimes, it's the quiet defiance, the calculated risks, the everyday acts of courage that rewrite the map.

Trailblazing is about carving your own road through landscapes that weren't designed with you in mind. Whether it's challenging gender norms, navigating unfamiliar cultural terrain, or speaking up in a room that wasn't built for your voice, every brave step forward expands what's possible - not just for you, but for everyone coming behind you.

Introduction: The Road Less Traveled

You don't smash through barriers in one dramatic moment. It's more often a series of small, deliberate choices - a step off the beaten path here, a risk taken there - that slowly shift the terrain.

For me, trailblazing has never been about applause or proving anyone wrong. It's been about carving a route where none existed, for myself and for others like me.

Whether it meant finding my voice in male-dominated industries, challenging cultural expectations, or standing up to my own inner doubts, every forward step called for courage, creativity, and the willingness to lean into the discomfort of the unknown.

The First Barriers: Gender and Expectations

Growing up in Norway, I was surrounded by strong women - my mother, my grandmothers, my aunts. Women who led, worked, volunteered, parented, cooked, and carried an almost invisible load with grace and grit. The stories they told, and the values we lived by, were full of fairness.

I grew up believing that everyone should have equal opportunities, regardless of gender. It was in our language. In our laws. In our books. So I expected the world to follow suit.

But reality told a more complicated story.

Even in our home, I noticed the quiet division of roles. The women often picked up the caregiving, even as they worked outside the home and gave endlessly to their communities. The men did other things. It wasn't said outright - but I noticed. There was a subtle mismatch between what I was told and what I observed.

I remember feeling a quiet envy at school watching friends unpack sandwiches lovingly wrapped by their mums - cut into triangles, maybe even with a note tucked inside. At our house, we made our own lunches. It was just how things were. But even then, I could feel the imbalance. My mum was juggling so much, and yet the expectation of care still fell on her shoulders. It didn't feel fair. My stepdad always made his sandwiches the day before as he was up at the crack of dawn (or earlier actually at 5am) to get to work in time.

But before fairness became a theme, that experience taught me something else: independence.

I could fend for myself, plan ahead, carry what I needed.

And even though I felt the weight of that quiet unfairness, I also learned early that survival - especially as a girl - sometimes meant figuring it out on your own.

Fairness became a theme. Not just in gender, but in every system I looked at.

I even went on women's rights marches with my mum in the mid-70s - tiny feet walking alongside loud voices. I think my stepdad came too. I was convinced we were going to fix it all. It was exhilarating for a tween with big ideas.

When it came time to choose my path, I only had a few clear criteria:

I wanted to prove that women could do what men could - and be paid well for it.
I wanted to study overseas, with people from different places, cultures, and stories. (England in the '80s was perfect for that.)
I wanted to do something that could create meaningful change.

I dabbled. Teaching - my parents, grandparents, and my wonderful primary school teacher. Hairdressing - my auntie. Carpentry - my stepdad. Medicine - Africa. Engineering - because I mastered math and science. Law - because the world needed fixing. Psychology - because our minds needed fixing. Then, one day, it clicked: technology would underpin everything. And I could be at the heart of it - building systems, connecting people, creating impact.

This was the early 1980s - no internet, no smartphones, no AI - although I first met AI in 1986. Tech wasn't sexy. It was niche, clunky, and deeply male-dominated. But something in me saw the future it could hold.

Where others saw wires and code, I saw connection. I saw the impact. I couldn't explain it fully - but I knew.

That decision was a line in the sand: I would not shrink to fit someone else's version of womanhood. I would carve out my own.

Student Daze: Expectations, Epiphanies, and Eye Rolls

Studying Computation in Manchester in the 1980s was fun - but mostly for what happened *outside* the lecture halls. Manchester had more students than any other city in Western Europe and was pulsing with music, fashion, and people from all over the world. Socially, I was in heaven.

Academically? That was more complicated.

Norwegian students like me had to complete a Foundation Year to level the differences in education systems - though it often felt like a clever way to extend our stay since the Norwegian government paid our fees. We were thrown into physics, science, chemistry, and two kinds of maths, taught by a revolving door of middle-aged, pasty, white men with limited social skills and even less interest in teaching. It felt irrelevant, rigid, and at times, ridiculous.

I remember calling my mum in tears one Easter break, declaring that all we did was "code, code, code" - no interaction, no connection, no psychology of any kind. I wanted out. But the drive that had brought me here - the belief that tech would shape everything and that I could make a difference - pulled me back in.

There were few women in my cohort, around 15%, and even fewer role models in the faculty. But those of us who were there were proud. We felt like we were at the front of something new - a gender-equal industry on the rise.

Spoiler alert: that prediction didn't quite pan out. The percentage of women in key roles has dropped over the past 35 years. Back then, it was closer to 35-40%. Today, I am told there are 25% women in technology roles and organisations. I don't trust the inflated numbers - because I'm on the ground, and I can see what's missing. I know that in Australia, the university that has the highest percentage of women studying information technology, only has 18% women with 95% being international students. And when they graduate, they are not getting job offers.

On a related note, when I speak with women who work in the creation of technology, the actual numbers are under 10% - if you look really hard.

I have a lot of theories on the broken recruitment system and what we need to do to get a more balanced industry, but that is an entirely different topic altogether. Even if we are part of the story.

Early Work Realities: Curiosity, Camaraderie, and Cracks in the Concrete

Fresh out of uni and brimming with optimism, I returned to Norway and landed a job at a large multinational tech company. It was everything I wanted: travel, innovation, and meaningful work. I even had my own half-office (shared, of course) and was greeted on my first day by the team's brilliant and under-credited team administrator.

Waiting on my desk were towering manuals on operating systems. These were not inspirational reads - they were ring binders packed with technical specs. By 9 am, my eyelids were staging a protest. At 10, I asked the secretary (yep, that's what her title was those days) about lunch. She raised her eyebrows - it was *way* too early for lunch, even in Norway. I was so bored, I had misread the time, which became a great source of entertainment as I got to know my way around the office.

Things improved quickly. Once I was given real problems to solve, I was hooked. I loved combining my creativity, empathy, and technical skill to design solutions. I was the only woman programmer initially, but was soon followed by a few others. I felt respected - for my technical know-how *and* my understanding of people.

The camaraderie was real. We were a little international family - working long hours, sharing jokes, and having each other's backs. It wasn't ideal for people who wanted families or children (especially women), but for me at the time, it worked.

I'd been interested in AI since university, but it was at Oracle in 1990 that I really got to explore more. What we worked on then was worlds away from the generative AI we see now - but it was foundational, and it was powerful. People are shocked when I say I've been in AI since the '80s. But I have proof.

One thing I noticed early - and never forgot - was that our department ran on the unspoken leadership of people like our highly efficient secretary. She was the one who kept us, and our bosses, afloat. She wasn't paid for that work. She wasn't recognised. But she led, nonetheless.

Later, when I stepped into formal leadership, I noticed a shift. I had always been respected for my technical and strategic thinking, for solving problems and connecting dots. But once I started managing teams and budgets, I hit what I call the *concrete ceiling*. The so-called glass ceiling wasn't just there - it was reinforced, heavy, and hard to crack.

It didn't matter how effective or innovative I was - there were rooms I suddenly wasn't invited into. My gender, my style of leadership, even my neurodivergent ways of thinking… they all became points of friction. But friction, as I've learned, is also what sparks fire.

Challenging Cultural Norms: Curiosity Without Judgement

Living in Botswana as a young Norwegian girl on the cusp of adolescence was, in many ways, an education far beyond the classroom. The contrasts weren't good or bad - they were just different. And for someone like me, wired for fairness and fascinated by people, they were deeply thought-provoking and exciting.

In many families I observed, roles were clearly defined - men were often at the bar drinking Bojalwa, the traditional sorghum beer, while women and even young girls prepared food, tended to children, and kept the home running. Sometimes, it felt imbalanced. Other times, it seemed like the women preferred it that way - like Kgabele, our maid and my sister's nanny, who used to laugh and say that having four children and no husband was a blessing. "A man would just be more work", she'd say with a twinkle in her eye.

And then there was Emily, our laundry lady. Her fury was volcanic the day she discovered that her husband of many years had taken another wife without telling her. I remember watching her navigate that heartbreak with a determination and fire that stayed with me long after. I thought she was an old lady then, but she was probably in her early sixties like me.

At home, there were quiet tensions around these same questions of gender and domestic roles. My mother, a full-time teacher, was resistant to the idea of hiring "help" - a resistance rooted in Norwegian values of equality and self-sufficiency. In our culture, outsourcing domestic work was often seen as elitist, even anti-feminist. The obvious thing to me was to share the chores and share the riches, but we know we still have a long way to go.

I've since seen this pattern in many migrant women's lives. Those coming from cultures where help is common often feel conflicted when they move to places like Norway or Australia.

They wrestle with what it means to be a "strong woman" in a new cultural context - yet somehow, the burden still always seems to fall back on the woman.

My mother, meanwhile, was constantly alert to the dangers young girls faced - especially the stories of sexual violence or the chilling whispers about witch doctors who targeted virgins for rituals said to boost a wealthy man's virility. Whether myth or reality, the fear was palpable, and I could feel her protectiveness tighten whenever I left the house.

One memory that really stayed with me was a traditional celebration - a multi-day feast for the baptism of Chief Linchwe's oldest son. Everyone in the village was invited. The air buzzed with energy and pride. There were songs, dances, and ceremonies that honoured history and culture in ways I found beautiful.

But I also noticed how the public proceedings - the Kgotla, a council traditionally led by male leaders - were entirely run by men. I wasn't judging. I just couldn't help but wonder: What if women ran the Kgotla? What might be different? That moment didn't spark defiance - it sparked a question. One of many I would carry with me as I began noticing power, structure, and inequity in every culture I touched.

Years later, walking through the *Terracotta Warriors* exhibition in Perth, I felt that same flicker of curiosity. Surrounded by row upon row of men cast in clay, I was struck by the absence of women - until I spotted a few female warriors, and the story of a Han Empress who had once ruled.

These are historical details. And they're patterns. Moments like the Kgotla and the Terracotta Warriors whispered the same deeper question: *Where are the women?*

It's a question I still ask - are we seeing the full picture? And if we don't see the women, who else are we not seeing?

Living in a vibrant and inclusive culture at such a formative age gave me more than stories - it gave me a hunger. A hunger to explore, to connect, to belong in unfamiliar places. That early sense of connection and curiosity shaped the way I move through the world. Whether I'm in a boardroom in Sydney, a marketplace in Hanoi, or a village in the Arctic Circle - I know how to listen, how to respect, and how to build bridges that span language, culture, and tradition.

That deep sense of global belonging has never left me. It's not rooted in sameness - it's built on curiosity, compassion, and the courage to meet people where they are.

The Intersection of Biases

For a long time, I knew I was different - I just didn't know how to express it.

I've always believed in a "different kind of normal". That we shouldn't all strive to be the same, but embrace what sets us apart. I knew I was different as a migrant, as a woman in tech, as someone who'd lived in several countries, as the daughter of an alcoholic, and later, as a woman over 50 still charting bold paths.

I didn't come across Crenshaw's Intersectionality Theory until 2018 while researching for a professional doctorate on gender diversity in the tech sector. Her words stopped me in my tracks. Here was a framework - finally - that captured what I'd felt for years but hadn't been able to articulate: that the layers of our identity don't exist in isolation. They intersect, overlap, and interact, creating unique experiences of both privilege and bias.

Crenshaw's theory helped me realise that many of the challenges I had faced weren't random or isolated - they were woven into the fabric of how society treats those who sit at multiple intersections.

It gave me language - and fuel - for something I'd long wanted to address: how we carry complex identities in spaces not built for complexity. In 2021, I initiated and chaired a panel titled *Same Same and Different* at a major conference, and for the first time, we brought intersectionality to the center of the conversation.

And then came another piece of the puzzle - one that hit closer to home.

After my siblings were diagnosed with ADHD and more, my brother challenged me directly whether I thought maybe I should get checked. I started exploring the possibility that my brain, too, was wired differently. The

signs had always been there - my intense focus, my pattern-seeking brain, my need for deep thinking, and my struggles with small talk and shallow systems. But I'd been masking so well, for so long, that I didn't even realise I was doing it. Discovering this was enlightening - it was a reframe. My neurodivergence was a lens through which I experienced the world.

And yet, these differences - when unseen or unsupported - can feel like weight. I firmly believe that we should embrace and celebrate differences. When people don't recognise your complexity, they often misunderstand your needs, your gifts and value, and even your silence. And that misunderstanding can be isolating.

But when those same intersections are recognised and embraced, they become a superpower. They give you perspective, insight, and empathy that others might miss. They allow you to bridge worlds - because you've lived in more than one.

That's why I speak up. Because when we acknowledge our intersecting identities, we stop trying to force ourselves into boxes that were never made for us. We begin to honour our full selves - quirks, contradictions, and all - and build spaces where others can do the same.

Becoming a Trailblazer

Trailblazing has never been about smashing through walls just for the sake of it. For me, it's been about walking paths where no clear roadmap existed - then quietly leaving markers so others might find the way a little easier.

I didn't set out to be a "trailblazer". I simply wanted to do good work, be treated fairly, and create positive change. But when the system isn't designed with you in mind, even ordinary progress can feel revolutionary.

And beneath it all, I held a bigger vision - a world where we celebrate differences rather than flatten them. A world that feels more connected, more inclusive. Where everyone feels welcome, valued, and inspired to bring their full self to the table.

That vision has guided me more than ambition ever did.

Over time, I learned to pick my battles - not every hill is worth the climb. But when it mattered, I showed up. I spoke up. I challenged outdated ways of thinking, even when my voice shook.

And I didn't do it alone.

One of the most rewarding moments came years into my career, when I had the chance to mentor a young woman just starting out in tech. She reminded me so much of myself - ambitious, thoughtful, full of ideas but unsure how to navigate a world that often mistook confidence for competence. I recognised that quiet fire in her. She just needed someone to reflect it back.

Watching her grow, succeed, and eventually lift others as she climbed - that was full-circle magic. That's what trailblazing is really about. Not spotlight. Not ego. Legacy.

Because the real power in breaking barriers is in turning around and holding the door open for the next person - not just crossing over them.

Tuning Up: Advocating for Your Place at the Table

It's not about fixing the women. It's about fixing the system.   Michelle Redfern

Fortune does favor the bold, and you'll never know what you're capable of if you don't try.   Sheryl Sandberg

I've had the privilege of knowing Michelle Redfern for several years, and I'm continually inspired by her unapologetic advocacy for women in leadership.

Through her work and her book *The Leadership Compass*, she reminds us that real equity isn't achieved by asking women to adapt, but by challenging systems that were never built for us.

Her compass calls us to navigate leadership with intelligence that's both strategic and human - blending business acumen, emotional awareness, and social connection. It's a reminder that progress isn't powered by perfection, but by participation.

Sheryl Sandberg, author of *Lean In* and former COO of Meta, has long championed the power of women stepping into leadership - often before they feel "ready." Her work reminds us that confidence grows through action, not perfection, and that many of us underestimate what we're capable of simply because we don't fit an outdated mould.

Sandberg's message isn't about waiting for permission. It's about taking a seat, speaking up, and creating space for others to do the same. Real advocacy begins when we recognise that visibility is impact.

Key takeaways from their work:

Lean into discomfort. *Growth often arrives wrapped in uncertainty. Step forward anyway.*

Don't go it alone. *Courage expands in connection. Seek out mentors, allies, and networks that lift you higher.*

Reframe bias. *When feedback feels unfair, use it as data - a reflection of system flaws, not your worth.*

Build a bigger table. *Advocacy isn't only about claiming space. It's about redesigning it so others can belong too.*

Trailblazing is about changing the landscape so others can follow with less resistance. Every time you speak truth, challenge bias, or hold the door open for someone else, you're helping reshape what leadership looks like.

Reflective Pause: Lighting the Way Forward

Advocacy starts in the room, but it grows in the quiet moments after - when you notice how your own courage might open doors for someone else.

Trailblazing is about showing up again and again - even when no one is watching.

Where have you taken a step, big or small, that changed your course?

What part of you is still waiting to be seen, heard, or valued?

Who might benefit from the space you've already cleared?

What if the courage you're building is already a signal for someone else?

You're further along than you think.
And you might already be someone's signpost.

Even trailblazers travel with allies - mentors, peers, and guides who help keep the path clear for those who come next.

STAGE ELEVEN
Harnessing the Power of Vulnerability

*Vulnerability is the birthplace
of innovation, creativity, and change.*

Brené Brown

For much of my life, I thought being strong meant standing tall, speaking with confidence, and never showing cracks. Vulnerability, on the other hand, felt like an unraveling - exposing parts of myself I'd worked hard to protect.

As a child, I never cried - I didn't want to be a bother. I ran away when people wanted to hug me (even if I secretly wanted the closeness). I remember coming home from university, and my friend who was picking me up came charging at me with a bear hug. I froze. I was extremely uncomfortable with public displays of affection. I was happy to pat a shoulder, but that's as far as it went. Looking back now, I can't help but wonder if that might be a neurodivergent trait - though I'm not going to speculate too much.

What I do know is this: for a long time, vulnerability felt dangerous.

But real strength? It's having the courage to be seen, especially when we feel most fragile.

It took years - and a lot of unlearning - to understand that vulnerability isn't weakness. It's a quiet kind of power. The kind that deepens trust, invites connection, and helps us embrace the beautiful messiness of being human.

Let's talk about that shift - from guarding to revealing. From perfection to presence. From fear to freedom.

The Masks We Wear

Growing up, I became a master of masking - a quiet kind of shape-shifting.

Not to hide my spark - that was always there. Bright, curious, full of energy. But I learned to turn the volume down. Because I noticed that not everyone could handle it, and to be fair, my shyness was inhibiting.

We moved a lot. And I knew, early on, that we were different. Aliens. Always the newcomers. So I studied the unspoken rules. I watched how others moved and interacted. And I adapted - just enough to blend in. I didn't talk about my family or the chaos at home. I didn't want pity. I wanted connection.

As I grew older and more confident in who I was, I carried some of that shape-shifting with me into professional spaces. But the context shifted.

Later in my career, I found myself working on a project with a team of introverted, methodical colleagues. They were thoughtful and brilliant - but not exactly comfortable with my high energy, quick thinking, or rapid-fire ideas. I could see it in their faces: the subtle pauses, the glances, the overwhelm. So, I slowed down.

I wanted them to feel heard. I've always known that listening is to make the other person feel truly seen. So I adjusted my pace, created space for them to contribute, and listened at their speed.

At times, I wondered if they understood how much of that shift was intentional. If they realised how hard it was to rein in that part of myself without losing my joy. But then, over time, something shifted. Trust built. Conversations deepened. And our collaboration flourished.

That experience reminded me: masking may not be related to hiding - it can be about care. But if the balance tips too far, if we contort ourselves too much, we lose the thread of who we are.

I've learned to ask myself: am I adjusting to connect, or am I disappearing to please?

Because I can adapt. I can meet people where they are. But I refuse to lose myself in the process.

The Connection Between Vulnerability and Strength

There's a paradox at the heart of vulnerability: it takes immense courage to let others see your struggles, your fears, and your imperfections. But when you do, the rewards can be profound.

In one of my first formal leadership roles, I was managing a diverse team - different personalities, different gifts, different needs. At first, I believed I had to lead from certainty. I thought being a good leader meant having the answers, staying composed, and never letting the cracks show.

Then came a high-stakes project. Tight deadlines, high expectations, and a whole lot riding on our success. I was overwhelmed and out of my depth. Instead of pretending to have it all under control, I took a breath and told my team the truth: "I don't have all the answers - but I believe we can figure it out together".

And something shifted.

Instead of losing confidence in me, my team stepped up. They shared ideas, offered support, and took ownership in ways I hadn't seen before. That honesty elevated me as a leader, and it deepened the trust between us. A few years later, a former team member called me out of the blue to strongly encourage me to apply for a role as his manager in a new company. I was honoured - and deeply moved. I'll wear that badge with joy for the rest of my life.

Vulnerability, I realised, is about creating space for others to bring their best. I did not have to have it all figured out - I just needed to be real, be open, and invite collaboration.

Vulnerability in Personal Relationships

For a long time, I was the strong one. I still am.

The one who held things together, looked after everyone else, and never dropped the ball. I took care of my siblings, my mum, and my friends. I knew how to be there for others. But somewhere along the way, I forgot how to let others be there for me.

It wasn't that I didn't want connection - I craved it. But real vulnerability? The kind where you let someone see behind the competence, the calm, the *"I've got this"*? That felt dangerous.

I thought asking for help made me a burden. I believed love had to be earned through doing. So I did. I over-functioned. And I became so good at looking after others that many stopped thinking I might ever need care in return.

It came to a head in a conversation with a friend and fellow coach. I told her I was tired of chasing clients - I wanted to become magnetic. She looked at me gently and asked, "How do you feel about receiving?"

There it was. The edge I hadn't wanted to face. It was about worth. About being valued for who I am, not just what I do. That moment cracked something open in me. I realised I had been avoiding the very thing I longed for - true, reciprocal connection - because I didn't know how to receive it without feeling exposed or undeserving.

And when that imbalance gets too much - when I feel taken for granted or like someone's leaning too hard without awareness - I can snap. I give sharp feedback, direct and unsparing. Unfortunately this sometimes happens with people who are a bit like me: high-functioning, human-doing, people-pleasing givers on the verge of burnout. I see them because I am them. Or at least, I've been them. And I want to help them step into their power.

I'm learning now that vulnerability is to allow yourself to be supported. To trust that your value is not superficial, and that real relationships have room for both giving and receiving.

I remember once, volunteering on a project where I felt deeply aligned with the mission. We were a group of smart, driven people trying to make real change - but every time I tried to articulate an idea, I could tell they didn't get it. I remember offering to write something up to explain it more clearly, only to be met with: "*Why can't you just say it now?*"

That moment stayed with me. It wasn't just a comment - it was a collision. Between how I process, how I communicate, and how easily those differences can be dismissed.

And here's the part I don't often say out loud: I feel deeply.

I can be bold. I can stand on a stage. But I also well up for strangers, for stories of injustice, for people less fortunate than me. That tenderness is a gift.

Yet when it comes to how I'm treated? I often just take it. Swallow it. Move on.

I've realised - that's not the advice I want to give.

We have to name it when something feels off. Even when that 'something' is us being sidelined, silenced, or expected to shape-shift beyond recognition.

The Cost of Guardedness

Of course, vulnerability isn't always met with warmth. There have been times when I've opened up and felt exposed - misunderstood, even bruised by someone's reaction. That kind of emotional hangover makes you want to retreat, to lock things up tighter next time.

But the alternative - keeping your walls up - isn't really safe. It's disconnection. It's loneliness wrapped in self-protection.

For years, I was the strong one. The go-to. The emotional rock for friends, family, teams. I rarely asked for help because I didn't want to burden anyone. I didn't think I could afford to fall apart, because someone always needed me whole.

Somewhere along the line, I'd internalised the message: *big girls don't cry*. So I didn't. Not in front of others, anyway. Not even by myself. I held it together with a smile, while the cracks quietly spread underneath.

Even now, I rarely talk about how hard the past five years of running a business have been - partly because I naturally focus on the positive, but also because vulnerability still feels uncomfortable.

But strength without openness becomes a fortress. And fortresses can repel connection.

Eventually, I started noticing a pattern. When I did get vulnerable - especially with people who mirrored my own people-pleasing tendencies - the relationship either deepened beautifully… or crumbled under the weight of unspoken needs and assumptions.

There's a tipping point. Being 'the strong one' becomes unsustainable. Sooner or later, you either burn out… or finally let someone in.

And when I don't let someone in soon enough - when I've ignored my own signals, stretched too far, or drowned in emotional noise - I've snapped. Sometimes, the ones I care about most get caught in the backlash.

It's not fair. It's not who I want to be. But it happens - especially when I've been running on empty, trying to hold it all together for everyone else.

I've had to learn that *not tending to my own overwhelm* doesn't make me noble. It makes me volatile. That lashing out isn't about them - it's a signal from my system that *I've abandoned myself*.

And so, if you've ever been on the receiving end of that edge in me - if you've felt my impatience or frustration when you deserved my presence - I'm sorry. And if you recognise that this is something you do too, be kind to yourself and the people around you.

I'm learning to name my needs sooner. To take a breath before the snap. To give the people I love the version of me that isn't just surviving.

That's what guardedness costs us. Not just intimacy, but ease. Joy. The relief of being seen without having to curate or perform.

Practical Steps to Embrace Vulnerability

So how do you go from being the fortress to being… well, real?

It doesn't require a dramatic reveal or a tearful monologue. It starts in the small, ordinary moments - the ones where you choose truth over polish, connection over performance.

Here are a few ways I've practiced softening the armour:

Start Small. Vulnerability might mean texting a friend when you're having a rough day instead of waiting until you're "fine again". It might mean saying, "Actually, I don't know", in a meeting instead of nodding along.

Reframe the Risk. If you've spent years hiding your messiness, vulnerability will feel risky. But what if the risk isn't in showing up - but in never being fully seen? What if hiding is the real gamble?

Listen Like It Matters. One of the gifts of vulnerability is that it's contagious. When someone opens up to you, resist the urge to fix. Just listen - fully, curiously. Let them feel held, not handled.

Give Yourself Grace. Letting your guard down might feel uncomfortable or even awkward at first. That's okay. Self-compassion is the companion to vulnerability. Be gentle with yourself as you navigate new emotional territory.

Notice the Relief. There's often a deep exhale that follows a moment of true vulnerability. Not because everything is resolved - but because you've stopped pretending. You've let yourself be known.

The Rewards of Vulnerability

For so long, I thought vulnerability was something you had to manage - contain, control, keep in check.

Now, I see it for what it truly is: one of the most liberating forces in my life.

Letting myself be seen - mess and all - has deepened my friendships, transformed my leadership, and brought more meaning into the quiet moments of connection. It's allowed me to stop striving to be the strong one all the time and start being the real one.

The kind who can say "I don't know", or "I need help", without shame.

The kind who laughs loud, cries when it matters, and tells the truth even when it shakes a little.

The kind who knows that cracks don't make you weak - they let the light in.

Vulnerability has made me a better listener, a more empathetic leader, and a more connected human. Not despite the shaky parts, but because of them.

Tuning Up: The Power of Vulnerability and Wholehearted Living

Vulnerability is the birthplace of innovation, creativity, and change.
Brené Brown

Brené Brown reminds us that real connection does not come from perfection. It comes from showing up as we are. Her work in *Daring Greatly*, *The Gifts of Imperfection*, and *Atlas of the Heart* has been a compass for those of us who spent too long trying to earn our place by being everything to everyone.

Vulnerability, she says, is courage in motion. It is what allows us to build trust, foster innovation, and create spaces where others feel safe enough to show up too.

And she is right.

I have lived it. Every time I dropped the armour - whether it was admitting I needed help, telling the truth when it was uncomfortable, or simply being honest about my limits - something shifted. I was met not with rejection, but with relief. With realness. With connection.

Here are a few takeaways inspired by her teachings, and shaped by the lessons I have learned on the road:

Courage over comfort. Vulnerability often starts with discomfort. Whether it is asking for help, setting a boundary, or sharing something real, these are acts of courage, not weakness.

Empathy dismantles shame. Shame thrives in silence. When we share our stories with those who meet us with empathy, shame loses power and we gain connection.

Boundaries protect vulnerability. Being vulnerable is not oversharing or leaking emotions. It is choosing who gets to see the real you, because your story is precious and not everyone has earned front-row access.

"I don't know" is a leadership superpower. Admitting you do not have all the answers does not diminish your authority. It humanises you and opens the door to collaboration.

When we show up fully, without the mask and without the script, we give others permission to do the same. That is how cultures shift. That is how trust grows. That is how real impact begins.

Reflective Pause: When Strong Isn't Enough

Have you been the strong one for so long that you have forgotten how to ask for help?

The one who holds space, keeps it together, makes it look easy. The one others rely on, but who rarely lets herself crumble, or ask, or rest.

What if being strong is not only in the holding, but in the unravelling?

What would it feel like to stop earning love through doing, and to trust that your presence, not your performance, is enough?

When overwhelm lashes out and the armour cracks with sharpness, can you forgive the ways you protected your heart in survival mode?

How could you begin again - more resourced, more aware, still worthy of love?

Let this be a gentler truth to sit with, not a task to complete.

Even the strong ones need soft places to land. Let others hold you, too: friends, mentors, guides who remind you that rest is also resilience.

FOURTH GEAR

Love on the Open Road - Navigating Relationships & Belonging

Love is not something you find. Love is something you build.
Unknown

Love has always felt like an open road to me - a journey with sharp turns, dead ends, unexpected rest stops, and unforgettable views. Not a straight shot to a perfect destination, but a ride full of lessons, longings, and self-discovery.

For those of us wired a little differently - sensitive, neurospicy minds without filters and big, tender hearts - relationships can feel especially complex.

How do you hold on to your truth while learning to meet others with grace?

How do you stay open in a world that often misunderstands or misreads your intensity?

It's about the quiet battles we fight to feel worthy - not just of love, but of belonging. About learning that being "good" isn't the same as being true. About the tiny gaps that let the light in when desire to be accepted and people-pleasing fall away.

You'll ride with me through stories of early relationships shaped by silence and survival. You'll meet the "good girl" I tried so hard to be.

And you'll witness the messy, beautiful unravelling of that persona as I learned that love - real love - doesn't need to be earned.

It grows when we stop doing and start being. When we say no without guilt. When we let ourselves be seen.

This is the stretch of road where I finally understood that I wasn't broken - I just needed to stop hiding.

So if love has ever felt confusing, conditional, or just out of reach... hold on to your helmet for a wild ride.

STAGE TWELVE
Human Being, Not Human Doing

Self-worth is not something we can earn by serving others. It's something we must claim by daring to serve ourselves.

Cheryl Richardson

Introduction: The People-Pleasing Pitfall

It's astonishing how early the seed of people-pleasing can take root. I've shared that for me, it started in childhood, nurtured by a need to keep the peace in a household that could swing from warm to chaotic. As the eldest of three young children with a father battling alcoholism and a mother juggling a career and a home, I learned quickly that being "good" was the safest way to navigate the world.

It became my default setting: keep things stable, make people happy, and avoid rocking the boat at all costs.

And when life felt too loud or unpredictable, I found ways to create order - some of which I only understood years later. I would make sure everything could be found where it belonged. I made sure my brothers did not bother the adults. I would intervene and speak up at school if someone was having a tough time. I would run as fast as I could to get tasks done to get the praise.

During my teenage years, I developed a very unhealthy relationship with my body and food became my way to control my environment.

Later, it was alcohol. Not as an escape, but as a kind of permission slip. A social lubricant in a world that felt like it demanded me to be less shy, less worried, more relaxed, more fun. It helped me step outside of my awkwardness. I could ignore what felt like rejection from people around me. I didn't need it - but I liked who I became after a glass or two. Freer. Funnier. Belonging.

It wasn't until much later, through a conversation with a wise coach, that I began to understand just how deeply I had tied my worth to what I could *do* for others, rather than simply who I was. More about that encounter soon.

The people-pleasing pitfall is insidious because it can masquerade as kindness. And in many ways, it *is* rooted in genuine care for others. But when you prioritise everyone else's needs over your own - when you measure your value by how much you give - you lose sight of who you are.

For years, I believed love was something I had to earn, not something I deserved simply because I existed.

I want to untangle those beliefs. Learn to say no without guilt and yes without obligation. To help us understand that love - true, authentic love - starts within.

You cannot pour from an empty cup. And you shouldn't have to.

The Roots of People-Pleasing

To understand how people-pleasing took hold of my life, we need to go back to the little girl who learned early that being "good" was the best way to feel safe.

My childhood was full of love, adventure, and laughter, but it also carried a shadow side. It wasn't simple, and it wasn't always safe. I saw myself as a kind of mediator. A buffer between the chaos and my younger siblings. I felt proud of that role - it made me believe I was strong, capable, and somehow responsible for holding the pieces together. I thought that if I was strong enough for everyone else, I wouldn't need help myself. I thought that was how love worked: you earned it by being dependable.

If I could smooth things over, anticipate needs, or fix the small things, then maybe - just maybe - the big things wouldn't spiral out of control.

I took on responsibilities far beyond my years, becoming the "good girl" who didn't make waves and rarely asked for help.

One of my funny, yet awkward memories is from an ordinary summer afternoon. I was playing with my brothers and the neighbour's kids. (Naturally, I was in charge - in my quiet and very adult way.) My mother walked past just as I stood up and orchestrated a scene that mimicked the adults, while "tippy toeing" and reminding them to be quiet so we didn't disturb them. She stopped in her tracks.

In that moment, she realised how much I was absorbing - of the worry she carried inside.

Children are sponges. I soaked up the unspoken rules of our household...

And I wasn't just soaking up what happened in the moment - I was absorbing patterns that ran deeper than our four walls. The women in my family were strong, resilient, fiercely capable. But their strength often looked like self-sacrifice. Like doing far more than was ever asked of them. They carried the emotional labour of entire households while working full-time, showed up with casseroles for sick neighbours, volunteered on weekends, and never - ever - dropped the ball.

I watched them. And somewhere along the way, I internalised the message that being good meant being needed. That love was earned through effort. That your worth came from how well you showed up for others - even at your own expense. They didn't say it. They lived it.

Stay quiet.
Be helpful.
Don't be a bother.

Nobody had said anything like that to me. But they were the rules I internalised. They shaped how I interacted with the world, how I navigated relationships, and how I defined my worth.

And then there was the day in my grandmother's kitchen. I was six, sitting at the table with my mum, grandma, aunties and maybe a cousin or two. My youngest aunt said lightly, "I've always thought I had a bit of a crooked nose - a little lump on it."

Without hesitation, I said, "But you do have a lump on your nose."

The table erupted. Everyone laughed.

I didn't. I was devastated. I hadn't meant to be rude - I just said what I saw. But I instantly felt the sting of shame. I thought I'd done something wrong. I didn't want to upset anyone. I wanted to belong. To be liked. To say the right thing.

Looking back now, I think that was one of the first moments I began to associate honesty with risk. That being accepted meant managing not just my actions, but the impact of my words - and learning to filter myself accordingly.

As I grew older, the habits of people-pleasing evolved. In school, I worked hard to be liked, to excel, to be seen as dependable. In friendships, I bent over backward to make others happy, often at the expense of my own needs. And in relationships, I sought love by giving more than I ever received.

Each small act of self-sacrifice felt like a down payment on the acceptance I so deeply craved.

It wasn't until much later - through therapy, coaching, and deep self-reflection - that I began to see the connection between my childhood experiences and my adult tendencies.

People-pleasing as a survival mechanism.

And like all survival mechanisms, it came with a cost.

The Wake-Up Call

Every journey toward change begins with a moment of reckoning - a spark that ignites the realisation that something needs to shift.

For me, that moment came in my early forties, during what I thought was just another coaching session. I'd been venting about my frustrations, my inability to say no, and the constant feeling that I was running around in circles. I was frustrated with my circumstances; I was frustrated with myself. Why couldn't I handle it all, like I always had?

My coach listened quietly, without judgment. Then she looked me straight in the eye and said something that cracked me wide open:

"Gry, remember - you are a human being, not a human doing".

It hit like a thunderclap.
Not an insult. Not advice.
Just a mirror, showing me what I had built my identity around without even realising it.

For decades, I had measured my worth by what I did for others. Was I helpful enough? Kind enough? Indispensable enough? The idea that I could simply *be* - without constantly proving my usefulness - felt almost absurd.

Her words didn't magically change everything overnight. But they planted a seed that I couldn't ignore. I started noticing how often I betrayed myself in small, almost invisible ways - saying yes when I meant no, apologising for things that weren't my fault, bending myself to fit into the spaces others had carved, even when those spaces were too small for who I really was.

There were plenty of examples from my past. One was working on a major project, pouring every ounce of energy into making it perfect. My boss was pleased. My colleagues were impressed. My customers were happy. On paper, it was a huge success. But inside, I felt hollow. Burned out. Disconnected from any sense of pride or joy.

That's when the realisation finally landed: no amount of external validation could fill the void created by abandoning myself.

The wake-up call helped me recognise the problem. It helped me decide to change. To set boundaries. To reclaim the parts of myself I had been so willing to trade for approval. To find value in who I was - and stop valuing myself by what I could produce for others.

It wasn't a straight line. It wasn't easy. But it was the beginning of a new chapter - one that asked me to live differently, with myself at the centre instead of the sidelines.

The Journey to Self-Love

Learning to love myself wasn't some grand, life-altering moment. It was slow, messy, and often uncomfortable. Like winding my way along unfamiliar roads, sometimes confident, sometimes second-guessing if I was heading in the right direction.

It will be a lifelong journey.

For most of my life, I'd measured my worth by what I did for others. The idea of prioritising myself felt alien, like veering off the safe, well-marked highway onto a narrow track with no signposts. Saying no was the hardest part at first. It felt like a betrayal of everything I thought made me good, useful, worthy.

That deep need to feel worthy had taken hold long before I could name it, leading to the very unhealthy relationship with my body that I touched on earlier. I developed an eating disorder. When I was 15, I weighed just 40kg at 172cm. Emaciated by most standards. Today, I stand at 176cm and weigh over 70kg - and even if I think I need to drop 5kg, I am reasonably slim.

It started in Botswana. My body started changing - late blooming buds that drew the attention of the "traditionally built" local women. They'd clap their hands in delight and say, "Ahhh, Grrryyyy (with their beautiful rolling R's), you are getting fat!" It was meant as a compliment. A sign of womanhood. But I remember shrinking inside. I didn't want to be seen like that.

I didn't want my body to change.

I had always tried to appear more like a boy than a girl. To me, it felt like boys got the better end of the deal - no pressure to be beautiful, no burdens of being "nice" or "proper." I recall an episode at the pharmacy when I was about 11 - short hair, stick thin, lined up with my brothers. The pharmacist looked at us and said, "You have got three wonderful, well-behaved boys there." I was so happy. Being a "boy" felt safe. It felt like permission to exist without performance.

But my mother - likely trying to protect my dignity - immediately responded, "No, this one is a girl." I was mortified. I didn't want to be different at that time. I didn't want to be seen.

Today, I realise that the pressures on girls and boys are simply different. Not easier or harder - just not the same.

This warped sense of self and not wanting to grow up, combined with the fact that I suddenly shot up 12cm in just 6 months, resulted in a body that I was happy with. A body that I was in charge of. Controlling food felt like the only thing in my world I could manage. Life felt chaotic and unpredictable as we were heading back to Norway - so I mastered the art of self-denial. It gave me a twisted sense of power and purpose.

When I moved to Norway, my extended family noticed immediately how thin I was. I was eating - but always just enough to keep control. My mum, gently but firmly, never named it directly. Instead, she nourished me with care, consistency, and patience. No shame. No lectures. Just presence. That mattered.

I joined the school orchestra. Played European handball (badly, but proudly). Rebuilt connections with old friends. Gradually, without fanfare, I began building myself - in my body, yes - but even more in my sense of self.

At the start, setting boundaries was clumsy and awkward. I would set one, only to apologise for it a moment later. But each time I stuck to a decision that honoured my energy - however small - I felt a little stronger, a little more grounded in who I was beyond what I could offer others.

Gradually, I began to celebrate my own wins, even when nobody else noticed. Completing a difficult project, protecting a weekend just for myself, speaking up even when my voice wobbled - these small victories became proof points. Evidence that I could trust myself again.

Another major shift came much later in life, with learning to be vulnerable. For so long, I had pretended everything was fine. It didn't occur to me that showing the parts of myself that weren't polished could actually deepen my connections with others. When I finally started opening up about my doubts and struggles, it was like removing a heavy helmet I'd been wearing for years. People didn't run away; they leaned in.

The road to self-love hasn't been a straight line. There have been detours, wrong turns, and plenty of times I've been tempted to turn back to old habits. But with every choice to listen to my own needs, to honour my own voice, I found a little more freedom. A little more space to just be.

Today, self-love isn't a grand proclamation. It's in the small, daily decisions: the way I speak to myself, the way I protect my time, the way I forgive my own imperfections. It's in giving myself permission to be a human being, not just a human doing.

Tuning Up: Learning to Be Enough

You're never going to feel ready. You're going to feel scared, and you're going to do it anyway.
Mel Robbins

You are responsible for what you say and do. You are not responsible for whether or not people freak out about it.
Jen Sincero, You Are a Badass

We've been taught that slowing down is lazy, that if we're not constantly producing, we're somehow falling behind. But speed doesn't equal progress. Sometimes the most radical thing you can do is pause - not because you've given up, but because you're tuning back in.

Jen Sincero calls this trusting your badass self - the part of you that knows when to rest, when to sprint, and when to coast.

Mel Robbins adds a practical twist: tools like her *5 Second Rule* and *High 5 Habit* remind us that confidence isn't built by being fearless. It's built by showing up, even when it's hard, and celebrating the small wins that keep you moving.

Simple rituals for returning to yourself:

5–4–3–2–1 and you act. *Because you've decided you're worth moving for.*

A high five in the mirror. *Don't fake joy; say "I see you. I've got you."*

Rest isn't a luxury. It's strategy. When you choose rest before burnout, you reclaim clarity and direction. You start acting from purpose instead of panic. That's what it means to be a human being - not a machine doing.

You don't need to prove your worth through exhaustion. You already earned your place on the road. Now the work is remembering it - and driving from that truth.

Reflective Pause: Being Is Enough

You've been tuning back in - slowing down to remember what already lives within you.

Think back for a moment:

When did you first get the idea that you had to earn love?

Was it through good grades? Helping hands? Smiling when you didn't feel like it?

What rhythms of doing *still hold power over your sense of worth?*

What if you didn't have to fix, achieve, or hustle to deserve care, joy, or belonging?

What if being you - right here, right now - was already enough?

No pressure to answer. Just an invitation to wonder - gently - as you journey this stretch of the road.

You never have to travel this part alone. Find the people, mentors, or coaches who help you rest in your worth when the world asks you to prove it.

STAGE THIRTEEN
The Good Girl Curse

We can do hard things, but we don't have to do all things.
Glennon Doyle

When you're riding through endless open country, it's easy to see the world for what it really is - wild, imperfect, beautifully untamed.

For a long time, I couldn't see life that way. I thought my role was to keep it all tidy, to meet every expectation, to be good enough to hold it all together.

But somewhere along the road, I realised: being perfect isn't the point. Being real is.

Introduction: The Weight of Perfection

Growing up, I learned early that being "good" was both a virtue and a survival strategy.

As the big sis, I naturally gravitated toward responsibility, keeping my younger siblings and cousins in check, defusing tension between adults (like when I sent my little sister into the room when my mum and stepdad had an argument), and excelling at school to make my parents and teachers proud.

On the surface, it seemed like a positive thing. I was praised for my maturity, my kindness, and my willingness to help. But the relentless pursuit of being "good" came with a cost. I felt the need to exceed expectations, to anticipate every potential problem, and to make sure everyone around me was okay, even when I wasn't.

There's a reason they call it a curse. Being good is endless. It demands constant vigilance, perfectionism, and an instinct to put others first, even at the expense of your own needs.

And when you grow up a bit different to people around you (or neurospicy as I see it now), that tendency to overcompensate often spirals even further: masking your quirks, editing yourself into acceptability, making yourself smaller to fit a world that feels too rigid and loud.

It took me a long time to see that the need to be good could also be a cage. Yes, it opened doors. But it also locked away parts of who I really was.

I felt like a butterfly pinned under glass - admired for being so capable, but unable to move freely.

Let's unpack the tension. Recognise that "goodness" does not have to mean being perfect, pleasing everyone, or fixing everything. It's about being whole - messy, beautiful, human - and letting yourself take up your full space in the world.

But even under the weight of all that goodness, there were moments of rebellion. In high school, I loosened the grip a little. There were parties, late nights, and laughter that felt deliciously free. Most of it was with my best friend - just the two of us navigating that world together. It never felt reckless, because we always had each other's backs. It was my first real taste of freedom, held safely in the anchor of deep friendship.

Good Intentions, Unintended Consequences

Being the "good girl" started as a survival strategy, a role I took on willingly, even enthusiastically, in my early years. It felt noble to be the one who brought calm to the storm, who anticipated needs before they were spoken, and who kept the peace when tensions threatened to boil over.

And honestly? It also felt good.

The smiles, the thank yous, the sense of being the steady hand in a swirling family - it was like being a tiny anchor in waters far too rough for a child. It made me proud. It made me feel needed. It made me believe that worthiness meant never needing help myself.

But pride, I would later learn, is not the same as peace.

In my child's mind, it was an honour to be trusted, to be needed, to make things better for the people I loved most.

But good intentions can have unintended consequences. In my quest to be everything to everyone, I unwittingly taught those around me that I could handle anything. That I didn't need help. That my needs were secondary - or even nonexistent.

At school, teachers praised me for being diligent and well-behaved. At home, I was the peacemaker, the helper, the one who could be counted on to make the right choice. In friendships, I was the confidante, always there to listen, always putting my friends' needs above my own. And while this earned me approval and affection, it also left me feeling invisible at times. I wanted to be seen for everything that I was, but I was hiding most of it to make sure we were all safe. Who was the real Gry?

Unlike the quiet internal rules I'd absorbed as a child, this was the grown-up version - harder to see, harder to shake. I'd been praised for being good so often that I didn't notice when that goodness came at my own expense.

In fact, it was my sister who inspired me to see things from a different perspective when she told me that she just wanted people to see her for everything that she is. Now, we are both a lot of things, so that might be a stretch for many people, but so important... Do you *really* see me?

There was a moment in my early twenties when a friend confided in me about a major life decision. She trusted me, sought my advice, and poured her heart out. When she finished, I felt a pang of sadness. I realised she didn't know me as deeply as I knew her. In my eagerness to be the dependable one, I had stopped sharing my own struggles, fears, and dreams. I had become a vessel for other people's stories, leaving my own untold.

The unintended consequence of being the "good girl" was a gradual erasure of self. I became so adept at molding myself to fit other people's needs that I lost sight of what I needed, what I wanted, and who I truly was.

Over time, this dynamic seeped into every corner of my life. In relationships, I often bent over backward to accommodate my partner's preferences, only to feel resentful when my own desires were overlooked.

In my career, I hesitated to advocate for myself, fearing that I'd come across as pushy or ungrateful. And in my personal growth, I struggled to separate what I truly wanted from what I thought others expected of me.

The irony is that my good intentions were rooted in love and care. But without boundaries or a strong sense of self, they became a double-edged sword. As I was giving to others - I was also giving pieces of myself away, bit by bit, until there was little left for me.

The journey to reclaim those pieces began with a simple, yet profound realisation: being good doesn't mean being selfless to the point of self-sacrifice. It means showing up authentically, with all your quirks, flaws, and boundaries intact.

Breaking the Chains of Perfection

I wasn't obsessed with perfection for its own sake. I craved the love and acceptance I thought it would unlock. If I did everything right, maybe everyone would come along for the journey.

It wasn't just about wanting things to be done well - it was about needing them to be flawless. Perfect grades, perfect behaviour, perfect solutions to everyone else's problems. Somewhere along the way, I had internalised the idea that my worth was tied to my ability to exceed expectations and always have it together.

The irony of perfectionism is that it promises control but delivers exhaustion. I thought if I could just do everything right, I could avoid criticism, disappointment, and failure. But the pursuit of perfection didn't shield me from those things; it magnified them. Every mistake felt like a personal failure. Every piece of feedback, no matter how minor, felt like confirmation that I wasn't enough.

I still remember a moment early in my career, when I had poured hours into a major project. I checked every detail twice, three times even. When I presented it, my boss was pleased - except for a small formatting error buried deep in the document. Instead of feeling proud of the 99% that was praised, I fixated on the 1% that wasn't. In my mind, that tiny imperfection eclipsed all the good.

In personal relationships, the story was much the same. I tried to be the ideal partner, the unwavering friend, the daughter who never needed anything. I anticipated needs, avoided conflict, and hid my struggles so I wouldn't seem "difficult". But perfection creates distance. It's hard to truly connect with someone who never lets their guard down.

The cracks eventually started to show.

And when they did, I began to understand that perfectionism was both unattainable and unsustainable. The harder I clung to it, the more isolated and exhausted I became. Like riding a never-ending highway with no rest stops, always chasing a mirage of "good enough" that kept moving further away.

Learning to let go of perfectionism for the purpose of acceptance was like easing off the throttle after miles of riding flat-out. I had to teach myself a different rhythm: one that allowed for mistakes, vulnerability, and softness.

I discovered that connection comes from being real. Asking for help made me human, not weak. Making mistakes meant I was growing, not failing.

Today, I remind myself often: good enough is good enough. I still strive for excellence, but I've learned to embrace the inevitable messiness of life. I've learned that there's beauty in the imperfections - in the wrong turns, the engine stalls, the unexpected detours.

And I've also stopped vilifying the way my brain works. For a long time, I beat myself up for what others called procrastination. But the truth is, I do a lot of processing internally. Things swirl around in my mind, taking shape quietly until - click - they arrive fully formed. My partner once said, "I don't know why you beat yourself up. You always get things done". And he's right. My timing isn't late - it's *just in time*. I've come to see this not as a flaw, but as a feature. My neurospicy brain doesn't need rigid lists or countdowns. It trusts its own flow. And when it's ready, it's ready.

Rather than striving for perfection, I've learned to release things into the world sooner - to test, to explore, to invite feedback. Not to prove my worth, but to co-create. It helps me stay aligned with what matters most: authenticity, connection, and meaningful impact. It also honours the way my brain works - fast, intuitive, and full of possibility. With AI as my creative co-pilot, I can now explore more options and iterate more freely. My ideas don't have to be fully formed before they're shared. They can be living, breathing works-in-progress - evolving in dialogue with others, rather than in isolation. NOTE: AI did not write this for me. She just tweaked it.

Breaking the chains of perfection is an ongoing journey, full of sharp bends and steep climbs. But the freedom it's given me - the freedom to be fully, unapologetically human - is worth every mile.

Redefining Strength: Vulnerability as a Superpower

It started with small cracks in my armour - hairline fractures that no one else could see, but I could feel them. A close friend and colleague, someone who saw beyond the polished surface I presented to the world, caught a glimpse.

"You know you don't always have to be okay, right?" she said, her voice gentle but steady.

Her words landed harder than I expected. For so long, I had worn resilience like a second skin. Holding it all together, carrying the weight without complaint, always showing up with a smile. But in that moment, something inside me shifted.

I felt exposed. Seen. And, oddly enough, relieved.

Maybe I didn't have to carry the whole world on my shoulders. Maybe I didn't have to believe everything was fine. Maybe I just needed to be real. Let others in. Trust that I didn't have to earn love by being endlessly capable or cheerful.

That conversation cracked open a door I hadn't even realised was locked. It gave me permission to stop performing and start living. Not as invincibility - but as authenticity.

In my professional life, that shift showed up during a challenging stretch in my volunteer work. When a project began to unravel, I stepped up - not because I had all the answers, but because the situation called for calm and clarity. I led gently, with steadiness and care. And together, we found our footing. But when things stabilised, I was asked to step back. The old me might have felt hurt or humiliated. But by then, I'd started to understand that leadership wasn't about control - it was about service. I let go with grace. I focused on what we'd built, on the people we'd supported, on the strength we'd uncovered in each other.

Vulnerability, I realised, wasn't just in admitting struggle. It was also in staying soft when it would have been easier to harden.

In my personal life, letting go of the mask was even harder. I had built so many walls, so many stories about being "too much" or "not enough", that it took real courage to peel them back. When I finally let someone see the parts of me that were messy, afraid, and imperfect, it felt like standing on the brink. Terrifying. Exhilarating.

I remember one December at our annual Danish Christmas lunch, surrounded by smart, worldly girlfriends. They'd all studied or lived in Denmark, and this was all traditional Danish food, rambunctious singing, hilarious laughs, and a few too many schnapps. I was fortunate to work with one of them and got included in the tradition. One friend - someone I didn't know all that well - turned to me mid-conversation and asked, "But how are you *really* feeling?"

I opened my mouth to answer and burst into tears.

I didn't even know I felt that way. Whatever "that" was. But clearly something inside me had been waiting for permission. For space. For someone to ask, without expectation or agenda.

It's happened more than once since - those emotional ambushes when someone gets past my polished surface and finds something raw, waiting.

And every time, it reminds me how much easier it is to feel for others than it is to feel for myself. But I'm learning.

Each of those moments taught me something: I don't have to understand my feelings before they're valid. I just have to let them through. And what I found was this: the right people hang around when you show them your humanity. They come closer.

One of the most healing moments in my life was when I finally voiced a truth I had carried in silence for years. I told someone I loved that deep down, I didn't always feel worthy of love. Saying it out loud felt like setting fire to a story I no longer wanted to live by. Instead of falling apart, the world opened up.

"You don't have to earn love", they said simply. "You just have to accept it". Those words oddly comforted me - and they changed me. They reminded me that vulnerability is a bridge. It's how we find each other, and how we find ourselves.

Today, I know that vulnerability and strength aren't opposites. They are twin flames. The more I allow myself to be seen - not just the polished parts, but all of it - the stronger and freer I become.

And if there's one thing this journey has taught me, it's that true resilience isn't about bearing the load alone.

It's about daring to let someone else walk beside you.

Embracing the Power of No

Saying *no* didn't come naturally to me. For much of my life, I avoided it - not because it was wrong, but because it carried the weight of guilt, rejection, and the fear of disappointing others. Saying *no* didn't feel like denying a request - it felt like denying a part of who I thought I needed to be: the good girl, the helper, the fixer.

But *no* is a boundary. It's a declaration. And sometimes it's the kindest thing you can say - to yourself or to someone else. Learning to wield that simple two-letter word became one of the most transformative lessons of my life.

The Cost of Saying Yes

My inability to say no came at a steep price. It cost me time, energy, and sometimes my sense of self. I'd agree to obligations I didn't have the bandwidth for, to relationships that drained me, to roles that didn't reflect my values.

Every *yes* to something that didn't serve me was, by default, a *no* to something that did. Over time, I realised my endless overcommitting was quietly eroding who I was at my core.

One particular moment still sticks with me. I had just said *yes* - yet again - to another project. I sat in my car afterward, hands on the wheel, trying to steady the flutter of excitement that threatened to spill over into anxiety. I was hungry to do more, but inside I felt stretched thin. Somewhere in that tension, I recognised how many parts of me were bending to hold it all together. I was depleted in quiet ways. I had lost sight of what I really wanted beneath all the expectations.

That was my "aha" moment. The moment I realised that saying *yes* to everything wasn't generosity. It was self-abandonment.

Reframing No

Learning to say no felt unnatural at first - like trying to write with the wrong hand. After decades of equating no with failure, selfishness, or rejection, it took time to see it differently.

No is not a betrayal of my kindness. It's not a weapon.

No is not self-preservation but not selfishness either.

No is simply a redirection - a way to honour both my boundaries and my relationships.

It's a way of respecting myself and respecting others - giving them an honest answer instead of a half-hearted, resentful *yes*.

And it's not just what you say - it's how you say it. A boundary shared with clarity and care can still hold compassion. You can be kind and clear. Firm and loving.

I started small. I declined invitations when I should rest. I politely turned down requests that didn't align with my priorities. I learned to say no to the critical voice inside my head that told me I was only valuable if I was useful. And it's still hard. Some days, the old patterns whisper louder than I'd like. But everything starts with awareness - with noticing the pull to say yes when I mean no, and choosing differently, one breath at a time.

And slowly, *no* became less scary. It became freeing.

The Empowerment of Boundaries

With every *no*, I reclaimed a little piece of myself. I began to understand that boundaries could be bridges to healthier relationships. They were declarations of where I ended and someone else began.

One of the most profound realisations was that people who truly cared about me respected my *no*. They didn't punish me for protecting my well-being. They accepted it. And those who didn't? Well, their response spoke volumes - and freed me even further.

I've also noticed that people often overstep by under-inviting. I *hate* it when someone assumes I'm too busy, too important, or too unavailable to be included. That kind of "courtesy" doesn't feel like care - it feels like erasure. It strips away my agency to choose. If you want to be inclusive, invite people. Let them decide if they have time. Don't make that call for them.

And yes, I'm still working on asking for help directly. It's a stretch for me too. But I've come to see that boundaries aren't just about saying no. They're also about saying *yes* - to support, to connection, to being seen.

Boundaries don't just keep people out. They can let the *right* people in - and let *yourself* show up fully, too.

A New Way Forward

Saying *no* gave me more time. It gave me back my agency. My energy. My joy.

I could finally channel my resources into what truly mattered: meaningful relationships, fulfilling work, and my own well-being.

Today, I still sometimes feel the tug of that old people-pleasing reflex, and a tiny dash of FOMO (fear of missing out). But more often than not, I can pause, check in with myself, and choose a different path. One that honours who I am, not just who others expect me to be.

Because here's the truth: you can still be kind. Still be generous. Still empower others - *without losing yourself in the process*. You don't have to disappear to make space for others.

That's not compassion. That's erasure.

No does not have to be a rejection. It's a *not now*. It's an invitation. An invitation to live more fully, more freely - and more authentically.

Tuning Up: Breaking the Good Girl Curse

You are not here to be consumed. You are here to be whole.
Emily Nagoski, Burnout

Let's talk about the script.

Be good. Be helpful. Be accommodating. Don't make waves. Don't take up too much space. And for the love of all things proper - smile.

For many of us, this script was passed down like a family heirloom. We watched our mothers, teachers, and aunties shape themselves to be liked, needed, indispensable. We learned: *that must be how to be safe. That must be how to belong.*

Emily Nagoski calls this the **Human Giver Syndrome.** In this framework, girls and women are expected to dedicate their lives to others - to be pretty, happy, calm, generous, and self-sacrificing - while suppressing anger, grief, or ambition.

It's no wonder burnout feels so personal. It's not just about doing too much. It's about **never being enough**, no matter how much we give.

Nagoski's work reminds us that burnout isn't weakness. It's **unresolved stress and unmet emotion** living in the body - that tight chest, that restless mind. Those are not flaws; they're signals from a system that's been overworked for too long.

To heal, we don't just change our calendars. We complete the stress cycle. We move. We cry. We scream in the car or dance in the kitchen to shake loose the static. Imagine if we, like other animals, released tension instinctively after escape.

You don't have to keep being a "good girl" to be good. You don't have to be palatable to be powerful. You don't have to earn rest, joy, or peace.

You are not a product. You are a person. You are not here to be consumed. You are here to be whole.

Reflective Pause: Reclaiming Wholeness

Let's pause and ask:

What were the "rules" you absorbed about being a good girl growing up?
Where in your body do those rules still live?
When was the last time you let yourself complete a stress cycle - without guilt?
What emotional needs have you deprioritised for the sake of being liked?
If you weren't trying to be good, what might you allow yourself to be?

You get to rewrite the script.
Wholeness, not perfection, is the destination.

And if the rewriting feels unfamiliar, reach for the people who remind you of your full story - coaches, allies, or mentors who help you live from your wholeness, not your wounds.

STAGE FOURTEEN
Lessons in Love and Loss

The wound is the place where the light enters you.

Rumi

* A Gentle Word Before We Begin
This chapter touches on experiences of domestic violence, abuse, and non-consensual encounters. These stories are not shared to dwell in pain, but to honour the resilience, strength, and healing that follow. Please read with care. If at any point it feels too much, it's okay to pause, skip, or return when you feel ready. Your well-being matters most.

Introduction: The Complexities of Love

Love, for all its beauty and potential, is rarely simple. It's shaped by the world we grow up in, the lessons we learn, and the expectations society places on us. For women of my generation, love was often tangled with compliance, silence, and an unspoken pressure to accept what we were given rather than what we truly wanted.

This wasn't the love I dreamed of as a girl. I imagined something tender, mutual, and empowering. But my early experiences taught me a different lesson: that love could be painful, that intimacy could be confusing, and that silence often felt safer than speaking up.

Despite all that, I believe deeply in love. I've been with Dave for more than 20 years, and what we've built together is grounded in respect, care, and choice. But it took me time to get here.

For a long time, even as I longed to be loved and accepted, I often ran at the first sign of attraction. Something in me pulled back, as though protection mattered more than connection - even when connection was what I most deeply craved.

Back then, we didn't talk about consent, coercion, or emotional abuse. These weren't terms in our vocabulary. What was expected was compliance - a quiet, unquestioning acceptance of what men wanted and what society deemed appropriate for women.

It's taken years to unravel the complex emotions tied to those early lessons. To understand that love isn't about submission or sacrifice, but about connection, respect, and choice. This chapter is a reflection on that journey - of facing the darker sides of love, learning to heal, and finding a sense of self-worth that could withstand the weight of the past.

Early Encounters and the Weight of Silence

The First Time: More Than Just a Moment

Even before intimacy entered the picture, I had always wrestled with visibility. I remember at 11, dancing at our neighbour's basement disco, secretly hoping the boy next door - the one I fancied - would notice me. I'd dance freely only when he wasn't looking, but as soon as he turned around, I would stop. Being seen, even in joy, carried a weight of risk. It was exhilarating and at the same time petrifying. That fear of exposure quietly travelled with me into adulthood.

The first time I was sexually intimate wasn't what I had dreamed it would be. It wasn't magical, intimate, or even consensual. It just... happened. I was 20 years old, a late bloomer by the standards of my peers, and yet the experience left me feeling anything but empowered.

By the time I found myself at that party, years later, that old dance of wanting to be noticed - and fearing what would happen if I was - hadn't left me. The boy I had a crush on was there, a different boy and older, and the situation felt exciting. But things did not go to plan. It unfolded in a way I hadn't anticipated, or wanted.

I was excited that he liked me back. For once, the attention I'd longed for was finally returned - and I thought that meant something. Maybe even that it would lead to something. But afterwards, he avoided my eyes. He never spoke to me again, never asked about me. That absence, that silence, hurt more than I expected.

In those days, consent was not even a known concept. No one prepared us for how to navigate intimacy, to express boundaries, or to advocate for ourselves. Feminism told us we had the right to claim pleasure just as freely as men, but it didn't teach us how to say *no* when pleasure wasn't what we wanted. For women like me, "freedom" sometimes blurred into silent resignation.

That first experience was marked by hesitation on my part and persistence on his. I didn't scream, cry, or push him away. I didn't know I could. And to be honest, part of me thought: maybe this is how I get a boyfriend. I'd had a few drinks to loosen the tension in my body - to feel less rigid, less awkward. I wanted to be wanted. So I did it.

Afterwards, I walked away that night feeling conflicted and ashamed.

I didn't know how to frame what had happened, only that it felt wrong. But society had no room for such nuances; women were either virgins or willing participants - nothing in between.

Somewhere deep down, I still craved real connection - tenderness, trust, mutuality - but I had already learned that opening myself up carried a cost. Love, intimacy, being seen: they all came with a flicker of danger.

Consent in a Culture of Compliance

My story isn't unique. For so many women, especially of my generation, the lines of consent were blurred by cultural norms that placed male desire above female autonomy. I knew I could say no. But I also wanted to be loved. And that longing sometimes blurred the lines between consent and compliance.

It wasn't about open coercion, not always. It was quieter, more complicated - a dance where stepping back was seen as rude, ungrateful, or even cruel. And when you grow up believing that being "good" means pleasing others, those moments of doubt and discomfort are easy to brush aside. You learn to silence your instincts and keep the peace.

I look back now and realise how many of us were navigating relationships with broken compasses. We didn't have the language of consent. We didn't know that "I'm not sure" or "I feel uncomfortable" should have been enough. Instead, we second-guessed ourselves. We internalised shame. We told ourselves we must have misread things, or worse, that it was somehow our fault for sending mixed signals or not speaking up sooner.

The boys around us weren't monsters, but there is a systemic, conditioned entitlement that we need to challenge daily. They were growing up in the same system, taught that persistence was romantic, that a reluctant yes was still a yes. And we, trying so hard to be liked, to fit in, to be normal, sometimes surrendered to that persistence without really understanding why it felt so hollow afterward.

It's only with distance and growth that I can see it clearly now:

Compliance isn't consent.
Silence isn't agreement.

And a culture where both young men and young women are not taught about boundaries, respect, and agency leaves everyone fumbling in the dark.

How do my experiences compare with what young people live today? My bet is that it is a bit same, same and different.

I often think about how different - and maybe harder - it must be for young people now. In my time, there were still places to hide. If someone judged you, it was often behind your back - not broadcast online. But today, with social media and cameras everywhere, even your mistakes can become permanent records.

Without going into intricate details, I am sharing a few experiences. I've been "walked in on". I've been misread and judged without people knowing the whole story. But at least back then, it wasn't all immortalised on someone's smart (not so smart) phone. There was no viral shame. No online echo chamber. And for that, I'm grateful.

The Repetition of Resignation

The second and third encounters followed a familiar pattern. There was no outright violence, no dramatic confrontation. Instead, there was a slow erosion of my boundaries, a gradual folding into situations I didn't want - but didn't know how to refuse. I didn't want these moments to happen; I felt that resisting felt harder than enduring. I was still desperate to fit in, to catch up with my peers, to feel normal in a world that made intimacy sound easy. And under it all was a quiet sense of shame - of wanting love, but not knowing how to get it. Every time I went along with something that didn't feel right, a little more of my voice disappeared.

I didn't end up in those moments because I didn't care. I ended up there because I did. I genuinely liked the people involved. I hoped that if I didn't push back, if I just stayed agreeable, it might turn into something more- something loving. Back then, I believed that being wanted was the same as being valued. That staying quiet might earn me closeness. But that silence didn't bring connection. It brought confusion, self-doubt, and a growing dissonance between who I was and who I thought I had to be to be loved.

Looking back, I don't place the blame on the boys or men involved. They didn't force themselves on me in ways that the movies or the media warned us about. They simply didn't stop to notice that I wasn't fully there - that my compliance was not the same as consent.

I drank with the others because it made me feel less rigid. Less outside. I wanted to be part of it all - the laughter, the connection, the ease. And yes,

I knew it dulled my judgment, but I told myself it helped me fit in. I wasn't a big drinker, but just enough to take the shyness off - to quiet the overthinking.

One morning after a big party at the student house where I lived, the boy I'd liked - the one I'd been intimate with - approached me in the hallway. He looked genuinely concerned and asked if I was okay. I was mortified. I mumbled something and fled. In hindsight, I think he wanted to get to know me better, to connect beyond the night before. But I couldn't handle the vulnerability. It felt too exposing. Too real. Too soon. And so I ran - back behind the armour I knew best: silence and withdrawal.

And I didn't have the language, the confidence, or the role models to say, *this is not what I want.*

What I carried from those early experiences wasn't fury toward the boys - or even society. It was a slow, heavy erosion of self-trust. Each resignation planted a seed of doubt:

Was I even allowed to want something different?

Was my discomfort valid?

Was there something wrong with me for feeling out of place in situations that everyone else seemed to navigate so effortlessly?

At the time, it didn't even occur to me that I had the right to question it. I told myself I was being too sensitive, too naive, too inexperienced. I folded myself into the expectations around me, hiding the discomfort under a mask of casual indifference. And the more I masked it, the more lost I became.

The Silent Struggles of the Late Bloomer

During my teens, I felt out of sync with my peers. Conversations among friends painted intimacy as effortless, a natural progression of relationships. I, meanwhile, felt like an outsider, still grappling with my own boundaries and fears, wondering why I felt so different.

Looking back, I think part of the disconnect was this: I understood the adult words, but not always the unspoken currents beneath them. I could follow the conversations, laugh at the jokes, track the plot lines. But the emotional undertones - the longing, the subtle invitations, the silent permissions - often slipped past me.

The pressure to "catch up" was both external and internal - it seeped into my own thoughts, turning self-doubt into a constant background hum. I wasn't inexperienced because I lacked opportunities; I was inexperienced because, deep down, I was scared. Scared of not belonging. Scared of getting it wrong. Scared that the parts of me that wanted to take things slow made me somehow *less than*.

On the outside, I kept up appearances - outgoing, curious, enthusiastic. I didn't want to seem like the only one who hadn't figured it all out yet. I smiled at the right jokes, nodded along, pretended to know what it felt like to be swept away by romance. But inside, I felt like a traveller without a map.

Reading (or rather listening to) *Strong Female Character* years later, I found myself deeply resonating with Fern Brady's reflections on navigating intimacy and social norms as someone who couldn't easily read subtext or unspoken rules. Her raw, unfiltered storytelling around erotic experience - marked by boundary confusion and a hunger to belong - mirrored so much of what I had felt but never quite named. Like her, I had often mistaken silence or retreat for safety. That recognition gave me a new lens to look back through - not with shame, but with compassion. Maybe I wasn't broken or naïve. Maybe I was just trying to survive a world that didn't come with a map I could read.

There were moments I tried to open up, tried to bridge the gap. I remember one afternoon in my final year of high school, tentatively voicing my confusion to a couple of my girlfriends. I admitted - half-laughing to cover the nerves - that intimacy wasn't as easy or exciting as the movies made it out to be. They shifted uncomfortably, glancing at each other. "That's just how it is", one said with a shrug. The other smiled awkwardly and changed the subject.

And so, I learned another lesson: Better to stay silent than to be seen as naive, prudish, or fragile. Talking about feelings has never been my thing - not because I don't feel them deeply, but because I've never quite known what to do with them once they're named out loud.

What made it harder was that to many of my classmates - especially those who knew me from high school - I probably didn't seem uncertain at all. I had always been outspoken, brave even, when it came to standing up for fairness or helping others. But when it came to my own heart, my own fears, I became invisible - even to the people closest to me.

A close friend from those years once reflected that I seemed conforming, even neutral, during high school. It wasn't until later that I "found my style", she said - my voice, my fire.

She wasn't wrong.

The truth was, I carried a deep-rooted fear of men - mixed with a fascinated attraction I didn't know how to navigate. I loved my father dearly, but I had also learned early that trust could be broken without warning. The tension between longing and fear became a quiet undercurrent in my early relationships, making intimacy feel both desirable and dangerous.

And so, I learned to wear the good girl mask a little tighter, sprinkled with a perfect dose of *I am strong and independent. I don't need you.* I learned to laugh when I wanted to cry, to say yes when I wanted to pause, to shrink myself to fit into a world that didn't seem to have space for uncertainty.

It would take many more years before I understood that the mask was isolating me.

Finding the Language

It took years before I found the words to name what had happened to me.

For the longest time, I believed those early experiences were just *normal*. Something to be tucked away, chalked up to "life lessons". I didn't scream. I didn't fight.

So how could I not have believed it was my own fault?

I didn't even have the framework to describe what had happened, let alone understand the impact it had left behind. Back then, we didn't talk about consent. We didn't talk about coercion. And we certainly didn't talk about the grey, murky places where doubt and discomfort lived.

When the language around consent and boundaries finally started to appear in conversations and headlines - I was in my 50s - it was like someone switched on a light in a room I didn't even know. Suddenly, there was a way to make sense of the unease I had carried for years - the quiet, persistent voice that had always told me something was wrong, even when the world around me insisted it was just "how things were".

It was freeing to finally have words like "coercion" and "non-consensual". But it was painful too. Because those words made the past real.

They forced me to face a hard truth. We had made silent agreements - to tolerate, to endure, to comply - because we didn't believe we had the right, or the power, to do anything else.

Hearing those stories cracked something open in me. I realised that what I had experienced wasn't clumsiness or confusion. It was a culture that taught girls to prioritise politeness over protection, silence over safety.

There was grief in that realisation. Grief for the girls who hadn't known they could say no. Grief for the women who had carried the weight of shame that was never theirs to bear.

But alongside the grief, there was also relief. Finally, I had a framework that made sense. Finally, I could stop twisting myself into knots trying to justify why something that had felt wrong actually *was* wrong.

Language gave me power. It allowed me to step outside the fog of self-blame and start weaving a new narrative - one grounded in truth, compassion, and dignity.

Not for me, but for every young woman who had been taught to shrink instead of shout.

I was still not in denial about my own status as a victim / survivor. That was yet to come.

Clarity Through Compassion

As I began to understand what had happened, I also started to understand myself. I realised that my fear of intimacy hadn't just come from awkward teenage experiences or cautionary tales whispered among friends. It went deeper. It had roots that stretched all the way back to my earliest memories of love.

As a child, I adored my father. But I could never fully trust him. It was confusing. It was heartbreaking. And it planted a seed deep inside me: a belief that men could be wonderful... but that love from men came with unpredictability.

That emotional safety was never a guarantee.

As I moved through the world, that belief shaped everything. I wanted to connect. I wanted to be loved. But some part of me was always standing just a little apart, watching for the moment the mask would slip. It made me cautious. Sceptical. Slow to trust anyone's intentions - even when they meant well.

Understanding this softened the shame. It helped me see that my fear wasn't weakness. It was a survival instinct - a tender self-protection I had long misunderstood, but was only beginning to honour.

And with that compassion, the work of healing could finally begin. I just needed to forgive myself for the ways I had learned to survive.

The Cycle of Harm

The Patterns We Inherit

Abuse and neglect, in all its forms, often feels like an echo - reverberating through generations, shaping the way we love, trust, and protect ourselves. For me, the cycle didn't begin with obvious violence or screaming arguments. It started subtly, in quiet moments of unease, power imbalances that felt normal, and an unspoken understanding about whose needs mattered most.

As a child, I watched my mother carry the burden of my father's alcoholism. She shielded us from the worst of it, but even her fierce protection couldn't hide the tension that hung in the air. I learned early that love came with compromise. That survival sometimes meant silence. And that you had to walk on eggshells to keep the peace.

Like water into soil, they soaked into my foundation, unnoticed until the weight of them showed up in my choices

Accepting What Shouldn't Be Acceptable

When I found myself in a seriously abusive relationship many years later, I didn't immediately recognise it for what it was. The intensity, the passion, even the temper - I rationalised it all as part of loving deeply. I was strong, independent, and determined not to need rescuing. Surely that meant I couldn't be in an abusive situation... right?

We met at a party with many of my work colleagues. He was handsome, funny and the life of the party - not unlike my father. I was smitten immediately, and he reciprocated my attention. Little did I know then that he was one of the people supplying party drugs. That had never been my scene, so I was oblivious to the tell-tale signs, but I don't know if it would have mattered because it wasn't his usual "profession".

The first few months together were wild, and there were plenty of warning signs, which I chose to ignore because I was convinced that I could help "fix him". However, I was not equipped to help someone with severe mental health issues who regularly decided to take himself off the prescribed medication.

When he started ignoring my boundaries, I told myself I hadn't been clear enough. When he belittled me or raged, I convinced myself it was stress, or maybe even my fault. By the time the violence escalated into physical acts - hands around my throat, my head against a wall - I had already lost so much of my sense of worth that leaving felt impossible.

But abuse isn't always explosive. It's in the gradual erosion of confidence. In the slow rewriting of your own reality to accommodate someone else's moods, their needs, their anger. It's the quiet resignation that this, somehow, is what love looks like.

The Invisible Scars

What's often overlooked about surviving abusive relationships are the invisible scars they leave behind. Long after the bruises fade, the doubts linger. The fear of being "too much", the questioning of your own memories, the instinct to apologise before you even speak.

For me, those scars showed up everywhere. In my work. In my friendships. Most heartbreakingly, in the relationships I ran away from - even when love was offered freely.

In relationship after relationship, I chose to disappear rather than have difficult conversations. It didn't matter who he was - my brain simply didn't know how to handle confrontations that didn't turn into a fight, a breakdown, or a goodbye.

Silence and running became my default survival tactics.

A Pattern of Running

Looking back, I see it clearly. I didn't trust love - not fully. I didn't trust that I could ask for what I needed and still be loved. I didn't believe that conflict could be navigated without catastrophe.

The sad truth is, in trying to protect myself from the pain of abandonment, I often created it myself. I left before I could be left. I withdrew before I could be rejected. I silenced myself before anyone else had a chance to silence me.

Each time, I thought I was doing the brave thing - choosing independence, control, self-reliance. But underneath it all was fear. Fear of not being enough. Fear of being too much. Fear that the people who said they loved me would change their minds if they really saw me - messy, scared, imperfect.

And maybe, at the heart of it all, was this: I didn't believe I deserved love. I feared abandonment not just because others might leave - but because deep down, I didn't know if I would stay with myself. I didn't yet know how to love the messy, scared, imperfect parts of me. And if I couldn't, how could anyone else?

A Moment of Realisation - the Breaking Point

Every cycle of harm has a breaking point - a moment when the weight of staying outweighs the fear of leaving.

For me, it was small. Almost ordinary. Another belittling comment, another wave of shame washing over me while he stood there, convinced of his own righteousness. But something shifted. I looked at him, really looked at him - not through the lens of fear or hope, but through my own, unfiltered strength.

I didn't scream. I didn't argue. I didn't beg him to see the damage he was doing. I just walked away. When he asked "what are you gonna do? Call the police?", I answered calmly "If that is what is needed, I will." When he followed with "they won't come", I shrugged my shoulders and said "wanna bet?"

It wasn't dramatic. It wasn't even loud. But in that quiet moment, something inside me - something I thought had long been extinguished - reignited. A deep knowing that I didn't deserve this. That whatever fear lay beyond leaving was less terrifying than what would happen if I stayed.

The moment itself was small. But it cracked the entire foundation wide open.

The Role of Society in the Cycle

Complicity Through Silence

It's impossible to talk about the cycle of harm without acknowledging the society that helps sustain it.

In my generation, silence was survival. You didn't air your dirty laundry. You didn't accuse "nice guys". You didn't question whether love should hurt.

Even now, echoes of those attitudes persist - the sideways glances when a woman speaks up, the whispered questions: "What did she do to set him off?" or "It couldn't have been that bad". I once overheard someone say, "She's just being dramatic" when I tried to explain why I left. But I also heard a lot of friends saying "thank goodness you're out" and "it was never your job to heal someone who is that broken by yourself".

In my most broken moments, I heard those voices in my own head. Was it my fault? Was I asking for too much?

It's hard to heal when the world around you keeps suggesting the harm you endured is somehow your burden to carry quietly.

Breaking the Chain

Ending the cycle isn't just about personal courage - although the higher power knows, that's part of it. It's about dismantling the myths that keep survivors isolated. It's about making space for the messy truth: that love can coexist with harm, that abusers can be charming, that victims can be strong.

It's about education. Empathy. Accountability. Teaching young people that consent isn't a grey area. Teaching ourselves that boundaries aren't selfish. Refusing to explain away cruelty as "passion" or "stress".

Change doesn't just happen inside us. It has to happen around us, too.

And right now, we're watching how deeply toxic masculinity still shapes our world - in politics, in media, in the corridors of power. Charisma is still mistaken for character. Strength is still equated with dominance. The same old scripts keep playing out: men rewarded for control, women punished for pain. It's not just individual men who harm - it's the culture that enables, excuses, and elects them.

We cannot break the chain without naming that.

Reflections and Lessons

Looking back, I don't just see scars. I see the woman who survived. The woman who refused - eventually - to let shame write her story.

I see resilience in every boundary I set. Every relationship I walked away from when I realised love shouldn't hurt. Every time I spoke the truth, even when my voice shook.

To anyone reading this who feels trapped in a cycle of harm: you are not broken. You are not weak. You are not alone.

The first step might feel impossibly small. It might just be a whisper inside you that says, "I deserve better". That's enough. That's the beginning of reclaiming your power.

Maybe you've taken that first step already - by reading these words. That's more than enough.

And you are so worthy of that freedom.

Healing and Reclaiming Power

Recognising What Was and What Could Be

For a long time, I didn't even name what I had lived through as abuse. In my mind, abuse was something that happened to other women - women who were less fortunate, dependent, trapped. I was none of those things. I was strong. Independent. Capable. So how could I possibly have been a victim?

It wasn't until 2024, standing in a crowd at a rally against domestic violence, that the truth finally broke through. As the speakers shared their stories - of coercive control, emotional manipulation, physical violence - I felt a deep, visceral recognition. These were not distant horrors. They were my memories. Strangulation. Verbal degradation. Physical violence in broad daylight. Friends who stayed silent, too afraid to step in.

There were also distant memories from my childhood. Memories that I had pushed to the side.

Even then, the part of me that had spent a lifetime being "the strong one" resisted. I told myself it hadn't been that bad. I made excuses: there were no children involved; it was "just me". Surely that made it different. Surely it didn't "count".

But it did. Abuse doesn't require an audience to be real. It doesn't need witnesses or bruises in the places people can see. It lives in the silences. In the shrinking. In the unspoken fear.

Naming it didn't erase the damage, but it was the first real act of reclaiming power. It was the beginning of seeing myself - not through the eyes of those who had hurt me, but through my own, clear, compassionate gaze.

The Unseen Costs of Staying

People often wonder and ask: 'Why does she stay?' , 'Why not leave at the first sign of harm?', or 'Why did you go back to him?'

The questions we should be asking are:

'Why does he keep hitting her?'
'Why does he not keep his promises?'

The truth is, leaving or staying away isn't a moment. It's a process. And leaving is the most dangerous time, increasing the risk of violence and abuse.

At first, there was love - real, messy, complicated love. The man who became my abuser wasn't a monster from the get go. He was vulnerable, charming, broken in ways that mirrored the brokenness I had grown up with.

I recognised the familiar. I thought I could fix it. I thought love could fix it.

By the time the red flags piled up - the unmanaged bipolar swings, the simmering rage, the casual cruelties - I was already deep inside the cycle. Strength became my trap. I wore it like armour, convinced that needing help, admitting fear, meant failure. That mindset kept me stuck far longer than I should have been.

In some strange way, enduring felt like winning. Like proving I was unbreakable.

But staying came with a cost - to my spirit, my self-worth, my dreams, and to him. It took years to see that survival wasn't enough. That I deserved more than simply enduring.

Finding Strength in Leaving

Leaving was a slow accumulation of tiny awakenings - little truths I could no longer ignore. Every time I said, "this isn't okay", even just to myself, it planted a seed.

The final decision to leave didn't come with fireworks or grand gestures. It happened quietly, in a deep place inside me that finally knew: I was allowed to choose myself.

I second-guessed myself constantly. Had I exaggerated it all? Was it really that bad?

The echoes of his words clung to me. "You're too sensitive". "No one else would put up with you". "You're the crazy one". Gaslighting doesn't disappear when you shut the door behind you. It lingers. It worms its way into the corners of your mind.

And when I did leave, the love and support from friends and family was overwhelming. They had seen the signs. They had been waiting. And they stood by me - steady and unflinching - as I rebuilt my life.

The Long Road to Healing

Healing didn't happen the day I left. It didn't happen after a month or even a year. It was a long, slow reclaiming of the pieces of myself that had been scattered along the way.

It was slow. Non-linear. Some days were filled with hope; others were heavy with grief for the years and parts of myself I had lost. But every small step forward was a victory.

Learning to trust again - trust myself, trust others, trust the world - was its own marathon. Some days, I felt powerful, certain I had made the right choice. Other days, the loneliness was suffocating, and I wondered if I had walked away from the only kind of love I was ever going to get.

At first, the silence was deafening. I had spent so long navigating chaos that stillness felt foreign, almost frightening. But it was in that stillness that I began to hear myself again - not the fear, not the doubt, but the steady, patient whisper of who I had always been.

There were setbacks, of course. Days when I wondered if I had imagined it all. Nights when the loneliness crept in and I questioned whether I would ever feel truly safe again. But healing isn't a straight line. It's a winding, messy, sometimes beautiful journey. And every small choice to believe in myself, every time I said no to something that didn't feel right, every time I reached out instead of retreating - they all mattered. They were all bricks in rebuilding a life on my own terms.

I learned to separate strength from silence. I learned that asking for help, setting boundaries, admitting vulnerability - these weren't signs of weakness. They were acts of radical self-love.

But slowly, step by shaky step, I began to remember who I was before the harm dulled my shine. A woman who deserved to be safe. To be seen. To be loved without fear.

Reconnecting Safely

About a year after we parted ways, my ex and I reconnected - not as partners, but as something simpler and safer: co-parents to our dogs.

By then, the urgency, the volatility, the dangerous pull between us had faded. I could show up for the dogs, for the version of him that was trying to heal, without stepping back into harm's way.

He moved into the granny flat on the property I was renting. Separate lives, shared responsibilities. Boundaries clear and unwavering. There was no more pretending that love alone could fix everything. Compassion, yes. Proximity, no.

Supporting someone's healing is very different from sacrificing your own to do it. This time, I chose differently.

The Men I Walked Away From

Not every man in my life was abusive. Some were kind. Patient. Even the exact kind of partner I thought I wanted - until the fear inside me said otherwise.

There was my kind-hearted university boyfriend, who came from a different world of privilege and ease. I adored him, but the deep-rooted belief that I didn't belong in his world gnawed at me. Instead of trusting the love we had, I ghosted him - disappearing without explanation, thinking I was sparing us both inevitable heartbreak.

There was the boy whose smile lit up when he first saw me, who moved into my life as easily as breathing. When his struggles with unemployment and self-worth surfaced, I didn't know how to stay and support him without drowning in my own fears. I ran again - out of sheer terror that I wasn't strong enough to navigate it without losing myself.

There was the one who saw the real me, even when I tried to hide. He spotted me on the dance floor - my happy space, where I've always felt free to be fully myself - and started to "pretend" to film me. If it were today, he'd have whipped out a smartphone, but this was 1989, so we had to store it the old-fashioned way: in memory.

He was from a different world. Exotic. Creative. And he made me laugh. We had so much fun that year. But it wasn't a "typical" relationship by any Norwegian standard. I wasn't ready to be seen the way he saw me. Not fully. So I pulled away.

Again and again, the pattern repeated: when things got too real, too intimate, too close - I'd disappear. I didn't know how to stay in the messiness of real connection without feeling overwhelmed by the fear of being hurt - or worse, seen as a burden.

These were good men. Some of them loved me, I think. But I hadn't yet learned how to love myself enough to let that love in.

Meeting Love Where It Found Me

It took decades. Years of unlearning the patterns that kept me stuck. Years of therapy, of false starts, of thinking I had it figured out, only to stumble again.

But eventually - blessedly - love found me. Not the kind that sweeps you off your feet with drama and fireworks. The kind that feels steady, grounding, and real.

When I met the man who would become my life partner at 42, it was both exhilarating and terrifying. We met at a place that I like to call the "second-hand market for divorcees" for fun. We were both tall and spotted each other across the room full of dancing bodies. Turns out he worked with one of my best friends and we were part of the same party, so not quite second-hand shopping. The attraction was immediate, and we have now been together for over 20 years.

For the first time, I allowed myself to say, "I love you". The words felt foreign on my tongue, clumsy and almost too vulnerable to speak aloud.

But they were real. And so was the love that grew between us - messy, imperfect, sometimes challenging, but rooted in deep respect and acceptance.

He didn't ask me to earn his love. He didn't require me to perform for it. He simply offered it, day after day, and little by little, I learned to believe that I was worthy of it.

Not because I was perfect. Not because I had finally "fixed" myself. But because I was human - lovable and enough exactly as I am.

I am not saying that there have not been challenges in our 20 years together, but we tackle them one by one as they appear. We walk away and come back together when we're calm. We are both fiercely independent, and I for one have had to learn to trust and that it is okay to share. No matter how difficult that is.

Since I accepted that my brain is wired differently and how much that has affected my livelihood, I have become more open about my struggles, and Dave is always there for me - even when he does not quite understand and has to drag the story out of me. And sometimes, I even ask for help. But most of the time, he simply sees me - often before I see myself - and he worries far more than he needs to. That's love too. The quiet kind. The steady kind. The kind that stays.

Reflections on Power and Healing

Healing isn't a destination. It's not a single moment where everything makes sense and the past stops hurting.

It's a long road - winding, sometimes lonely, sometimes breathtakingly beautiful. It's a thousand tiny choices to show up for yourself when it would be easier to hide.

And it's the reminder, over and over again, that you are not broken. That surviving isn't something to be ashamed of - it's a testament to your strength.

Today, I carry the scars not as burdens, but as proof. Proof that I made it through. Proof that I'm still here, still growing, still open to love in all its beautiful, messy forms.

To anyone reading this who has endured hurt, loss, or betrayal: You are worthy of healing. You are worthy of peace. And you are worthy of a love that lifts you, not one that breaks you.

Always.

Conclusion: Moving Forward with Strength

Looking back on the twists and turns of my journey - the heartbreaks, the silence, the small rebellions, and the giant leaps - I'm struck not by the weight of the pain, but by the sheer resilience it took to keep moving forward.

For a long time, I thought surviving was just what you did. You grit your teeth. You get through it. You carry on. But surviving is not automatic. It's a choice. A quiet act of rebellion against the forces that tried to diminish you.

Every scar, every hard-won truth, every moment I chose to get back on the road when it would have been easier to stay stuck - they all form the map of who I am today.

Healing never erases the past - it stops it from defining me.

Today, I ride forward with optimism and with clear-eyed hope. Hope that acknowledges where I've been, honours what I've survived, and trusts that there are still breathtaking vistas ahead.

Love, for me, isn't the shiny destination at the end of the roadtrip. It's the quiet campfires along the way - the honest conversations, the safe hands, the moments when you can finally exhale and know: You are safe. You are loved. You are home.

To anyone still navigating their own journey: It's okay to stop and rest. It's okay to reroute. It's okay to stumble. What matters is that you keep choosing yourself, mile after mile.

Strength is in showing up, again and again, even when the road is rough.

And I promise you: The adventure - your roadtrip - is still waiting for you, full of possibility.

Keep going.

Tuning Up: The Healing Power of Self-Compassion

Having compassion for ourselves means that we honor and accept our humanness.
Dr. Kristin Neff

When we think about strength or being strong, it's easy to imagine resilience as being hard, tough, or impervious to pain. But true healing often begins with tenderness - a willingness to meet yourself with the same compassion you would offer a dear friend.

Kristin Neff, a pioneering researcher on self-compassion, teaches that recovery from hardship is about recognising your pain without judging yourself for it. Her work reminds us that self-compassion is not self-pity or weakness - it's courage in its most grounded, enduring form.

Some key insights from Neff that resonate with this chapter's journey:

Self-kindness over self-criticism. *When we meet our struggles with harsh judgment, we double the pain. Choosing kindness toward ourselves eases the weight of suffering and opens the door to healing.*

Common humanity over isolation. *Pain can make us feel alone. Neff's research shows that recognising suffering as a shared human experience helps us feel connected rather than cut off.*

Mindfulness over overidentification. *Mindfulness recognises what hurts and, at the same time, holds those experiences with gentle awareness - without letting them define your entire story.*

Self-compassion is a practice that grows stronger every time we treat ourselves with the same dignity, patience, and care we so easily extend to others.

In learning to love and trust again, the greatest journey we can take is back to ourselves.

Reflective Pause: Pulling Over to Recalibrate

On every long journey, there comes a time when you need to pull over - because the road has been rough and your body, mind, and soul need a moment to breathe. Healing is much the same. It's not about racing ahead; it's about recognising when you need to stop, reassess, and offer yourself a little grace.

As you sit by the side of your own metaphorical road, ask yourself:

What are the silent burdens you've been carrying without realising it?
Where might you be holding onto blame that was never yours to begin with?
What boundaries were crossed, subtly or overtly, that you've since normalised?
How have unspoken power dynamics shaped your understanding of intimacy or safety?
What would it feel like to meet your story, all of it, with kindness instead of judgment?

You don't need to have all the answers. Just the willingness to ask the deeper questions.

There's no prize for pushing through at full throttle. Sometimes, the greatest act of courage is pulling over, opening the windows wide, and letting in the air of compassion and possibility.

And remember - you don't have to rest alone on the roadside. Reach for the people who know how to pause with you, who remind you that stillness can be shared too.

FIFTH GEAR

Full Throttle - Celebrating Uniqueness and Advocacy

Visibility is not a privilege, it is a right.
Laverne Cox

There's a difference between being seen and choosing to be visible.

For most of my life, I'd ridden along trying to earn a place at the table - to be seen for my skills, my ideas, my drive. But visibility on my own terms? That took something else entirely. A different kind of ride.

In 2023, as I approached my 60th birthday, I decided to take a new road. Something bold. Something raw, public, and purposeful.

I launched a campaign called *Celebrating Differences* to raise awareness and funding for mental health projects supporting girls and women. As part of it, I made a very public promise: I would shave off my waist-long hair - a symbol of my identity for decades - to spark conversation, visibility, and change.

It was one of the scariest rides I'd ever taken.

On New Year's Eve, I shared my heart with the world: the why, the hopes, the urgency behind it all.

And then... silence.

A few donations trickled in. A handful of kind messages. But nothing close to the wave I had imagined.

Within 24 hours, I found myself at an unexpected crossroads. I spiraled - felt exposed, embarrassed, and above all - invisible.

I didn't post. I didn't follow up. I pulled off the road. I shrank.

And yet, something inside me refused to stay stalled for long.

I realised that if I could only show up when it was easy, I wasn't honoring the girls and women I had set out to advocate for. So I turned the ignition again - awkward, imperfect, but determined to keep moving.

I launched *#60QuirksIn60Days* - a daily practice of visibility and authenticity. Small steps. Wobbly at first. But real.

On 2 April 2023, I honored my promise. I shaved my head - on camera, on purpose.

In the end, we raised over $9,000. We sparked honest conversations around mental health. I reclaimed not just my voice, but my visibility - and my resilience.

But the part I'm proudest of? I came back. I kept riding. I kept showing up.

This story is a continuation of that campaign. It's about what it really means to live full throttle.

It's about risking vulnerability, falling down, and choosing to get back on the road louder, stronger, and more yourself than ever before.

In the chapters ahead, we'll explore how embracing your uniqueness - and advocating for others - creates wavelets of change that are bigger than any single voice.

It's not always easy. It's not always a straight road. But it's always worth it. Because when you dare to show up for yourself, you open the door for others to show up too.

This is the real heart of Full Throttle living: Not perfection. Not constant fearlessness. But the courage to keep returning - and keep riding.

STAGE FIFTEEN
Amplifying Voices

I raise up my voice - not so that I can shout, but so that those without a voice can be heard.

Malala Yousafzai

Introduction: The Power of Speaking Up

After the raw ride of *Celebrating Differences* - putting myself out there, stumbling, and finding my way back - I realised something deeper about visibility. I had the choice to keep showing up, even when it would have been easier to pull over and hide.

In a world that often seems designed to drown out quiet truths, speaking up can feel like pushing against the wind. For me, the process of finding and amplifying my voice was a winding road, filled with setbacks, triumphs, and revelations.

Some of the deepest revelations came from watching people I love struggle. When both my brother and sister were diagnosed as neurodivergent after years of mental health challenges, it cracked something open in me. Suddenly, neurodivergence wasn't a distant concept or a quirky label - it was personal. It lived in my family. And it made me look harder at the world around me: a world often too quick to judge, too slow to understand.

Around the same time, a close friend confided that she suspected she had ADHD - struggling to cope as menopause shifted the ground under her feet. I answered too quickly: "You probably do". In my eagerness to celebrate the gifts of differently wired brains, I missed the grief that came with her realisation. She didn't speak to me for weeks. And when we finally spoke, she confided that she wasn't ready to share and build bridges. "I didn't realise that we had bridges to mend", I said.

Turns out she was upset with me for not telling her that I thought she had ADHD. The thing is, it had never occurred to me until she mentioned it - and to me, it was just a different kind of normal. One of the many reasons I love her so much. I also had to gently remind her that I'm not qualified to assess or diagnose anyone.

And it taught me something essential about advocacy: That listening is just as important as speaking. That not everyone arrives at acceptance at the same speed - or with the same scars.

We don't live in the same place anymore, and our lives have taken very different turns. She left the workforce and only took on occasional contract roles. But those roles never ended well. Time and again, she was told she was "too much", even as she quietly excelled. She felt unseen, undervalued - despite knowing, deep down, that she had done the job well.

What struck me most was how familiar her experience was. It mirrored what I'd encountered too - in employment, in running my own businesses, even in volunteering. Over time, I felt like a squeaky wheel. Not because I was looking for conflict, but because I couldn't ignore what was broken or could be done better..

This same friend, years earlier, had sparked a grassroots movement to shift gender balance in one of the most male-dominated fields out there. I was lucky enough to work alongside her on a major event that raised both funding and visibility for women in the field. It was a massive success - not just for the cause, but as a testament to our kind of leadership.

Leadership that doesn't always tick traditional boxes, but leads with inclusion, innovation, and impact. Where "business as usual" isn't even on the agenda.

Leading with a mind that solved complex problems in flashes but stumbled on office politics, I quickly learned that being heard wasn't just about speaking louder. It was about timing. Strategy. Persistence. And it was about resilience - being prepared for the reality that sometimes, your voice would be dismissed, misattributed, or met with resistance.

It wasn't until much later - through advocating for mental health awareness in others - that I truly began to open my own eyes to the ways my brain worked differently. Reluctantly, at first. I had long celebrated the creative bursts, the fierce focus, the ability to connect unlikely dots. But it took standing up for others to finally accept that it wasn't just my background and upbringing - I was very likely neurodivergent too.

And that realization, though uncomfortable, gave me a new kind of power: the power of naming my difference without shame.

I was fighting to be heard for myself, driven by a deep sense of justice - a need to challenge unfair practices and create spaces where others could speak without fear.

The journey wasn't without costs. I've been labeled difficult, confrontational, too passionate. I've been sidelined, patronised, made to feel like the squeaky wheel that needed oiling - or needed removing altogether.

But through these experiences, I've come to understand the true power of speaking up. Not as a weapon of dissent - but as a bridge to understanding, collaboration, and change.

This leg is about the lessons I've learned in using that power wisely: Lessons in amplifying my voice - and helping others find theirs.

Reclaiming the Mic: From Frustration to Influence

Reclaiming your voice isn't always a dramatic, slam-your-hand-on-the-table moment. Sometimes it starts with something much quieter: a conversation, a suggestion, a nudge toward possibility.

Although sometimes, that dramatic moment is necessary too. But often, it begins with a whisper rather than a roar.

One of the greatest joys of my journey has been mentoring women who are finding their place in spaces that weren't designed with them in mind.

I first met this young woman through an incredible leadership program for diverse women here in Perth. She had recently moved into a new role - a field where most of her colleagues were privileged men over forty. Coming from a previous role where she had worked alongside many women and other migrants, she had once felt part of a team that was equal - seen, included, valued.

Now, she found herself feeling invisible. Her self-esteem, once solid, had sunk deep underground.

In our first mentoring conversation, she confided that she felt like she didn't have a voice at all. Meetings rolled on without her. Decisions were made around her. She didn't know how to step in - or even whether she was allowed to.

I suggested something simple: "Ask your manager if you can sit in on meetings, just to listen and learn". A small suggestion. But for my mentee, it was a spark.

She decided to take the advice immediately - marching into work the next day, asking her manager for the opportunity.

His answer was an unconditional yes. No hesitation. No question.

And in that moment, something shifted. She felt valued. She felt seen. She felt strong. She hadn't needed to fight or prove herself - she had simply asked. And the act of asking gave her back a piece of her power.

Helping this incredible woman in tech reclaim her mic reminded me that advocacy can be most effective by creating small openings - quiet doorways where someone else's courage can walk through.

Sometimes it's about planting a seed and watching someone else grow into their own space, in their own way.

I cannot move on these pages without a shoutout to the manager and sponsor who saw what she couldn't yet see - who championed her voice when it was tentative, advocated for her in rooms she didn't feel she had earned access to, and gave her the confidence to keep showing up.

The Cost of Staying Silent

Not every story of reclaiming your voice is simple or joyful.

There have been plenty of times when I stayed silent for too long - waiting for the right moment, hoping that my work would speak for itself. Believing, deep down, that if I just kept my head down and did good work, the right people would notice.

For years, I convinced myself that working harder and staying in my lane would earn me respect. That competence would create visibility. That someone would eventually pull me into the room where decisions were made.

But silence doesn't make waves. In settings built around louder voices, quieter ones too often default to invisibility.

The cost of staying silent wasn't always obvious at first. It crept in quietly - like a slow leak in a tire. Eroding confidence. Flattening ambition. Making the ride feel narrower and narrower.

It wasn't just professional frustration. It was personal.

I often *did* put my ideas forward - sometimes 'forcefully' - but it didn't always land. And I knew that not everyone felt able to do even that. Still, the result was the same: the fear of being too much, too loud, too inconvenient, left so many of us muted.

Every time I swallowed my ideas instead of speaking them, every time I watched someone else get credit for a thought I had buried out of fear, I felt a little smaller. A little more invisible. A little more disconnected from the reasons I loved the work in the first place.

And I saw it happening not just to me - but to so many brilliant people around me. Women who had all the expertise, all the heart, but who struggled to be heard in systems that weren't built for them.

I found that when I raised my voice, the room reacted not to the content but to me as a woman speaking. The same tone, the same force, would pass cleanly for others - but for me, the room tilted. I learned how gender and voice are never neutral.

The world wasn't designed for voices like ours. Which meant we couldn't afford to keep waiting for permission to speak.

We had to learn to take the mic. Even when our hands shook. Even when the room fell silent in response.

Because the real cost of staying silent isn't just missing opportunities. It's missing yourself. It's forgetting, piece by piece, that you had something worth saying in the first place.

Speaking Up: A Double-Edged Sword

Reclaiming my voice turned out to be about more than just me - it became about creating room for others, too. Yes, maybe I was the squeaky wheel - but what about those who didn't have the luxury of being heard, even when they squeaked?

The first few times I pushed back, it didn't go well.

When I pointed out that my ideas were being appropriated by others, I was met with awkward silences or smirks. In one instance, after calling it out in real time, the room shifted uncomfortably, and the meeting wrapped early. I was labeled "too confrontational".

It didn't matter that I was right. What mattered was *how* the message landed - and how the room responded to it.

I realised that if I wanted to create change, it wasn't just about fighting harder. It was about being strategic - finding ways to stay true to my voice without letting frustration speak for me.

Instead of reacting with anger, I practiced redirecting the conversation:

"Thank you for supporting and expanding on my idea. I love your build and think it can add great value. Why don't we workshop it together?"

When I shifted the tone, something incredible happened: The room began to recognise my ideas as valuable from the start, and collaboration became a shared victory instead of a silent battle.

It wasn't about being softer. It was about being smarter about when and how I used my influence and power.

Learning to hold both truth and strategy in the same breath became a new kind of power.

The Shift to Influence

Over time, I realised that reclaiming my voice meant that I could take up space for myself, and through that create space for others too.

Once I started speaking up more confidently, I began to notice who else in the room wasn't speaking - and why.

In many spaces, the loudest voices still carried the conversation, while quieter, equally brilliant perspectives were lost. And in some cases, the more exuberant, extrovert voices were also ignored - maybe because they were too frequent. It wasn't always intentional. Sometimes it was just the rhythm of old habits - the ones that reward dominance over thoughtfulness.

Ironically, I was often one of them. I spoke up, I had a voice that carried - and still, I wasn't always truly heard. Visibility didn't always translate into influence.

So I set a new precedent. It was a concept that was developed by an amazing colleague and usability advocate I had the pleasure of working with.

In meetings, I made a conscious effort to acknowledge contributions immediately - with a simple, neutral response: "Thank you for that idea".

No instant judgment. No immediate critique or praise. Just acknowledgement.

Sometimes I forget to say it out loud, but I hear them. And when I don't know how to move the idea forward myself, I've started simply asking: *What would taking this further look like for you?* That small question - posed with curiosity - has become another way of honouring what was said.

That small shift created a tiny wave of movement. When people knew their ideas would be received with basic respect - even if not agreed with - they were more willing to share. More voices entered the conversation. More perspectives shaped the solutions. And slowly, the room changed.

I also began insisting on having at least two underrepresented people (typically women in tech) in important meetings wherever possible. Because representation changes the conversation. The balance of voices gave others permission to contribute without fear.

As my influence grew, I modeled another practice: always crediting the source when building on someone else's thought: "As Jane just pointed out...", "That's a brilliant insight from Tom; let's build on it".

Recognition creates visibility. And visibility builds confidence - not just in individuals, but in entire cultures. The more I practiced these small shifts, the more others followed.

Leadership, I realised, includes speaking up, but just as importantly it's about creating conditions where more voices can be heard, valued, and trusted.

Creating Space for Others: Lifting as You Climb

Amplifying my own voice was powerful. But creating space for others is where true impact lives.

Throughout my journey, I've learned that leadership is about stepping into the spotlight - and sharing it. By lifting others as I climb, I've fostered inclusion, sparked innovation, and left a legacy that is bigger than any individual success story.

The day before I launched *IT Girls Rock* in 2022, something devastating happened that I've carried with me ever since. While visiting my parents in Norway, I received an unexpected call from the leader of another advocacy group in Australia. I was asked to attend an extraordinary meeting - not to collaborate, but to justify what I was doing.

They questioned my motives for creating a global coaching community and raised concerns about a potential conflict of interest and competition. I was blindsided. *Flabbergasted*. What I had hoped would be a moment of celebration - of lifting others as I climbed - instead felt like a call to defend my worth.

We did eventually come to an agreement: there was no actual conflict of interest. But there *could* have been a perceived conflict, and we resolved things professionally. On the surface, it ended well. But privately? It didn't just break my heart. It broke my back.

It crushed the intention that had fuelled the creation of IT Girls Rock. My energy, my momentum, my hope - all of it collapsed under the weight of that moment. I felt shut down before I had even begun. And the sting of that still sits with me, even now.

I have been anonymous in my pain forever, cautious about naming names or events. But to be true to the story, and to the cost of raising your voice and creating something new, this moment has to be acknowledged. Because it's not always resistance from external enemies that derails us - sometimes it's silence or suspicion from within our own communities.

And yet, I know now: that moment didn't undo me. It marked me. It shaped how I've continued to lead - with more compassion, with clearer boundaries, and with a deepened awareness of how powerful (and painful) visibility can be.

Visibility and leadership is about building broader stages where more voices can stand and be heard. And the stage does not need to be scary and daunting, but inviting to people from all walks of life.

The Power of Representation

Throughout my career, I often found myself in rooms where my voice blended into the background - not only because I was softly spoken, but because it didn't sound like what people were used to hearing. Even when I spoke up clearly and passionately, I wasn't always heard. My ideas were often echoed later by others, more familiar voices, and only then taken seriously.

It took me years to realise that it wasn't about how loud I was. It was about who was *already* in the room - and who the room was designed to hear.

That's why representation matters. Not just in a tick-box way, but in the kind of soul-deep recognition that comes when you see someone who looks like you, thinks like you, or has walked a path that mirrors your own. It's about feeling - sometimes for the first time - that you're not alone, not an anomaly, not asking for too much.

It's also about advocacy. When people in power use their position to create space for underrepresented voices - to listen, to sponsor, to make room - it changes everything. Especially for those still finding their voice.

This understanding shaped my commitment to ensuring that *everyone* - especially women, migrants, and neurodivergent individuals - has a seat at the table. Not just a symbolic one, but a meaningful one.

One memorable moment came when I introduced a simple but powerful rule after an infamous "stolen ideas" incident: there must always be at least two diverse representatives in the room where important decisions are made. I called out the inequity, and I helped build systems to uplift others - so history wouldn't repeat itself.

It wasn't enough to speak up once. I needed to change the conditions so that more voices could thrive - long after I had left the room.

The Importance of Active Sponsorship

Mentorship is valuable. But I discovered that sponsorship - actively advocating for others when they're not in the room - can be life-changing. I've championed colleagues by using my influence to recommend, endorse, and create opportunities. In addition to giving advice, I was paving a path forward.

I remember the quiet pride I felt when watching a former mentee I had sponsored step up to lead her first major project. Instead of hoarding knowledge or protecting my own turf, I had equipped her with the tools and confidence she needed to succeed - on her terms, in her voice.

That moment wasn't about ownership. It was about legacy. A living reminder that leadership means creating new leaders, not just gathering followers.

Leading by Listening

Another pillar of creating space for others has been mastering the art of listening.

I know that for some people, it might not seem like I listen. My brain moves fast - really fast. I often process a problem before the other person has even finished describing it. I might jump in early with a solution that feels completely unrelated to what they brought up. I understand how that can feel jarring. But I want to say, clearly: I *do* listen. I listen deeply. What's happening inside my mind is rapid synthesis - my brain connecting dots, reaching for possibilities, often at lightning speed. It's not a lack of care, it's just a different way of processing.

After my own experiences of being silenced or misunderstood, I developed a sensitivity to people who hesitate to speak up. But it wasn't just about paying attention to the words. I had to learn to slow down my own mind - one that can process ideas at a million miles an hour - and create genuine pauses in conversation. Space where other people's words could land and grow, instead of getting swept away.

Listening, I discovered, isn't just about understanding content. It's about reading between the lines. It's about observing non-verbal cues. It's about making the other person feel heard and seen.

Growing up in a lively family where we all spoke over each other, I didn't realise until much later how hard it can be for quieter voices to break through. We weren't trying to shut anyone out - we were just passionate, animated, always chasing the next idea. But for the introverts in the room, it must have felt like standing on the banks of a fast-moving river - never quite able to step in.

It took years - and many lessons - to understand that real listening sometimes means holding back your brilliant next thought, resisting the urge to fill every silence, and creating a stillness where someone else's voice can rise.

By fostering a culture where questions and concerns are welcome, I've helped quieter voices step forward. I've seen firsthand that real leadership isn't about having all the answers. It's about making it safe enough for the real questions - and the real people - to surface.

Balancing Confidence and Collaboration

Creating space for others has never meant diminishing my own light.

I've learned to balance confidence in my ideas with a collaborative spirit that invites others into the process. Sometimes that has meant navigating egos, misunderstandings, or clashing communication styles. But my resilience and empathy have helped me stay authentic - standing my ground without bulldozing, and lifting others without losing myself.

It's not a perfect science. It's a daily practice. A choice to believe that power shared is power multiplied, not divided.

A friend and fellow community member once told me, 'You always bring your full, inclusive self.' I took it as one of the highest compliments. It reminded me that I didn't need to shrink to lift others. When we lead with authenticity, we create space where others feel seen, welcomed, and empowered.

Tuning Up: Creating the Conditions to Speak - Inside and Out

You can't be courageous without first feeling safe enough to take the risk.
Amy Edmondson

Imposter feelings are not a reflection of your ability. They are a reflection of your inner narrative. Valerie Young

Amplifying your voice is brave work. It's about self-trust as much as self-expression.

Amy Edmondson, a Harvard researcher and author of *The Fearless Organization*, describes **psychological safety** as the belief that a team or group is safe for interpersonal risk-taking. It's the foundation of inclusion, innovation, and growth. In unsafe environments, people stay quiet - not because they have nothing to say, but because they fear the cost of saying it.

That silence can cost teams ideas. And it can cost you your voice.

Even in psychologically safe environments, many women still hesitate to speak up - not because the room isn't safe, but because the **inner narrative** says they're not ready, not credible, not enough.

Valerie Young's work reframes this as **imposter syndrome**, showing that even highly capable people can question their right to belong. But this isn't a flaw - it's a conditioned response. Years of being "the only" or "the first" can plant that doubt.

Still, we must be careful not to pathologise those feelings. What we call *imposter syndrome* can also reflect real exclusion - environments that fail to recognise or include difference.

In *Conquer Your Imposter*, Alison Shamir offers simple, practical steps to shift the inner story: **name the feeling without shame, check the evidence that supports your worth, and take one visible action anyway.** Each act of courage strengthens self-trust - and helps your voice grow steadier.

When safety grows both inside and outside, something powerful happens:

You speak, even if your voice shakes. You share, even if it's not perfect. You own your story, even if it's still unfolding.

Your voice tells the world: *I belong here.*

Reflective Pause: Open the Mic, Even When Your Voice Shakes

Speaking up isn't just one act of courage - it's a pattern we practice. A risk we take.

Not just to be heard, but to be *seen*. As we are.

There is no perfect moment to speak the truth.
Sometimes it sounds like a whisper.
Sometimes like a crack in your voice you let through anyway.

What shuts your voice down faster: outer resistance or inner doubt?

When have you chosen silence to stay safe - and what did it cost you?

What would building "psychological safety" inside yourself look like?

What's one thing you've wanted to say (or create, or claim) that deserves amplification - even if it's imperfect?

You don't have to roar. You just have to speak with truth.
And trust that your voice was never too much - just waiting for space.

And if the space still feels too big, borrow courage from your crew - the mentors, coaches, and allies who remind you that every voice grows stronger when it's echoed in good company.

STAGE SIXTEEN
The Power of Connection Across Differences

It is not our differences that divide us. It is our inability to recognize, accept, and celebrate those differences.
Audre Lorde

Introduction: Building Bridges on the Open Road

Sometimes, the horizon looks like an endless stretch of differences - cultural, generational, ideological. The easy thing is to turn around, find a road more familiar, stay with those who look and think like we do.

But the real adventure - the real growth - comes from daring to cross the bridges that connect what seems impossible to bring together.

I've always believed that meaningful progress happens when we learn to honour our differences while finding common ground. That belief didn't come from a book or a classroom. It was shaped in the long rides through unfamiliar places, through personal experiences both rewarding and confronting.

Inclusion is a word that gets thrown around easily. Real inclusion is about recognising and valuing the richness that different perspectives bring - and knowing that the strongest bridges are the ones that leave both sides standing strong.

I've sat at tables where I was the only woman, the only neurospicy brain, the outsider to the established power structure. I could either shrink back or throttle forward. I've done both.

But the moments that changed everything - the real turning points - were the ones where I chose to stay visible. Where I chose not just to speak, but to make space for others to step onto the bridge too.

In addition to professional victories, we want to celebrate the personal miles travelled - the detours, the potholes, the unexpected friendships built along the way.

Because the more we connect across differences, the more we break down walls of fear, bias, and exclusion. And every bridge built makes the next journey easier for those who come after.

Bridging the Gap: Stories of Connection

While bridging gaps between differences can feel like grand, abstract goals, it's a series of small, gritty, courageous actions. It's the conversations that happen around long tables and on winding roads, in the quiet moments when someone dares to lean in a little closer.

Over the years, I've experienced firsthand how small moments of connection can change the entire trajectory of relationships, projects, and even careers. But those moments didn't happen by accident. They came from a commitment to show up - to risk discomfort, to ride through the storms of misunderstanding, and sometimes, to be the one stubborn enough to keep knocking when the door stayed half-closed.

Connection doesn't always come easy. It asks us to stay visible even when shrinking feels safer. It asks us to trust that the road we're on will lead somewhere better, even when we can't yet see the next bend.

These are some of the stories that shaped me. Moments where the bridges weren't obvious - or easy - but were absolutely worth building.

The Idea That Wasn't Mine (Until It Was)

Some moments on the road hit harder than any pothole.

One that still stings happened during the planning of a major conference. I'd taken the lead on the program - coordinating topics, working closely with speakers, and stepping up to carry more than my share when others needed to step back.

It was emotionally heavy work. Some of my peers were going through personal challenges, and I wanted to hold the ship steady - for the team, for the mission. That's what I do. But when the praise came - in wrap-up meetings, public thank yous, and email chains - my name was left out.

It wasn't the first time. But something about that moment, how it erased the work I'd done with such intention and care, cracked something in me.

I wasn't looking for applause. I just wanted it to be fair.

And I realised that if I kept holding the mic for others without ever using it myself, I'd always stay invisible.

Another situation that sticks with me happened during a leadership meeting in a different organisation - a cross-functional gathering designed to align strategies. As the only woman at the table, I knew that my ideas would need to come with recipes. I had spent days refining a novel solution to a critical issue, excited to present it. I spoke up and shared my thoughts. The room went silent - blank stares, a few polite nods.

I chalked it up to timing and kept listening. A few minutes later, one of the senior leaders spoke up: "I really liked John's idea about..." - and went on to repeat my proposal almost word-for-word.

Something in me snapped. I stood up, placed my hands firmly on the table, and said, "That was my proposal". The room froze. Then came the awkward laughter and the dismissive mutters: "Sure it was".

I wish I could say I handled it gracefully. The truth is, I was livid. It wasn't just the "stolen" credit - it was the casual dismissal of my voice. That moment became a fork in the road.

There is also another invisible rule no one had taught me: The *real* pitching didn't happen in the meeting. It happened before.

In my world, if you had a strong idea you could bring it to the group and be heard - openly, together. That's how I was raised. That's the cultural rhythm I moved with.

But in this context, I was missing something. I hadn't learned yet that influence was often built *quietly*, in one-on-one conversations *before* the official discussion ever began.

Once I understood that, things started to shift. I didn't change the boldness of my ideas - but I changed how I brought them into the room. I started having pre-conversations. Making sure my voice had support *before* it ever hit the air.

Not because I wanted to play politics. I realised that being strategic meant I could be both authentic and be heard.

Instead of shrinking into silence, I started taking deliberate steps to make sure my contributions - and those of others who felt invisible - would not be erased.

These days, when I'm in rooms where decisions are made, I set a clear expectation early: more than one underrepresented voice belongs at the table - always.

It's a small move. But small moves pave big roads. And every road we pave makes it a little easier for the next woman - or the next outsider - to ride further than we did.

The "Squeaky Wheel" Moment: When Speaking Up Cost Me

Some breakdowns on the road you can fix with a quick patch. Others leave you sitting alone in the dark, wondering if you'll ever find your way back.

One of the hardest parts of my advocacy journey happened inside a space that should have been safe - a group advocating for diversity, inclusion and equity in my field of work, built on the promise of inclusion and support. On the surface, everything looked right. Beneath it, something harsher that I did not agree with, had taken root. Despite all the talk of welcoming diverse perspectives, elitist behaviours ran unchecked. Invisible lines were drawn around who truly belonged - and who didn't.

At first, I spoke up carefully. Not to shame, not to attack - but to bring awareness. I pointed out patterns of exclusion. I offered ideas for change.

Each time, I was met with resistance - or worse, silence. A shrug. A "that's just how things are" tossed out like a dusty map to nowhere.

I was not so gently nudged, again and again, to "fall in line", to "stop rocking the boat". But I couldn't. I wouldn't.

I kept believing that persistence, passion, and patience could shift the culture. It didn't. Instead, it shifted me.

Phone calls that once felt collaborative became heavy with unexpected tension. Messages from leaders I trusted triggered a pulse of anxiety deep in my chest. Direct, full frontal attacks in meetings when I presented ideas that did not toe the line. I found myself checking the caller ID and hoping it wasn't them - an ache of dread I couldn't explain to anyone who hadn't been through it.

And yet, these weren't strangers. These were people I had once called my tribe. My people. The environment where I felt I belonged. Where I should feel respected and supported.

The silence and exclusion cut deeper than any corporate slight ever could.

This wasn't just a professional setback. It was a fracture in belonging - a loneliness that no amount of logic could soothe.

When I finally resigned, I didn't burn bridges. I finished my projects, tied every loose end, and left with as much dignity as I could muster. But inside, it felt like riding away from a home I had built with my own hands - only to find the door bolted shut behind me.

The grief was real. Grief for the role, and for the community and friendships I thought were real - and for the part of myself that had believed it always would be.

But the road didn't end there. It never does.

In time, I realised I didn't have to keep knocking on closed doors. I could build new ones - stronger ones. I could create communities where belonging wasn't a privilege granted by gatekeepers - it was a birthright.

And I have.

The wheels kept turning. The road kept calling. And somewhere between the silence and the scars, I found a stronger kind of belonging - the kind you build yourself.

But even the strongest bridges can carry hidden cracks. Even after moving forward, some old roads have a way of pulling you off course - especially when you least expect it.

When Playing by the Rules Still Isn't Enough

There's a particular kind of heartbreak that comes from being invited in, only to realise the invitation was never real.

I'd been asked to assess a contentious initiative - something with strong feelings on both sides. The goal was to bring clarity, find a win-win path forward, and help the team move past tension toward alignment. I stepped in with care. I hosted the first conversation, facilitated openly, and captured the key points in a written summary. No AI tools back then - just my own two ears, my intuition, and a deep commitment to neutrality.

So when one of the leaders, who hadn't even been in the meeting, accused me of bias, I was floored.

Dumbfounded, really. I'd gone out of my way to be balanced. To check myself. To make sure no sentence leaned too hard in either direction. Just to be sure,

I even sent the notes to a few trusted advisors - without context - asking, "Does this read fair to you?" Their answers were clear. Neutral. Measured. Spot on.

Still, I didn't defend myself. Instead, I did what I thought a good leader should do. I met individually with every team member. I listened. I asked questions. I stayed open. And gradually, something surprising surfaced: it seemed we were all on the same page.

So when we regrouped for the decision, I was hopeful. The leader who had been most opposed to the alternative option spoke first - and I was curious.

But what came out of their mouth shocked me.

They passionately argued *against* the very motion they had, just days earlier, told me they supported "hands down".

I blinked. Breathed. And gently asked, "What happened between our one-on-one and now?"

There was no real answer. Just a shrug. A pivot. A change of tune that left me standing there wondering why I'd been asked to spend time, energy, and trust on something that clearly had already been decided behind closed doors.

The sting wasn't just the reversal. It was the realisation that no matter how diplomatically I'd played it, no matter how fairly I'd tried to lead, the outcome had never been mine to shape. I had been asked to run a project for which the outcome was already decided, wasting both my time and everyone else's.

That moment carved another groove in the story: that sometimes, no amount of skill, care, or emotional labour will change a room not ready to listen.

It also taught me this: when your voice gets dismissed not because of how you speak, but because of who you are - it's not your failure. It's a systemic fault.

And it's not a reason to stop. It's a reason to speak louder, build differently, and keep your compass steady.

When the Past Pulls You Off Course

Healing is rarely a clean line. Sometimes it's a winding backroad you thought you'd finished travelling - until something reminds you that the road still has work to do.

Over a year after I had walked away from that organisation, I believed I was doing well. I had poured my energy into new projects. I had built communities where I was seen, valued, and supported.

And then, during a conversation with one of my mentors, a simple suggestion hit me harder than I expected.

"Why not reach out to communities that serve your audience and propose a collaboration?"

I froze. Completely.

In an instant, the memories came rushing back - how many times I had tried to build bridges with the group that once felt like my tribe... and how often I had been met with silence, deflection, or invisible walls.

It was a physical reaction. My breath caught. My chest tightened. I realised I hadn't fully reckoned with the depth of the hurt and rejection I had felt.

That moment forced me to slow down and listen - not just to the coach's question, but to the ache underneath it.

This was about more than fear of rejection. It was about the scar tissue left by broken trust.

And it taught me something important: True resilience is about recognising when old wounds still shape your choices - and choosing to heal anyway.

Since then, I've found new spaces where inclusion is real, not just promised. Places where we celebrate differences. Places where I can ride both within and along the boundary, with full awareness of what's happening inside me.

But along the way, I noticed something. The loudest pain often gets the most comfort. The people who cry in meetings, who fall apart publicly - they're offered soft landings. And I'm glad they are. But that's never been how I fall.

As we have established, I don't cry - ever. I go quiet. I shut down. I keep moving. And then I replay it all a thousand times in my own space, where no one can see it. That doesn't make the hurt less real. That's just how I bleed. Maybe it is my resilience, maybe it is because I just don't get incongruence.

Big girls don't cry, they say. I think some of us just cry differently. Some of us rebuild in silence. Some of us need to be asked, twice. That, too, is vulnerability. That, too, is worthy of support.

Maybe the real wisdom is this: Inclusion means making space for every kind of hurt. Every kind of healing.

The feeling of being both part of and apart from communities hasn't disappeared. Maybe it never will. But now, instead of letting it isolate me, I ride with it. I notice it. I name it. And I choose, again and again, to keep showing up - with open eyes and a stronger heart.

Finding the Humanity in Hierarchies

Not every roadblock on the journey is about terrain. Some of the hardest ones are built into the structures around us - the invisible forces of power, status, and control.

One of the most painful lessons I learned in advocacy was realising that good intentions aren't always enough to move a system that wasn't built to listen.

Early in my career, I believed that standing up for my team was simple: see injustice, speak out, protect your people. I thought transparency and honesty would speak for themselves - that results would prove the worth of the path I was riding.

But the road was trickier than I first understood.

There's a difference between advocating for others and unintentionally disrupting the system by not navigating leadership expectations. I didn't realise, back then, that while I was fiercely protecting my team's dignity, I wasn't always aligning with leadership's priorities. And without sponsorship from those holding the maps and the keys, my efforts often went nowhere - or worse, were seen as rebellion.

In hindsight, I also see that some team members learned to play on my protective instincts, knowing I would charge ahead without hesitation. I was riding solo, thinking loyalty alone would carry us through.

It didn't.

The lessons cost me - opportunities, credibility, and sometimes peace of mind.

Now, I approach advocacy differently. I still stand fiercely for fairness. But I do it with a deeper understanding that real change isn't a solo ride - it's a convoy. It's about building coalitions, securing alignment, and ensuring that directness is matched with collaboration.

Humanity is still there - mine and theirs. It just took a few hard miles to learn how to navigate the road.

The Unseen Cost of Isolation

It's easy to believe that standing up for what's right will be met with applause and appreciation. That if you ride true, others will fall in behind you.

But the truth is, advocacy can be lonely. Sometimes it feels like cresting a hill, only to look around and realise you're riding alone.

You might lose the backing you expected. You might lose relationships you thought were unshakeable. You might even lose a sense of who you are, in the spaces where you once felt most at home.

I've learned that losing your people isn't just a professional disappointment. It's grief. A raw, aching grief that comes not from losing titles or status - but from losing belonging. From losing the shared purpose that once fuelled every mile.

And like any true grief, it doesn't heal overnight. It asks you to reckon with the gap - and then decide how you'll fill it.

Just as you can lose a tribe, you can find - or build - one.

You can gather riders who value the journey as much as the destination. You can find new companions who see your differences as gifts. You can build spaces where belonging isn't earned through silence - but through showing up, scarred and whole, exactly as you are.

The road can get lonely. But it never runs out of possibilities.

Breaking Walls: Challenging the Status Quo

Being a justice warrior means speaking up when things go wrong. It also means refusing to accept systems that favour the status quo at the expense of equity, innovation, and humanity.

It's about facing down barriers that others pretend don't exist - or are too afraid to challenge. It's about knowing that sometimes, the price of progress is the discomfort that comes with naming the truth.

I've lost count of the times I've been told to "fall in line" or "let it go" for the sake of keeping the peace. But keeping the peace isn't the same as keeping things fair. Sometimes, to clear the trail, you have to rattle the foundations others are too scared to shake.

When Standing Alone Is the Only Option

One of the hardest lessons I've learned in advocacy is that sometimes, you're the only one willing to take a stand. It's isolating. It's exhausting. It's often thankless.

There was this project where I found myself the lone dissenting voice in a room full of yes-people. The issue wasn't a small oversight - we had overlooked a fundamental requirement that could make or break our product, and nobody was willing to step up and own it. It was a fundamental flaw that would spread outward, affecting the team and the people we were supposed to be serving.

When I raised it, the room went silent. People shifted uncomfortably in their seats, avoiding eye contact as if my words carried a weight they couldn't bear.

I could feel the tension rising like steam in a pressure cooker. But I held my ground.

Later, someone whispered, "You were brave to say that". And while part of me was grateful for the acknowledgment, another part couldn't help but think: Why does bravery feel so lonely?

Some rides you take with a convoy. Others, you ride solo because the destination matters too much to abandon.

The Cost of Courage

Speaking truth to power often comes at a cost - sometimes a steep one.

I've been excluded from meetings I once led. Overlooked for opportunities I had helped create. Accused of being "difficult" simply for advocating for fairness and transparency.

I used to think being a truth teller would be enough - that naming the problem with clarity and care would spark change. But I learned that truth alone doesn't always open doors. Sometimes, it closes them. Speaking up can shrink you in the eyes of those protecting comfort zones, especially when you name what they'd rather ignore.

But over time, I've come to understand something critical: My value isn't tied to my approval rating in someone else's eyes. It isn't tied to how comfortable I make the room feel. Navigating this is difficult when all you want is love and

acceptance. If you spend your life shrinking to fit someone else's comfort zone, you end up abandoning your own truth - and that's a price I'm no longer willing to pay.

The road to real change isn't paved with popularity contests. It's paved with integrity, and sometimes, with scars.

Breaking Barriers Together

Despite the isolation that often comes with challenging the status quo, I've also experienced the incredible power of finding allies - those rare and brilliant people who hear you and say, "You're not crazy. And you're not alone".

One of the most rewarding moments in my advocacy journey was seeing the ripple effect after I spoke out. Others, inspired by the same hunger for fairness, began to find their voices too. How they started to first bring issues to my attention, and then with my support were able to stand up and carry it themselves.

Real change rarely happens overnight. But when people come together - when they stand shoulder to shoulder instead of shrinking back - the walls that once seemed unbreakable start to crumble.

And the road ahead, once blocked and broken, starts to clear.

Breaking Down Barriers with Courage and Curiosity

One of the most powerful ways to bridge divides is by stepping forward with an open mind and heart, even when fear or uncertainty whispers in the background.

Courage does more than roar - it often shows up as a quiet, steady determination to ask questions, to understand, and to connect.

The Power of "Why?"

In my life, curiosity has been my greatest asset in breaking down barriers. Whether I was the outsider in a new country or the lone woman in a boardroom, I found that asking "Why?" - genuinely and without judgment - could shift the entire energy of the room.

"Why is this policy important to you?" "Why do we assume this is the only way?" But make sure you personalise the way you ask the questions.

By digging deeper and inviting others to share their perspectives, I created conversations that led to real progress. Design thinking has always been my friend. No judgement. Just process.

But curiosity is only powerful when paired with humility. It's about listening to understand, not just to respond. It's about being willing to hear hard truths and sit with the discomfort they bring. And sometimes, it's about accepting that the answers you receive may challenge your beliefs - and push you to re-route your course.

Courage in Confrontation

Courage is about how you approach conflict. There have been moments when I had to challenge the status quo, even at the risk of standing alone. I've questioned leadership decisions, advocated for marginalised voices, and raised my hand when it felt safer to stay silent.

One instance that stands out is when I saw a team member's work consistently overlooked in favour of others. Instead of tiptoeing around the issue, I addressed it head-on with leadership, using data to highlight the discrepancy. I wasn't confrontational, but I was clear. I asked questions that couldn't be ignored and framed the conversation as a way to strengthen the team. This approach supports the individual, and it challenges others to re-examine their blind spots and be more intentional about inclusion.

Meeting People Where They Are

A crucial part of building bridges is recognising that not everyone starts from the same point on the road. Some are miles ahead in their understanding of inclusion and advocacy. Others are just starting to learn the map.

Rather than dismissing those who "don't get it", I've learned to meet them where they are - and guide them forward.

I never tolerate harm, but I extend patience to those willing to learn, turning "I don't know how" into "Let's figure it out together". And it also means knowing when to set firm boundaries and ride on without apology when growth isn't possible.

The journey toward equity is a long ride - and every voice willing to learn and lean in makes the pathway a little stronger. I am always on a mission of bringing everyone along for the journey.

Creating Collaborative Pathways

In the professional world, we're often taught that competition is healthy - that it drives progress, fuels ambition, and raises the bar. But what if the real fuel for lasting change isn't competition at all? What if lifting each other up, rather than racing each other to the finish line, is the key to progress that sustains rather than exhausts us?

I much prefer the term *coopetition*, where we both collaborate and compete in healthy ways.

In my early career, I absorbed the idea that I needed to prove my worth by being the best. I thought being the most prepared, the fastest, or the loudest would secure my place at the table.

But over time - and over miles - I came to see that my greatest successes came standing out authentically and from riding alongside others who carried unique powers I didn't. Aligned with my natural tendency of collaboration and co-creation.

A Shift in Mindset

Collaboration doesn't mean you stop being ambitious. It doesn't mean you lower your standards. It simply shifts your mindset from asking, "Who do I need to outperform?" to asking, "Who can I grow with?"

This shift became crystal clear when I joined a cross-disciplinary team working on an ambitious project. Instead of gatekeeping ideas or guarding credit, we asked:

"What does each of us bring to the table that can make this even better?"

The result was a level of innovation none of us could have reached alone.

When you view collaboration as a strength rather than a compromise, you move from scarcity to abundance. When others shine, it amplifies your light, and it lights the road for everyone.

The Challenges of Collaboration

Of course, collaboration isn't always an easy ride. It demands clear communication, vulnerability, and a willingness to compromise without losing the heart of your own voice.

There were moments when I felt frustrated - unsure if my ideas were being valued, unsure if I was yielding too much. But true collaboration is about creating spaces where different voices make the whole stronger.

It's about building bridges wide enough to hold real weight - not just polishing the surface.

From Competition to Connection

Many of us have felt that gut-punch moment when someone undermines us to get ahead, or takes credit for work that isn't theirs. Those moments sting - and they can make collaboration feel risky.

But when we model collaboration instead of competition, we set the tone. We show others there's another way to travel the road. We build trust. We attract the right companions for the journey.

I've also learned the quiet power of calling out great ideas that aren't mine - acknowledging others without losing my own voice. It strengthens connections. And often, it creates a butterfly effect where others start championing your voice too.

From Ally to Accomplice

Recently, I found myself in three separate conversations with senior men - good men - who care about fairness and equity. Each, in his own way, told me that he didn't really see a gender equity problem. Not anymore. One said we just needed to "fix the system". Another assured me that women just needed better mentors. The third explained how his workplace was already "pretty balanced".

I didn't argue. I just stared.

These men support the women close to them - daughters, wives, female colleagues. They're what many would call allies. But none of them have lived the experience of being judged and underestimated before they even open their mouth. Of being told they're "too much" when they speak with conviction. Of having ideas ignored until someone else repeats them in a deeper voice.

Supporting women in proximity is not the same as understanding systemic barriers. Good intentions aren't the same as shared risk. And mentorship, while valuable, doesn't replace investment.

We don't just need allies. We need accomplices - people who are willing to step up and shake things up for good.

An accomplice understands that equity isn't charity - it's justice. They don't just cheer from the sidelines. They step in. They take on some of the weight. They speak up in rooms we're not in. They shift resources, share access, and push for change even when it's inconvenient.

Fixing the system is both strategy and practical, gritty work - like providing real opportunities, sponsoring real women, and staying when the conversation gets uncomfortable.

And when accomplices show up - not just allies - the celebration becomes collective. We win louder, together.

Celebrating Wins as a Team

One of the most powerful lessons in collaboration is that celebrating collective wins matters just as much as individual ones.

Individual credit has its place. But in the ecosystems I've worked hard to build, mutual respect and shared success shine brighter.

When we cheer for our peers, we build cultures where recognition is abundant. Where no one has to hustle alone for visibility.

And we don't sacrifice our own success in the process. We expand the meaning of the win - to honour the journey and the riders who helped get us there.

Because at the end of the road, it's not about who got there fastest. It's about who we became - and what we built - along the way.

Tuning Up: Belonging Through Brave Conversation

While no single conversation is guaranteed to change the trajectory of a relationship, any single conversation can.
Susan Scott, *Fierce Conversations*

Connection doesn't begin in agreement - it begins in honesty. When you step into a conversation that matters, your body knows it before your mind does: the quickened pulse, the breath that catches, the urge to retreat. Staying present through that moment is its own kind of courage.

Susan Scott's work reminds us that belonging isn't built by smoothing over differences or avoiding conflict. It grows through conversations where truth meets compassion - when you speak with clarity, listen with curiosity, and stay grounded long enough for understanding to take root.

We've been taught to make conversations "nice."

But niceness often hides what's real. Brave conversations are different: they are direct, kind, and accountable. They demand that we bring our full selves - not just the polished version - to the table.

Scott teaches that each conversation is a microcosm of our larger relationships. When we choose authenticity over avoidance, we strengthen the fabric of trust. And when we listen not to reply but to connect, we create the safety that allows others to do the same.

So here's what this means on the road:

Notice where silence has replaced sincerity - and choose to speak what's true.
When your voice shakes, speak anyway.
Stay curious longer than feels comfortable.
Remember that honesty not harmony is what sustains real connection.

Because belonging isn't about avoiding tension. It's about learning to stay in the room - heart steady, truth intact.

Reflective Pause: Stay in the Room

Connection isn't always comfortable - but it's worth it. The bravest conversations often start where comfort ends.

What situations or conversations tempt you to stay quiet when you know you need to speak?

When have you softened or sidestepped truth to keep the peace - and what did that cost you?

How do you react when someone's truth challenges your own? (Defensiveness? Curiosity? Compassion?)

What might it look like to stay open - even when the air feels charged with tension or truth?

Presence in conversation isn't passive. It's active listening, grounded honesty, and respect - even when disagreement stays on the table.

You don't have to fix every moment. You just have to stay long enough to understand. Stay in the room - especially when it would be easier to walk out. That's where real connection begins.

And if the air feels too heavy to breathe alone, lean on your crew - the coach, the ally, or the friend who can hold steady ground beside you until clarity returns.

STAGE SEVENTEEN
Owning Your Spotlight

*I don't want to be invisible because I'm a woman.
I want to be seen because I'm me.*

Viola Davis

Introduction: Stepping into Your Power

Stepping into your power can be a single, triumphant moment, but more often it's a series of small, often uncelebrated choices. And your "spotlight"? It doesn't have to mean stages or microphones. Visibility looks different for everyone. For some, it's the quiet courage to speak in a meeting, to press 'send' on a bold idea, or to advocate for yourself when it's easier to stay silent. For others, it might be stepping onto a literal stage. Both are valid. Both matter.

It's the resolve to stay visible when you feel invisible - and the courage to keep showing up despite uncertainty.

For me, the journey to owning the stage was filled with resistance. I doubted myself, questioned whether I deserved to be in the rooms I entered, and often braced myself for rejection. The fear of being "too much" or "not enough" was a constant shadow.

I still remember standing on the TEDx stage - heart racing, exhilarated, finally feeling seen for who I truly was. I finally had the opportunity to share my vision for how we need to incorporate AI and tech into our lives by combining with diverse, human perspectives.

It felt like stepping into my power, claiming my space.

But when a close friend's talk from the same event went viral, and mine did not, the crash came swiftly. I retreated into the background - organising, supporting, amplifying others - while slowly easing off my own throttle.

But one truth became clear: I had to accept that my brilliance, quirks, and unique perspectives were gifts - not burdens. And that retreating, while sometimes necessary for healing, wasn't where my journey was meant to end.

There's something transformative about deciding to show up fully, even when the world hasn't made space for you. When you do, step into your own power - you're setting a precedent. You're inviting others to embrace their own brilliance too.

As you move through this chapter, I invite you to reflect on the spaces where you've made yourself smaller, and where you've already taken courageous steps toward owning your worth.

The Courage to Be Seen

Conscious and intentional visibility is about being noticed and known for who you truly are. But stepping into that visibility can feel like standing on a stage with all eyes on you. Every flaw seems magnified. Every whisper of self-doubt amplified. For highly sensitive people with less "oomph" than I possess, stepping up can feel unsurmountable, until you do - with the support of your community.

The internal voice of imposter syndrome asks, *"Why me?"* even as the world desperately needs exactly what you have to offer.

I vividly remember moments where I hesitated before stepping up. Sometimes it was because I felt like an outsider in rooms full of polished experts. Other times, it was fear that if I spoke, I'd confirm my worst fear - that I didn't belong there.

One moment stays etched in my mind: standing backstage at a conference, clutching my notes so tightly my knuckles ached. I could hear the hum of the audience beyond the curtain - confident voices, polished laughter. My heart hammered so loudly it drowned out everything else. For a breathless moment, I thought about slipping away, about choosing invisibility over vulnerability. But then I remembered why I was there. Why my voice mattered. And even though it shook, I stepped into the light anyway.

Over time, I learned that courage doesn't come from the absence of fear - it comes from showing up despite it.

From "Why Me?" to "Why Not Me?"

I've always hungered for external validation - waiting for someone to notice me, to hand me permission to lead, to tell me I was ready. I still do, but I am getting better at noticing when I do. I thought if I worked hard enough, stayed quiet enough, someone would eventually tap me on the shoulder and say, *"Now it's your turn."*

But that permission never came in a way I could read.

What I didn't realise was that the permission I craved had to come from within. The moment I shifted my mindset from "*Why me?*" to "*Why not me?*" everything changed.

I still remember one of the first moments I caught myself spiralling - even in the middle of something I had created. I'd proposed the panel, shaped the topic, and knew I was the right person to lead it. It was my project.

But as the event drew closer, that old voice crept in: *Surely there's someone more qualified. Who am I to lead this conversation?*

I didn't back out, but I noticed the wobble. The second-guessing. The quiet hum of imposter thoughts playing in the background.

And then, after the session, a woman came up to me - eyes filled with tears. "Thank you", she said. "Thank you. I never knew there was a name for my lived experience".

That was the moment the spiral broke. Because I remembered: the reason I'd created that space was for women like her. And for women like me. The truth is, most people who succeed aren't free from doubt - they're just willing to try anyway. They acknowledge the fear but choose action over perfection.

This realisation helped me embrace the moments when I felt small - and remember that stepping into discomfort is how we grow.

Imposter Syndrome vs. Your Truth

Let's be real: Telling women they have imposter syndrome often just reinforces the idea that we don't belong. It shifts the burden from broken systems onto individuals - when the real problem is often the culture that wasn't built to include us in the first place.

Yes, I've felt it. The deep-rooted doubt. The feeling that no matter how hard I worked, one day someone would realise I didn't deserve to be there.

But what I've learned is this: Feeling like an imposter doesn't mean you are one. It means you care. It means you're standing at the edge of growth, not stuck in comfortable mediocrity.

I started asking myself a different question: *"What's more powerful - this fear of failure, or my desire to make an impact?"*

That question became a compass. Whenever fear flared up, I didn't pretend it wasn't there. I acknowledged it - and then I asked myself what mattered more: my discomfort, or my mission.

And almost always, the mission won. Because when I looked beyond my own fears, I remembered the bigger picture - the people I wanted to uplift, the stories that needed to be heard, the change I wanted to ignite.

Imposter syndrome is loud. But your truth - your lived experiences, your unique voice, your hard-earned wisdom - is louder, if you let it be.

You don't have to wait until you feel "ready". You don't have to be perfect. You just have to keep showing up, bringing your full, flawed, extraordinary self to the adventure.

Defying Expectations and Stereotypes

The world often has a script ready for people like us - a map that was drawn without ever asking who we were or where we wanted to go. A set of expectations stamped onto our identities based on gender, background, or quirks that don't fit the "norm".

We're told where we belong. How far we're supposed to go. How loud we're allowed to be.

And when we dare to deviate from that script, the road gets bumpier. We're met with skepticism, side-eyes, criticism - or worse, dismissal cloaked in politeness.

I've felt it firsthand: the stiff smiles when I challenged the unspoken rules, the conversations that turned colder the moment I chose to show up fully instead of shrinking into "palatable".

One moment still rides with me. I had just delivered a keynote at a leadership conference - a talk filled with honesty, humour, and fire. As I stepped offstage, an older executive pulled me aside. *"You're very... passionate"*, he said, with a smile that didn't quite reach his eyes. *"Maybe a little too much for this crowd."*

For a heartbeat, shame flickered inside me - an old, familiar ghost. But then a younger woman, waiting nearby, caught my eye and whispered, *"Thank you. I needed that."*

In that moment, I realised: stereotypes are only powerful if we accept them as our truth. And sometimes we do - because we long to belong. We round off our quirks, turn down the volume, try to fit the mould, hoping it'll earn us a place at the table.

Breaking free is both loud rebellion and steady refusal. It's choosing not to shrink, not to apologise for occupying space, not to trade authenticity for acceptance.

Every time you ride beyond the map they tried to hand you, you carve a new road - not just for yourself, but for everyone who follows.

Owning the Room When You're Not Invited

I've always had a knack for seeing what needs doing - and just getting on with it.

Even in the early days, when a big group of us would go out for dinner, I was the one who took charge of the order. I didn't need or even want to be in control. But I knew how these things could spiral into chaos. Someone would forget to order. The vegan would get chicken. The loudest voices would win. So I'd confidently pull it together - check preferences, scan the menu, and make sure everyone felt looked after.

It was second nature to me. Organising things. Holding space for others. Making sure the table worked for everyone sitting around it.

Years later, that same instinct showed up on the football (the World Game aka soccer) field.

When our coach unexpectedly left the club, there was no plan. No handover. Just a gap where leadership used to be.

I didn't wait to be asked. I stepped in. I organised sessions. Found a co-coach. Got certified. Took the role seriously - because I knew how much it mattered. Not just to me, but to the team.

But leadership without invitation doesn't always land softly. I could feel the side-eyes. The unspoken questions. *Who does she think she is? Isn't that a bit much?*

Some of my teammates - who I'd trained with, played with, laughed with - carried a discomfort I couldn't always name. Maybe it was the perceived imbalance. Maybe it was the way I claimed space in a role that had previously been handed down, not stepped into.

But we did well that year. Really well.

And what I know now is this: Owning the room sometimes looks like showing up before you're asked. Taking responsibility. Holding steady, even when others aren't sure they want you to. Asking others if it will help if you step up or in. Does someone else want to do it?

People often tell me I "light up the room". But truthfully? I usually walk in bracing for impact - hoping to be seen, but expecting to be misunderstood.

And yet, I show up anyway.

Because leadership does not ask for permission. It means stepping into space and refusing to shrink when the air gets tense. It's about trusting that belonging doesn't always come first - sometimes, it follows courage.

Sadly, I didn't celebrate our team's success as much as I could have. My rejection sensitivity - always waiting in the wings - stepped forward and took the lead.

In the following season, when an experienced coach offered to take over, the team discussed whether we should continue with our current coaching structure. One of the senior players, perhaps trying to be kind, said they thought we should say yes to the new coach - because it wasn't "fair" to ask me to do it again.

I know they meant well. But all I heard was that my leadership hadn't been enough. That I wasn't enough.

And as we've already established, I have little patience for people making assumptions about what I have - and don't have - the capacity to do.

I kept showing up. I kept playing. But I always felt a bit out of place after that.

The Invisible Standards

One of the hardest things about navigating spaces where you don't "fit" is the rules you can't see but are expected to obey.

The invisible standards. The unspoken expectations that decide who gets a seat at the table, the mic, or the benefit of the doubt.

Standards that often prioritise conformity over creativity. Silence over questioning. Loyalty over authenticity.

I've felt those invisible weights press down the moment I opened my mouth to challenge the status quo. The side-glances. The tight smiles. The subtle shifts in energy that said, *"We don't do that here."*

It's like riding down a straight, open highway - and suddenly hitting a patch of invisible black ice. You didn't see it coming. You weren't prepared for it. And for a moment, you question whether you should have stayed safely in the lane everyone else was riding in.

Progress doesn't happen inside the lines drawn to keep things predictable. Diversity of thought isn't a buzzword - it's the fuel for real innovation.

When we bring our authentic selves into the room - even when it feels like an act of resistance - we remind the world that change doesn't come from staying quiet.

It comes from being willing to ride a different road, even when it hasn't been paved yet.

Creating Ripples: Impact Beyond Self

When we step into our power and embrace visibility, something incredible happens - we become a mirror for others. Our courage sends out ripples, creating waves of possibility for those watching quietly from the sidelines.

Advocacy and authenticity are contagious. Every time you dare to be seen, you widen the road for those still waiting at the crossroads.

Your Visibility Is Someone Else's Permission Slip

I'll never forget a conference participant who pulled me aside after a talk. She stood there, nervous but smiling, clutching her notebook like a lifeline. *"I've never seen someone like me up there before - thank you"*, she said, voice cracking a little with emotion. She had finally seen someone who she could see herself in.

It hit me harder than any applause.

For all the moments I had questioned whether it mattered - for all the nights spent doubting if showing up as my full, quirky, defiant self was worth it - this moment answered it loud and clear.

Simply by being visible, I had given someone else permission to dream bigger, to speak louder, to believe that there was room for them too.

This is why visibility matters. It's about paving a path for those who come after us, not the headlines or accolades. When we own our brilliance unapologetically, we create space for others to do the same.

Passing the Mic and Sharing the Stage

Advocacy is about speaking for others, and simultaneously lifting as you climb, sharing the road, and making sure nobody gets left behind at the last pit stop.

I've learned that true leadership does not require you to have all the answers. It's about knowing when to step back and listen, when to elevate someone else's idea, and when to shine a light on someone who's been overlooked.

Sometimes, it's as simple as saying in a meeting, *"I love that point Sarah made - let's build on it"*, or *"thanks for raising that, Jamal - your insight just changed my thinking."*

Small acknowledgements. Tiny moments. But they create seismic shifts in who feels they belong.

And sometimes, those ripples grow into waves that reshape the whole journey.

Staying True to Your Values

Stepping onto the metaphorical stage can sometimes feel like walking a tightrope across a canyon nobody else seems to notice. There's a fine balance between self-promotion and staying grounded, between visibility and authenticity.

The pressure to "play the game", to iron out your kinks, to fit the mould - can feel overwhelming. Especially when the easy road promises comfort and acceptance.

But true power comes from staying aligned with your values - even when the road gets rough. Especially then.

In a world where shortcuts and compromises are tempting, integrity is what keeps your wheels steady when everything around you feels slippery.

I've found that when decisions align with my core values, they bring clarity - even when the outcome is uncertain.

There was a time I was asked to "tone down" my opinions during a high-profile leadership event. Smile more. Filter my words. Pick the right time. Play nice for the brand.

I was torn. Speaking up might cost me opportunities. But staying silent would cost me something bigger - myself.

I chose to speak authentically. Not with anger. Not with rebellion. But with clear, unwavering truth.

Not everyone applauded. Some people turned away. But the right people leaned in - and that was enough.

Navigating the Line Between Confidence and Humility

Advocating for yourself means standing firm enough in your story that others feel permission to stand firmer in theirs.

When you lead with empathy and authenticity, confidence and humility don't cancel each other out - they fuel each other. You can own your presence without dimming anyone else's.

Owning your space means riding forward - scars, quirks, uncertainties and all - because leadership's real map is paved by those who dare to ride fully, flaws and all.

Embracing Your Spotlight

Stepping onto the stage is about showing up as your full, unapologetic self - flaws, brilliance, quirks and all. It's about celebrating your journey, owning your wins, and letting others see what's possible by simply watching you thrive.

In a world that often tries to shrink those who stand out, choosing to be visible is a revolutionary act. It's a reminder that you belong at the table - not by anyone's permission, not by ticking all the right boxes, but by your own decision to pull up a chair and claim your space.

Whether you're speaking up in a meeting, sharing your story online, or advocating for someone else, your voice matters. Your presence matters.

Every time you show up as yourself - imperfect, courageous, real - you make it easier for someone else to do the same.

Step forward. Take up space. Ride your own road, even when the signs are missing.

And remember: You're not just taking a stance for yourself - you're showing the path for others who are still finding the courage to step into theirs.

Tuning Up: Redefining Visibility with Courage

You're not here to play small. You're here to play true.
Tara Mohr, *Playing Big*

Visibility is about daring to share your worth, even when fear whispers that you're not ready.

Tara Mohr reminds us that fear doesn't mean you're unprepared - it often means you're exactly where you need to be. Her work shines a light on the truth that confidence doesn't come before action. It follows it.

Some key insights from Mohr that align with this chapter's journey:

Taking Action Before Feeling Ready. *Fear is a natural companion to growth. Stepping forward while afraid teaches your brain - and your heart - that you are capable.*

Inner Mentor Over Inner Critic. *Instead of letting self-doubt drive, Mohr encourages tuning into your inner mentor - the future, wiser version of you who already knows you belong in the room.*

Visibility as Contribution, Not Exposure. *Visibility isn't about performance or perfection. It's about offering your perspective and talents to the world as an act of service.*

Owning your spotlight doesn't demand flawlessness. It asks only that you bring your truth to the ride - messy, brave, and unapologetically real. Even when it's imperfect, it's progress. And every step forward is part of your evolution.

Reflective Pause: Trusting the Road You're On

Sometimes the road ahead feels wide open. Sometimes it disappears into fog.

Choose to keep stepping into your power, again and again. Especially when the path is uncertain, and fear tugs at your handlebars.

When doubt creeps in, remember: you are not lost. You're riding into new territory - and the map is being drawn with each brave mile.

Where in your life right now are you being invited to ride forward, even without all the answers?

Where can you trust that the next marker will appear when you need it most?

Breathe.
Throttle steady.
Trust the road you're paving with every courageous mile.

And remember - even the most fearless riders have a crew beside them. Coaches, mentors, and allies who remind you to lift your chin, check your mirrors, and keep going when the fog rolls in.

SIXTH GEAR

The Road Less Traveled - Embracing Change and Adventure

The biggest adventure you can take is to live the life of your dreams.

Oprah Winfrey

There's something magnetic about the unknown. It hums along the borders of our comfort zones, daring us to let go of the map and follow the call of possibility.

The unknown holds both promise and uncertainty, and stepping toward it often feels like riding into fog without a clear view of what's ahead. But within that first, shaky throttle twist lies the potential for growth, transformation, and breathtaking self-discovery.

Let's stop playing it safe or sticking to the script. Let's start saying yes to the detours - the unexpected turns that stretch you, challenge you, and awaken something wild and wonderful inside you.

Life has a way of nudging us toward the unknown - an unplanned move, a surprising opportunity, a whispered invitation to change direction. And while fear is a natural passenger on these rides, those who answer the call discover something extraordinary: An inner resilience they didn't even know they carried.

They become architects of their own lives - navigating not with certainty, but with the steady compass of curiosity, courage, and grit.

This section is an invitation to take the road less travelled. To find joy in the unmarked paths, build resilience when the storms roll in, and celebrate the stories that unfold when you choose adventure over expectation.

Whether it's a journey across continents or a deep dive into your own reinvention, every twist and turn offers a chance to grow, to evolve, and to live full throttle and on your own terms.

So take a deep breath. Throttle steady. Trust yourself. The greatest adventures aren't always the ones you plan - they're the ones you say yes to when the road disappears from the map.

STAGE EIGHTEEN
The Allure of the Unknown

Life is either a daring adventure or nothing at all.
Helen Keller

Introduction: Riding into the Great Unknown

The pull of the unknown has always been like a low rhythm or beat in the background of my life - steady, insistent, impossible to ignore. It wasn't the loud roar of rebellion; it was the quiet rumble of curiosity calling me off the beaten track.

While some people found comfort in the well-worn and familiar, I was pulled toward the unfamiliar - the thrill of new air in my lungs, fresh colours streaking past as if the world itself was in motion.

For me, adventure isn't about grand, cinematic moments or conquering mountains. It's about following curiosity wherever it leads, embracing the discomfort of change, and discovering new parts of myself along the way.

I still remember with excitement the first time I answered that call - knocking on strangers' doors in Vikane, heart hammering in my chest, introducing myself and my siblings as "the new kids in town". Every smile, every awkward silence, every open or closed door taught me something about courage and connection.

Later, when I boarded a plane to Botswana with little more than excitement and nerves in my suitcase, it felt like throttling into thick mist. No guarantees, no maps - just a deep belief that growth lay somewhere on the other side of uncertainty.

Or packing up my life in Norway to move to Sydney, sight unseen, and again when I moved to the 'Wild West' of Australia on a whim.

These moments weren't always glamorous. In fact, they were often messy, uncomfortable, and occasionally terrifying. But each time, the unknown taught me something important: The road you don't yet know often leads to the parts of yourself you haven't yet discovered.

Curiosity as a Compass

Curiosity has always been my true north. Where others might have hesitated, I leaned in, trusting that asking "what if" was often the first step toward something extraordinary.

It was curiosity that pushed me to explore new cultures, to leap into careers I didn't yet fully understand, and to say yes to leadership roles when the trail ahead felt anything but certain. Even when the stakes were high and the map was missing, curiosity whispered, *"Go. See where this leads."*

When I landed in Botswana as a teenager, curiosity was a companion, and it was my guide. I didn't just passively absorb the new environment; I threw myself into it. I made friends across cultural and social divides, soaking in every sight, sound, and story like a sponge. I didn't wait for invitations to belong. I carved my own adventures into the landscape. I'd persuade my parents to let me explore the bustling local markets, where the colors, smells, and rhythms of a new world lit up my senses and sparked new parts of me awake.

That same restless spirit carried me into adulthood. I built teams and businesses without a blueprint, navigated industries where I didn't tick the traditional boxes, and dreamed up projects that didn't come with step-by-step instructions.

I was an inventor, not just of things - but of ways forward. An innovator by necessity and instinct, always willing to follow an idea before I knew where it would land.

For me, adventure has always been as much about internal expansion as external exploration. I have an internal compass. And every time I trust it, even when the landscape blurs into the unknown, I discovered something new about the world - and about myself.

Answering the Call

Uncertainty has never held me back. The weight of being the reliable one, the one with the well-paid job, the steady hands, the socially acceptable path, did. There's a strange kind of push-pull that lives inside me: the compliant rebel. The one who dreams wildly but still double-checks the rules. The one who longs for liberation but doesn't want to disappoint the people I care about.

The call of adventure has always been there - an itch under my skin, a whisper in quiet moments. It wasn't safety I craved. Quite the opposite. I've always

been drawn to new horizons, different ways of living, the draw towards the excitement of foreign cultures. But still - I stayed, out of obligation. Out of the quiet pressure to be responsible. To not rock the boat.

When I did leap - when I chose the road less mapped - I did so with little fear and trepidation. The fear that nobody would like me and that I would not be enough. The fear that I would be judged. I did it because the ache to live fully, to follow curiosity and honour my own rhythm, became too loud to ignore.

What I've learned is that courage doesn't always look like rebellion. Sometimes it looks like a quiet *yes* whispered under your breath. A decision made not in defiance, but in devotion - to yourself, your evolution, your unlived dreams.

And every time I've answered that call, even hesitantly, I've come home to more of myself.

Saying Yes to Change

It's no secret that change has always been the oxygen I breathe. From a young age, when life meant packing up and moving to new towns, I learned that each shift carried its own kind of magic: new people, new places, new stories waiting to unfold.

I didn't wait for change and transformation to knock - I invited it; I threw open the door.

As I grew older, I sought out the roads less travelled. A friend once asked "what are you running from?". "Nothing", I said. "I am flying towards something that draws me in with excitement".

I was hungry to grow, to stretch, to become. Saying *yes* to adventure has always been my compass - sometimes guiding me to breathtaking discoveries, sometimes dropping me into challenges I never saw coming. But even the hard landings taught me something: that transformation comes from choosing to move - even when the route ahead isn't marked.

The Courage to Say Yes

Some *yeses* have been neat and planned. Others came wrapped in spontaneity and jet lag.

Like the day I decided to study in the United Kingdom, chasing the curiosity that whispered: *There's more to learn out there.* Or the bigger leap - moving to Australia without ever setting foot on its soil. It was meant to be a short detour, two or three years at most. Nearly three decades later, it's the place where my roots found surprising depth.

The Power of Pivotal Decisions

Some *yeses* came with less thinking and more leaping. Like the frantic call that sent me racing to South Africa with barely a few hours' notice to fix a tech crisis at a mining site. Or rather a crisis in expectations where I was there to engage and turn around the senior leadership team who were threatening to throw our product out.

This time, I got to travel six hundred metres underground, headlamp cutting through the darkness. The miners were surprised and excited to see a foreign, white woman that far underground, but I loved it. And the best thing was that I got to visit Botswana and reconnect with Bannye, my "sister" from school - almost 30 years after we were roomies. Adventure has a way of bringing old pieces of your story full circle.

Or the *yes* to building offshore teams in India - an experience that stretched my professional skills, and deepened my emotional fluency across cultures.

An early encounter happened in a training room in freezing Sweden, where I was tasked with onboarding a team of young South Indian professionals in the dead of winter. Poor young men, wrapped in layer after layer of jumpers and scarves, looked like they might shatter from the cold.

It took me half a day to realise that the constant headshakes weren't disagreement - they were agreement. Before long, I was nodding and shaking my head right along with them, much to their cautious amusement. Carefully though - not in mockery, but in mirrored respect. A natural instinct I have to connect across cultures by tuning in closely and adjusting, sometimes unconsciously.

Connection is more about presence than language - about sensing your way across the gaps until something clicks.

Balancing Risk and Reward

Of course, not every leap has been without its challenges. Travelling solo in Brazil taught me that no amount of textbooks prepares you for a language spoken with an entirely different rhythm than what you expect.

Having spent time in Portugal and picked up the language, I was mind boggled at how different Brazilian enunciation and culture were. I spent two frustrating weeks feeling isolated and invisible. But stubbornness - and

kindness - bridged the gaps eventually, and I built connections that didn't require perfect Portuguese, just patience and openness.

Every *yes*, even the messy ones, stretched me. Every challenge sharpened the instincts I didn't even know I had.

Your *Yes* Doesn't Have to Be Loud

Some *yeses* came as grand leaps onto planes or into new careers. But some have been quiet and deeply personal: "*Yes, I will trust this feeling*". "*Yes, I will try again even though I'm scared*".

In the end, every *yes* was a commitment to living more fully. To letting adventure, not fear, set the route. To keeping the throttle open, even when the road ahead disappeared into mist.

Navigating the Fear and Joy of Uncertainty

Change and uncertainty often come along for the ride - not in the driver's seat, but riding shotgun - with a far more stubborn passenger: the quiet fear that maybe, just maybe, *I'm not enough to handle what's coming*.

For me, the fear was more about the weight I carried into the unknown than the unknown itself - the questions about whether I was ready, worthy, or deserving of the opportunities unfolding. Whether it was what I was "supposed to do".

The Inner Dialogue of Doubt

We all have that inner voice that whispers worst-case scenarios: *What if I make the wrong choice? What if this ruins everything?* Fear can be persuasive, but I've come to learn that it's often loudest right before something amazing happens. The key isn't silencing the fear entirely - it's understanding that you can hold fear in one hand and courage in the other.

My doubts were never loud screams. They were small, persistent whispers:

"*Am I good enough for this?*"
"*Did I really earn my place at the table - or did I just get lucky?*"
"*What if they realise I'm not as capable as they think?*"

I worried about whether I was enough to ride on these new, inviting roads.

From Anxiety to Action

In moments where that inner noise got deafening, I learned a simple truth: action quiets doubt. Not big, showy action. Small, steady, everyday decisions that chipped away at fear's hold.

I had been asked to lead a cross-cultural project team - people I admired, people I feared wouldn't see me as enough, people I knew might think they were better for the job than me. Inside, I questioned everything: *Was I capable? Had I earned it?* But instead of letting those doubts take the wheel, I broke it down into small steps. One conversation. One planning session. One brave moment at a time. And slowly, action stitched a bridge strong enough to carry me across the fear. Each step whispered louder than my doubt: *You belong here.*

When I launched other projects that felt far bigger than me, I didn't conquer fear by pretending I wasn't scared. I moved forward anyway - plotting tiny milestones like pins on a map. Every step was a reminder: *I don't have to feel ready to be ready.*

Seeking Comfort in Curiosity

Curiosity became my co-pilot.

Instead of asking, *"Am I worthy?"* I started asking, *"What might I learn?"*

Instead of wondering if I deserved the next adventure, I wondered what new parts of myself I might discover along the way.

Over time, those small shifts in curiosity became trust in my own capacity. I learned to lean into moments where others looked to me for answers - not because I had all the proof, but because I had done enough work in private to believe it. Once, when I was laid up at home with illness and unable to travel, I saw a request for information from a large manufacturer. On a hunch, I replied - using only what I had in my head at the time - and secured a multi-year contract.

In another project, I flew to Georgia and South Dakota to lead a digital transformation initiative for a major computer manufacturer. I showed up not as a project and change manager, a curious partner - asking questions, listening deeply, inviting others into the process. These moments were invitations to show up as I am - flawed, steady, open to learning.

Curiosity turned fear from a stop sign into a stepping stone.

Holding Space for Both Fear and Growth

The biggest shift came when I realised: I could ride with fear and still move forward.

I didn't need to banish doubt to make progress. I didn't need to be fearless to be worthy.

Some of my most important journeys - both literal and internal - started with a shaking hand on the throttle.

Fear doesn't mean you're not ready.

It means you're about to ride somewhere new.

The Rewards of Choosing the Unconventional Path

When you take the road less travelled, you don't just find new landscapes - you find new versions of yourself. Walking an unconventional path isn't about chasing risk for the adrenaline. It's about choosing authenticity - especially when the world offers you a safer, smaller script.

It's about trusting that there are rewards waiting for those who dare to listen to the quiet, persistent tug of their own soul.

Unexpected Wins

Some of the greatest gifts in my life came wrapped in uncertainty. Saying yes to moving continents when everything in me screamed "this is going to come back and bite me in the butt." Jumping into industries where I didn't have the neat resume or the traditional qualifications - only heart, hunger, and curiosity. Starting businesses, building projects, raising my hand when my brain whispered, *someone better will do it*.

The friendships I formed. The opportunities that stretched me. The unexpected moments of deep pride and belonging. None of them were part of the "perfect plan" I thought I needed.

They were waiting just past the horizon of what felt possible.

The road less travelled doesn't guarantee easy wins. But it promises a life full of stories, meaning, and the deep satisfaction of knowing you showed up fully for your own adventure.

Lessons from Missteps

Of course, not every leap landed gracefully. There were moments when I belly-flopped so hard I wondered if I had made a colossal mistake. The job that wasn't the right fit. The initiative that didn't catch fire. The idea that sparked beautifully but fizzled just as fast.

As a small business owner, I've made more missteps than I care to admit. But I keep showing up - trying, learning, and finding new ways to guide people on their journeys. One of my coaches once said he was blown away by how quickly I move from idea, to concept testing, to finished product.

I've fully embraced the startup-world mantra of *fail fast, fail often* - or as I like to call it, *flearn*: fail and learn.

One such flearning moment came during a digital transformation project where I was brought in as the change manager. My role was to guide people through the transition - to bring them along on the journey. But the project was led by someone without the experience or openness to do the work collaboratively. I could see the obstacles early, but the culture didn't allow for influence without hierarchy. Despite the challenges, we got there in the end.

It wasn't a total belly-flop, but it wasn't a clean landing either. And yet, even in that tension, I grew - learning not just how to navigate broken systems, but how to preserve my integrity when the work doesn't go the way my heart hoped it would.

And still, I bring everything I've learned into the next project. When you mix that growth with my neurospicy brain and a bit of AI? Let's just say, it looks like I'm running on steroids. I can stand up a new concept in under an hour, and set up the systems to support it in a day.

That's the power of learning how to adapt, pivot, and build - fast and strong, even when things don't go to plan.

Full throttle and torque.

Each misstep hurt. But each one also offered something more valuable than comfort: resilience. Self-trust. A deeper understanding that failure isn't a verdict - it's part of the process.

Sometimes the paths that dead-end simply sharpen your sense of direction for the next one. That's full throttle and torque in action - learning as you go, failing forward, and choosing momentum over perfection.

Living a Life True to Yourself

The real reward of living unconventionally can be about ticking boxes or reaching predefined milestones. In parallel, it's about waking up most mornings knowing you're living a life that feels like your own - not a life built out of obligation, expectation, or fear.

For me, choosing the unfamiliar has always come with moments of doubt, discomfort, and vulnerability. But those moments pale in comparison to the joy of living with curiosity, creativity, and courage. There's no map for the life you're here to create. There's only the call - and your willingness to follow it.

18. The Allure of the Unknown

Tuning Up: Trusting Curiosity Over Fear

Fear is always going to be there, riding shotgun. You just have to make sure curiosity is driving.
Elizabeth Gilbert, *Big Magic*

Elizabeth Gilbert reminds us that creativity and courage aren't about fearlessness. They're about learning to live with fear without letting it take the wheel.

Fear will always come along for the ride when we embark on something new or uncertain. The work is not to banish it, but to make sure it doesn't decide where we're going.

Some key insights from Gilbert that resonate with this chapter's journey:

Curiosity over Fear. *Instead of demanding that every leap makes sense, Gilbert invites us to follow the gentle pull of curiosity. She describes it as a quieter, less intimidating guide than passion - one that can lead us toward the most extraordinary paths.*

Permission to Be Bold. *You don't need anyone's permission to live a vivid, brave life. The act of being here, alive, is already an invitation to explore your questions, your ideas, and your dreams - even if no one else understands them.*

The Inevitable Fear. *Fear doesn't vanish when you grow. It just changes shape. Gilbert encourages us to recognise its presence without giving it control, to let it sit quietly in the backseat while curiosity and courage steer the ride.*

When you choose curiosity over fear, you say yes to discovery. You step into a way of living where every unknown road holds the possibility of expansion - because you're more loyal to your growth than your comfort.

That's the essence of choosing the road less traveled. Not because it's easy, but because it's yours.

Reflective Pause: Trusting the Unmarked Road

Sometimes the bravest move is following a road that's still shrouded in fog.

Because something in you - a spark, a question, a longing - whispers, *there's something here for you.*

You don't need a perfect map or a guarantee. You just need the willingness to take one small step at a time.

Maybe the path will be wild. Maybe it will be winding. It may stretch you, surprise you, or change you in ways you can't yet see.

Take a moment to reflect:

What unknown or unmarked road are you standing before right now?
What would it look like to choose curiosity instead of control?
Where could a single small step open something new for you?
How might fear be trying to protect you - and how could you thank it, then move forward anyway?

That's the gift of the unknown. Breathe. You're already braver than you think. Every great adventure begins with a question, not an answer.
Trust the road you're drawn to, even if you can't see where it ends yet.

And remember - even explorers travel with a compass. Find your guide, mentor, or crew - the people who help you keep faith when the fog feels thick, and remind you that courage grows in company.

STAGE NINETEEN
Pivotal Journeys

The journey of a thousand miles begins with a single step.

Lao Tzu

Introduction: Defining Moments on the Open Road

Every journey, whether literal or symbolic, holds the power to redefine who we are. Pivotal moments rarely announce themselves. They sneak in through quiet walks, unexpected conversations, or one brave leap into the unknown. Some shake us to our core; others nudge us gently toward transformation.

For me, the open road has always been more than a pathway - it's been a metaphor for freedom, possibility, and the untold. From the icy winds of winter in Vardø, to the vibrant streets of Gaborone, to the sun-drenched, eclectic charm of Walyalup-Fremantle ("Freo" to those of us lucky enough to call it home), every new place has shaped my worldview, tested my resilience, and and shaped me in ways no classroom ever could.

These pivotal journeys were never about reaching a destination; they were about discovering new layers of myself and others, learning to navigate differences with curiosity, and redefining what "home" truly means.

The stories that follow are chapters of travel or change, they are milestones, markers on the ever-winding, adventure-filled road of my life.

A World Beyond Borders

My journeys were always about stepping into new ways of thinking, feeling, and belonging. Every new adventure, whether through bustling cities or quiet coastlines, taught me something profound about resilience, connection, and the quiet courage it takes to build a home in unfamiliar places.

I learned early that the world is bigger, messier, and more beautiful than any single map can hold. Whether it was knocking on strangers' doors in a tiny Norwegian village, navigating dusty roads in Botswana, or studying technology in England before tech was even a "thing," every step was a conversation with the unknown.

Other adventures took me much farther from home. Winning a place at Oracle's Quota Club (recognition for top performers) sent me to Hawaii twice in the early '90s - a world away from the grey skies of Europe. Those trips opened my eyes not just to wealth and possibility, but to a dazzling array of colleagues from every corner of the globe.

It was there I first rode pillion on a Harley. One of my French colleagues saw me drooling over the bikes and invited me for a ride around Maui. The weather was too beautiful to worry about protective clothing and helmets, so there I was - living the dream (well, almost; I would've preferred to ride one myself) - scantily dressed in a suede mini skirt and matching boots under a beaded waistcoat. An unexpected thrill that eventually led me to get my motorcycle licence and buy my own bike years later in Sydney.

Landing in Sydney (and Landing Hard)

Moving to Australia was another giant leap into the unknown. That same Frenchman had introduced me to the CEO in Sydney, which led to a one-way ticket and a job. I arrived expecting to stay two, maybe three years. I'd never even visited before. But I fell in love - with the climate, and with a dog - and now, 30 years later, I'm still here.

That first year in Sydney was a shock in ways I hadn't anticipated: chronic colds from a damp, drafty terrace house, and a harsh confrontation with overt sexism in the workplace. I arrived on the 1st of February - mid-summer by Australian standards - but still found myself freezing. I hadn't packed any warm clothes or even a bed cover. My suitcase was full of summer clothes, and Sydney's unexpected 15-degree chill cut right through them. When I left Oracle, I found a fresh start with a pioneering e-business venture, shaking up traditional industries and carving a new path.

The Wild West Calls

Eventually, a new opportunity pulled me west - to Walyalup (Fremantle), Western Australia. The move was not about the sunshine nor the slower pace of life. I saw the chance to grow professionally, work with innovative teams, and still enjoy the benefits of better weather. The eclectic, creative spirit of "Freo" fit me. It gave me a new rhythm and the space to feel less like I was chasing something, and more like I was arriving.

Movement has never been about ticking countries off a list for me. It's about connection, curiosity, and the small but profound ways every new place - and every new person - changes you.

Unlikely Lessons from a Hong Kong Barstool

Not every lesson arrives neatly wrapped or in predictable form. Sometimes, insight shows up wearing bright lipstick and broken English. Sometimes it hums through ancient roots beneath your feet.

I once found myself on a three-month assignment in Hong Kong, helping implement what was then one of the world's largest logistics systems. Most nights, I was out with my male colleagues - the only woman in the crew - learning fast how to navigate the unspoken rules of social dynamics in unfamiliar places. One evening, we ended up in a "ladies bar" - the kind of place I had no reference for. I naively offered to buy one of the bar staff a drink, not realising it came with a "service" attached and cost ten times the price. My shock and surprise were palpable, and we quickly clarified and negotiated the situation.

It was awkward - and I wasn't moving from my barstool to follow her behind the bar - until she offered me a neck massage and, miracle of miracles, fixed a problem none of the doctors or health professionals had been able to solve. In that unlikely moment, I realised: healing, insight, even connection can come from the most unconventional sources - if you stay open.

Pace and Peace in India

That same spirit of openness took me all over India during another project, where every side trip became a story. One of the most unforgettable was a last-minute night bus ride from the misty hills of Kodaikanal to the coastal town of Pondicherry. The driver gently shifted a man so I could sit next to a young woman - safety first. She turned out to be a Person of Indian Origin, with parents from Europe and a former French colony. She'd grown up in Auroville, a unique intentional township built on the dream of human unity in diversity.

That visit changed me. Sitting beneath the roots of an ancient Banyan tree near the golden Matrimandir temple, I experienced a rare, profound peace. It was the first time I felt what I can only describe as a spiritual download - a deep, humming sense of wholeness. I hadn't gone seeking transcendence. I'd just followed a thread of curiosity. But the road, as always, had something far greater to offer.

These travel anecdotes - they were moments of transformation. They were pivots. Whether it was an unplanned neck massage in a Hong Kong bar or a spiritual stillness under a Banyan tree in Auroville, what these experiences taught me was simple but powerful: when you lead with curiosity instead of certainty, the world meets you with unexpected gifts.

Not every lesson arrives neatly wrapped or in predictable form. Sometimes insight shows up wearing neon lights and broken English. Sometimes it hums through ancient roots beneath your feet.

What matters most is the openness with which you arrive. The courage to say yes. The willingness to be surprised. And the trust that even in the most unfamiliar places, you can find pieces of yourself waiting to be remembered.

The Power of Perspective

Each place I've lived gifted me a different lens through which to see the world. The stark beauty of Northern Norway with the "long evenings" in summer and the Northern Lights in winter, taught me independence, imagination - and the deep, enduring warmth that thrives in communities touched by hardship and isolation. Even when the days were short and the nights stretched long, there was a spirit of resilience and hospitality that wrapped around you like a thick wool blanket. I loved how neighbours would just drop in for a chat and the kettle was always on brewing strong black coffee.

Later, Africa cracked open my heart in an entirely different way. Living under expansive skies and surrounded by the unfiltered rhythms of Botswana, I learned about communal living, resilience, and the profound richness of diverse perspectives.

Those experiences gave me a kind of cultural fluency that no textbook could teach - an emotional passport that made me comfortable with discomfort, willing to sit with difference, and able to adapt to any room or conversation.

But it came with a cost too. Belonging everywhere can sometimes feel like belonging nowhere - a particular ache that many global wanderers know.

Still, every place stitched itself into me like patches on a rider's jacket - signs not of where I passed through, but where I learned to belong, even briefly, to something larger than myself.

Memorable Moments on Foreign Soil

Some memories are tucked into my mind like roadside postcards - small, vivid flashes that changed the journey forever. In my twenties, I spent nearly a decade traversing Europe by rail - often with nothing but a backpack, a wide-open mind, and no map. I'd wander foreign cities with only curiosity as my compass, finding joy in getting lost.

Paris: Standing in Truth

I still remember one freezing Easter afternoon in Paris, walking down Rue de St Denis and suddenly realising the lightly clad women standing in doorways weren't shopkeepers. They were working women - something my young, naïve self had never encountered. But I didn't feel fear or judgment. I smiled, nodded, and greeted them with the same curiosity and respect I would have offered anyone else. They were just women, standing in their truth, in a world that had shaped their choices differently than mine.

Mumbai: The Guide I Didn't Expect

Years later, on a long layover in Mumbai after a work trip to India, I debated whether to stay at the airport or explore. On a whim, I grabbed my luggage and hailed a taxi. What pulled up wasn't just a cab - it was a car with two men: a driver and an older gentleman who introduced himself as Hari. He claimed to be a former Bollywood producer, and whether or not that was true, he turned out to be one of the most entertaining, insightful guides I've ever met. For under fifty dollars - a fortune for many Indians, but great value for Australians - I got a full-day tour of Mumbai, peppered with stories, wisdom, and laughter.

I could have said no - two men, unfamiliar city, a sense of risk. But something in me trusted the moment. It turned out to be one of the best days of my life.

Botswana: Cardboard, Curiosity, and a Calculator

And then there are moments even earlier, like in the science club at my school in Botswana. We built a solar cooker from cardboard and alfoil, armed only with a library book and a wild sense of curiosity. No internet. No templates. Just hands-on trial and error.

We cooked bacon and eggs at the annual fair and I ended up winning a scientific calculator for my work. I still remember standing on that stage - awkward, proud, and just beginning to believe that this strange, curious brain of mine had something to offer. Who would've thought a shy girl from an island in the far north of Norway would be demonstrating solar science to a crowd that looked nothing like her?

Every moment taught me something essential: If you meet the world with curiosity instead of fear, it will open doors you didn't even know existed.

Travel has always been my greatest teacher. No classroom could replicate the lessons learned through lost luggage, broken translations, spontaneous road trips, or unexpected friendships across oceans of difference.

I learned that kindness is a universal language. That community can sprout up on dusty backroads, sunlit cafés, or crowded marketplaces if you're willing to be open. I learned that survival isn't just endurance - it's adaptation, community, and a fierce belief that wherever you are, you can find or build connections.

Home Isn't on a Map

Most of all, I learned that home isn't a fixed place on a map. It's a feeling. It's in the laughter of new friends, the rhythm of a language just beginning to make sense, the moment you realise you're no longer just passing through - you're part of the story.

And some stories never leave you.

Africa carved its own groove in my memory - like gentle postcards and wild, thundering beats all blended into one joyful mixing bowl. These were the stories that didn't ask permission to lodge themselves in my bones. They just did.

Giraffes and Undercurrents

Like the time in Nairobi, when all six of us plus the driver - limbs folded like origami - squeezed into a tiny Toyota Corolla taxi for a tour of the national park and watched giraffes fight, their long necks swinging with shocking force like medieval flails. Or the time my 10-year-old brother was nearly dragged out to sea by the undercurrent of the Indian Ocean in Durban. None of us dared blink until my dad managed to grab him and pull him back to dry land. Let's just say, we have a lot of ocean around Norway - but that was something else entirely. And of course, there was always the lurking threat of sharks.

Roars at Dusk

The Okavango Delta gifted me one of the most surreal lessons in calm. Picture this: rainy season, mud roads, a 1966 Toyota Land Cruiser packed to the brim with six of us, plus a 200-litre drum of petrol. We got stuck at dusk, and my dad - always the practical problem-solver - was guiding us, trying to heave the 4WD out. My youngest brother and I were 10-15 metres from the car in the muddy bushland, holding a makeshift branch winch, when we first heard the lions' territorial roars.

I'd love to say there was no panic. That would be a lie.

But my dad stayed calm. And I held my brother back so we wouldn't split up.

I still don't know how close the lions were, but I can tell you - we were very happy to end the night crammed into the back of that truck, swarmed by mosquitoes but alive.

Monkey Business and Charged Encounters

A couple of days later, came a scream I'll never forget. High-pitched, piercing. My little sister had been ambushed by a monkey who decided the pot she was rinsing was fair game.

I've slept under the stars on real hunts, surrounded by firelight and the untamed sounds of the African night. Once, a massive alpha male elephant charged toward our Land Cruiser - a vehicle that suddenly felt toy-sized. His herd was on the other side. We learned fast who had the right of way.

The Shot that Got Away

And how could I forget the lions mating just metres away - right as my dad's camera jammed, out of film. Some moments are meant to be witnessed, not captured. Though we've never let him live it down. Imagine: instead of thousands (well, at least hundreds) of moonrise photos, we could have had lions. Up close. In action. But the speed at which things move near the equator fascinated him more than the drama just metres away.

These memories don't fade - they roar, stomp, and dance through the dusty corridors of my mind. And they're not done with me yet.

When Life Throws a Curveball

The measure of intelligence is the ability to change.
Albert Einstein

Life's twists and turns don't come with warning signs. Sometimes they're sharp bends you never saw coming - moments that force you to slow down, recalibrate, and figure out how to keep moving forward without a clear map.

My journey has been filled with these unexpected curves. Plans derailed. Dreams delayed. Opportunities disguised as detours. And while it would be comforting to say I navigated them with steady hands and clear vision, the truth is more complicated - and far more human.

Some of the most transformative chapters of my life weren't ones I chose. They were thrust upon me: a sudden move across continents, a career I loved grinding to a halt, my realisation that my brain does not necessarily work the way our society expects, and accepting that as my superpower.

At first, I fought the disruption. I gripped the handlebars tighter, tried to steer the road back to what I thought it *should* look like. But the more I resisted, the harder the ride became. Somewhere along the way, I learned a different kind of navigation: not fighting the bad weather, but adjusting my stance to ride it out, decision by decision, breath by breath.

I learned that resilience is forged in unexpected conditions. And resilience doesn't always roar like thunder; sometimes, it's the quiet persistence of getting up one more time when every part of you wants to stay down.

The moments that cracked me open - the project that failed, the friendship that ended, the opportunities that slipped through my fingers - didn't break me. They redefined me. They taught me that failure isn't a dead end; it's a bend in the road that sharpens your skills, your spirit, and your trust in your own ability to adapt.

If there's one lesson I carry with me, tucked safely under the jacket for the next unexpected bend, it's this: You don't have to control the road. You only have to stay willing to ride it, wherever it leads.

Building a Life You Love

We often think that life happens to us - but every decision we make, big or small, shapes the framework of the life we live.

From the giant leaps of faith to the quiet, seemingly inconsequential choices, each moment becomes a brushstroke in the bigger picture of who we are and what we value.

I didn't always know where the road would lead. But whether I was boarding a plane for a new continent, deciding to walk away from a job that drained me, or simply choosing to take a different route home one afternoon, every choice became part of building a life that felt meaningful - and mine.

The Power of Intentional Choices

Looking back, it's the intentional choices that shine the brightest.

Some felt monumental - like moving across the world or leaving behind relationships that no longer fit the person I was becoming. Others seemed small at the time - choosing a book that shifted my worldview, saying yes to a

coffee invitation that would later spark a lifelong friendship, or hitting pause instead of pushing through exhaustion.

Not every decision was perfect. There were plenty of detours, second-guesses, and u-turns along the way. But even the stumbles shaped me. Every step, every choice, every course correction reinforced one truth: life isn't something we find - it's something we create.

Crafting a Life Aligned with Your Values

Living authentically may not happen automatically. It takes courage. It takes clarity. And it takes the quiet, everyday bravery of saying "this matters more" when the world around you is shouting for something else.

There was a time when I felt trapped by the need to perform, to fit in, to chase milestones that didn't feel like mine. I wore success like a heavy jacket that didn't quite fit.

It took stepping back - and peeling off layers of expectation - to realise that my version of success was different. It wasn't about checking off boxes or earning gold stars. It was about building a life stitched together with joy, connection, and purpose.

A life I didn't have to escape from. A life I was proud to live every day.

The Journey is Yours to Shape

Building a life you love doesn't guarantee easy roads. There are still unexpected detours, potholes, and wrong turns.

But when your journey is grounded in your own truth, even the rough patches make sense. You trust yourself to navigate. You trust that the road - even when it disappears for a while - is leading you somewhere worth going.

I'm still on that road. Still making choices. Still adjusting the map when needed. And that, I think, is the most beautiful part: Life isn't about arriving. It's about riding - with heart, curiosity, and the guts to keep going.

Tuning Up: Expanding Your Worldview Through Stories

The danger of a single story is not that it is untrue, but that it is incomplete.
Chimamanda Ngozi Adichie, *The Danger of a Single Story*

Chimamanda Ngozi Adichie, in her powerful TED Talk, reminds us that our understanding of the world deepens when we move beyond first impressions and fixed narratives. Growing up in Nigeria, she shared how the only books available were British and American stories - and how easy it was to mistake a narrow lens for the full picture.

Her work highlights something every traveller, adventurer, and bridge-builder eventually learns: true connection requires seeing beyond the surface.

When we embrace multiple perspectives, we don't just expand our view of the world - we expand our view of ourselves.

Some key insights from Adichie's storytelling wisdom that resonate with this chapter's journey:

Beware of the Single Story. *It's easy to flatten complex places, people, or even parts of ourselves into one label. Real life - and real connection - is richer, layered, and often messy.*

Stories Shape Dignity. *When we hear and share diverse stories, we affirm the humanity and complexity of others - and invite the same grace for ourselves.*

Curiosity Creates Connection. *Approaching new cultures, communities, and experiences with curiosity (not judgment) transforms travel into transformation.*

We Are All Storytellers and Story-Hearers. *Each time we listen with openness - or share a piece of our own story - we help dissolve barriers of misunderstanding.*

Your journey across continents, cultures, and countless inner transformations echoes this truth: the road isn't just about the places you visit - it's about the stories you gather, the perspectives you reshape, and the humanity you deepen along the way.

Reflective Pause: Beyond the First Glance

When you step into a new place - or even a familiar one - with fresh eyes, what do you notice first? The differences? The similarities? The stories written between the lines?

It's easy to stop at the surface. But deeper connection starts when you linger long enough to listen for what's underneath.

Next time you meet someone new, travel somewhere unfamiliar, or find yourself in a situation that feels different, ask yourself:

What stories might I not yet see?

How can I stay curious rather than certain?

Where have I grown the most because I allowed a single story to expand into a fuller truth?

The road less travelled may cover vast distances. And sometimes, it's about daring to see - and be seen - more fully.

Breathe in the unfamiliar. You might just find a new home inside yourself.

"Every detour, every pivot, every step off the beaten path - I wasn't getting lost. I was writing the most extraordinary parts of my story."

And if the road feels lonely, find your storytellers - coaches, mentors, and companions who help you see the narratives you might have missed, and remind you that your journey is richer when shared.

STAGE TWENTY
The Art of Reinvention

And the day came when the risk to remain tight in a bud was more painful than the risk it took to blossom.

Anaïs Nin

Introduction: The Power of Reinvention

There's something deeply empowering about realising that we can choose who we become. Reinvention isn't about changing careers or moving cities - it's about growth, courage, and the willingness to let go of what no longer serves us. It's about standing at a crossroads, recognising that staying small is no longer an option, and daring to imagine a different way forward.

In my life, reinvention has rarely come wrapped in a neat, shiny bow. Sometimes it came in the aftermath of a curveball - the unexpected job loss, losing my crew, the dream that didn't unfold as planned, the sharp realisation that what once fit now felt like a cage.

Other times, it started with a quieter tug: the feeling that I'd outgrown the story I was living, that something deeper was calling me to evolve.

What I've learned is that reinvention doesn't always roar onto the scene with a grand announcement. Sometimes it starts like a storm building on the horizon - unsettling, thrilling, impossible to ignore. Other times, it's softer - a whisper that says, *there's more for you.*

And whether the catalyst was sudden or slow, each reinvention has brought me closer to the person I was meant to be. Each one has been an invitation to honour who I've been, to release what I've outgrown, and to step, sometimes trembling, into new possibilities.

The need for reinvention isn't always sparked by external disruption. Sometimes it's internal - a persistent, subtle vibration that something isn't quite aligned.

For me, that hum has often come from a deep feeling of disconnection. Even in spaces where I was included, even when others saw me as part of the fabric, I felt like an outsider. Because of the way my brain is wired. Rejection sensitivity, the quiet sting of not quite belonging, often made me feel like I was always orbiting, never landing.

The only places I've ever felt truly "home" were where everyone was new. Where connection was the point, not the proof. That's why reinvention, for me, has also been about seeking - or creating - spaces where that kind of openness exists. Where I can breathe freely. Where we all arrive as we are.

If life has taught me anything, it's this: you're never stuck. Reinvention isn't a one-time event - it's a mindset. A commitment to evolving, expanding, and choosing, again and again, to bet on yourself.

This stretch is an ode to those pivotal moments. The messy ones. The bold ones. The ones that didn't look like "success" at first glance but turned out to be the stepping stones to a life that feels truer, freer, and more alive.

Turning Points

In 2018, I attended an entrepreneur retreat in Bali, not knowing it would become one of the most quietly pivotal experiences of my life. We were asked to rate ourselves across eight life areas, and when it came to *wealth*, I froze. I felt hollow. I had poured years of effort into work I cared deeply about - but in that moment, all I could see was a bank balance that didn't reflect the depth of my commitment.

I felt like a failure.

Then the mentor leading the session said something that landed like lightning in my chest: *"Wealth is what you have left when you have no money left."*

It stopped me in my tracks. Because suddenly I could *see* it - the relationships I'd nurtured, the skills I'd honed, the trust I'd earned, the courage it had taken to keep showing up. That was wealth too.

Overnight, something shifted. The next morning, I danced into the room, radiant and light, and my cohort stared at me like I'd grown wings. "What happened to you, Gry?" they asked. I just smiled. The weight had lifted. I wasn't empty - I was equipped. I wasn't behind - I was exactly where I needed to be.

And then, as if the universe wanted to seal the shift, I got an email later that day. I'd been accepted to deliver a TEDx talk. The theme? Turning Points.

Shedding Old Identities

Reinvention often starts with a shedding - a deliberate, often uncomfortable act of letting go. But unlike the effortless slide of a snake's skin, real change can feel more like excavation. It's messy, emotional, and full of questions. We hold onto old identities, not because they still fit, but because they feel familiar, like a well-worn jacket that's fraying at the seams.

For a long time, I found a sense of worth in the roles others expected of me: "The high achiever". "The reliable one". "The fixer". I wore those labels like armour - shields that helped me navigate the world, but also trapped me inside expectations that no longer fit.

There came a moment when I realised I wasn't just living my life - I was performing it. I was chasing validation, ticking boxes, wearing a mask that no longer matched who I was becoming. Letting go of those roles wasn't easy. They had been stitched into my identity, woven into how others saw me - and how I saw myself.

The hardest part wasn't the shedding. It was the silence that came afterward. Who was I without the accolades, the expectations, the well-practised answers?

Shedding old identities isn't about disowning who you were. It's about honouring that version of yourself for getting you here - and then having the courage to evolve beyond her.

You're allowed to outgrow the dreams you once had. You're allowed to want more, even when others don't understand. You're allowed to rewrite the story halfway through the journey.

And every time you do, you clear space for a life that fits you now - not the one that fit you back then.

Letting Go of Roles That No Longer Serve

Letting go of these roles has never been a clean, celebratory act. Often, it felt like a slow unraveling. A series of realisations that holding on - whether to a job, a title, or even a dream - was no longer an act of loyalty or perseverance. It was an act of self-abandonment.

I think back to some of the pivotal times I chose to let go:

When I left my first role three years after I graduated, it was because they didn't deliver on the promise of working in France. I later found out that they had been working on the opportunity behind the scenes without telling me. It was too late, I had already accepted a role at Oracle by then, stepping toward a new chapter. Moral of the story? Even when you care deeply, you can't cling to decisions made without your voice in the room.

When I packed my life into a crate and moved to Australia - a culture that looked so familiar on the surface, but soon revealed itself to be deeply different. I had to reinvent how I worked, how I related, even how I understood belonging. It wasn't just about location; it was about identity.

When I walked away from Oracle after facing overt sexism and a rigid system that wouldn't bend. Instead, I said yes to becoming a founding team member of a Swedish company bringing eBusiness innovation down under - pioneering, scrappy, creative. Reinvention was not only survival; it was breathing space.

Choosing to step away from stability and from the golden handcuffs yet again - into consulting, into startups, into crazy pivots like building a bartering platform for mums, diving into HealthTech, chasing dreams bigger than my immediate reality.

Each time, it would have been simpler to stay - to keep performing the same role, even if it no longer fit.

But staying would have meant shrinking. And I was no longer willing to shrink.

Letting go of the roles that no longer serve you isn't betrayal. It's an act of fierce self-trust.

It's standing at the crossroads, hearing the familiar call of "But you've always been this..." - and answering back, "Not anymore".

The Courage to Disappoint Others

One of the hardest lessons on the road of reinvention is this: Sometimes, in order to be true to yourself, you have to disappoint others.

When you start to change, not everyone will clap. Some people will pull back. Some will question. And a few - the ones who benefited most from your old roles - might resist your evolution altogether.

For much of my life, I tried to keep everyone happy. I was the problem-solver, the go-to, the one who would make things better and make life easier for everyone else. It was a role I wore with pride - and exhaustion.

But every time I moved forward - whether by stepping out of rigid workplaces, choosing adventure over predictability, or walking away from titles and identities that once defined me - I had to reckon with the reality that not everyone would understand.

I disappointed bosses who expected me to stay. I surprised colleagues who thought I was "too good" for the risk of reinvention. I even confused friends who wondered why I couldn't just be content.

Each decision to change cost me something: Approval. Familiarity. Easy belonging. Financial security.

And yet... each decision also gave me something far greater: Freedom. Truth. A life that felt real, not performed.

There's a unique kind of loneliness that comes with disappointing others. But there's also an undeniable power in standing firm - in saying, "I choose me".

It's not an act of rebellion. It's an act of self-respect. It's recognising that their version of you doesn't have to be your future.

And over time, you realise: The people who truly love you - the ones who see you, not just the role you played for them - they'll find their way alongside your evolution.

The rest? Maybe they were only meant to walk part of your journey with you, not the whole way.

Embracing the New You

Shedding old identities leaves a strange kind of silence behind. No longer defined by the labels others gave you - or the ones you clung to for safety - you're left standing at the crossroads of possibility.

It's exhilarating. It's terrifying. And it's one of the most powerful places you'll ever find yourself.

For me, embracing the new versions of myself was like flipping a switch and allowing myself to choose, over and over again, to trust the unfolding - even when it was messy, even when I didn't know what the next chapter looked like.

When I left corporate roles that no longer fit, I didn't have a detailed blueprint or roadmap. When I moved across countries and cultures, I didn't have a guarantee that I would pick up the foreign rhythm. When I stepped into entrepreneurship, I didn't have a roadmap - only a gut feeling that it was time.

At each pivot point, I had to get comfortable with being a beginner again. I had to meet myself with curiosity instead of judgment.

Sometimes, that beginner's energy felt like a tidal wave of new ideas - powerful, unrelenting, and forward-focused. I'd follow sparks of inspiration into new territory, sometimes abandoning an idea before it had the chance to fully take root. Not because it lacked promise, but because I was already ten steps ahead, chasing the next glimmer of possibility.

I've learned to hold space for both: the momentum of vision, and the discipline of patience. That's why so many of my ideas live on the backburner - still simmering, still alive.

Who am I without the job title? Without the comfort zone? Without the applause? Without the money?

I didn't abandon everything that came before. I layered growth over experience, like rings in a tree - each one representing a season of evolution.

Some seasons were expansive. Some were brutal. But all of them added something to the woman I was becoming.

Embracing the new you is reframing the past and recognising that you are allowed to keep growing, even when others want you to stay the same.

It's about letting possibility be your co-pilot, not fear.

It's about choosing, again and again, to believe in the next version of yourself - even before anyone else sees her clearly.

Redefining Myself Through Growth

Reinvention means expanding who you can become, not discarding or erasing who you are. Growth means adding new layers, new colours, new dimensions.

One of my earliest and most vivid experiences of this came when we moved to Botswana. True, I was stepping into a new country, and I was stepping into a whole new way of being. Gone were the thick winter coats of Northern Norway. In their place: sun-drenched uniforms, dusty playgrounds, and the music of a language I didn't yet understand. At first, I clung tightly to the familiar - my Norwegian roots, my habits, my assumptions about the world.

But slowly, curiosity and necessity pulled me forward. I learned new words, new customs, new ways of connecting. I learned that belonging isn't about blending in perfectly - it's about showing up with respect and heart.

That early journey taught me something that has stayed with me through every pivot, every reinvention: You don't have to erase your roots to grow new branches.

Throughout my life, I've continued to say yes to expansion - even when it felt awkward, even when the path was invisible. Studying technology in England in the 80s, decades before "women in tech" became a buzzword. Moving to Australia without ever having set foot there before. Jumping onto planes with barely a day's notice to solve systems crises in Africa.

Each leap didn't erase who I was - it layered new strengths onto my foundation. I wasn't abandoning anything. I was building. Evolving. Growing wider, deeper, stronger.

Sometimes reinvention looks like bold moves across continents. Other times, it's quieter: deciding to believe in yourself when the world expects you to shrink. Choosing possibility over fear. Trusting that you can be both rooted and reaching at the same time.

Every reinvention in my life has asked me one thing: Are you willing to become more of who you really are?

And every time I've answered yes - even trembling a little - the road ahead has revealed more magic than I could have imagined.

When Reinvention Still Doesn't Equal Belonging

Stepping into entrepreneurship was answering a deeper call to build something meaningful, to lead boldly, and to do it differently. I brought that same full-throttle energy I always had - diving in, hands-on, head-first, heart-aligned.

But even there - in a space I helped shape - I didn't always feel like I belonged.

I was building something novel and innovative. We were getting results, securing funding, moving the needle. But the undercurrent was familiar: I still felt like an outsider. Like I had to prove myself, over and over again. And even when the outcomes were clear, the credit didn't always follow.

I remember one moment vividly - I was driving from Sydney to Canberra to sort out my passport. The team chat kept going off: topic after topic, questions flying, ideas exchanged. I knew I could add value. So I kept stopping to reply, juggling the road and responsibility. But eventually, I had to let go. The thread rolled on without me. And with it came that familiar ache - of being outside something I was building.

And then there were the digs that cut deeper than they should have. Like the time a co-founder was asked, *"What's it like working with Gry, who constantly wants to take your place?"*

I didn't. I never did. But I did challenge a system where only one person was allowed in the room - a system where my voice, my lens, my presence would inevitably change the conversation. I believed we were equals. But somehow, being assertive was interpreted as being threatening.

Here's the beautiful part: my business partner and I are still great friends. We don't see each other often, but when we do, it's like time never passed. And the person who asked that question? Also a good friend. That's the power of staying open. Of not letting one uncomfortable moment define an entire relationship. We were all doing our best with what we knew at the time.

Another time, a different peer - with no tech background - told me I wasn't technical enough to be CTO. They said they'd "heard" I was a bad presenter. That I didn't connect well with teams. None of it was true. But still... it scratched the same old wound. The one that whispers: *Maybe they're right. Maybe you're too much. Too loud. Too intense.*

What made it worse was what happened next. Instead of questioning their motives, I started questioning everyone else's. I found myself trying to figure out who had supposedly said those things, wondering who I could no longer trust - when, in reality, it was not someone else. The very person who had shared the "feedback" was the one trying to get to me - the person I considered to be a friend.

Looking back, I can name it now. That was gaslighting. It was narcissistic behaviour disguised as constructive input. What made it harder was that I genuinely tried to work through it. We went to counselling. We tried to rebuild. But when the lines between what is real and what is projected blur, it's hard to tell what's actually being challenged - the facts, or your very sense of self.

I knew better. But that doesn't mean it didn't sting.

That's the thing about being wired the way I am - with rejection sensitivity, people-pleasing tendencies, and a lifelong desire to be liked. I can *know* something isn't fair, and still feel it like a bruise.

I'm not sharing this to call anyone out. I'm sharing it because this is what it means to be human. To navigate leadership, innovation, reinvention - while still carrying our own stories, our own scars, our own programming.

Because even when you're at the table, *how* you're seen can still make you feel invisible.

Owning My Story

There's a moment in every reinvention when you realise: you're not changing, you're claiming. Owning your story isn't about pretending it's all been easy or perfectly planned. It's about standing tall in the beautiful, complicated, messy truth of who you are.

In the past, I wore titles like the high achiever, the reliable one, the fixer. They were true, but they weren't *all* of me. They were the safe, acceptable pieces that made others comfortable - and, if I'm honest, made me feel useful and valued. But inside, there was a wilder truth. A woman who wasn't just surviving systems, but questioning them. A dreamer who believed that life could be bigger, braver, more expansive than the boxes we're handed. A world where everyone is welcome and valued.

Owning my story meant peeling back the layers I had built to fit in - and finding power not despite my differences, but because of them.

It meant honouring the moments that stretched me almost to breaking:

The startups that soared and crashed, teaching me resilience.
The boardrooms where I was shut down, but still daring to stay visible anyway.
The times I walked away from "success" because it cost too much of my soul.

It meant recognising that my story isn't neat and it isn't linear. It has wild detours and unexpected victories and hard-won wisdom stitched through every chapter.

And it meant learning that the parts of me I once tried to minimise - my sensitivity, my stubborn hope, my neurospicy wiring - were not flaws to fix. They were fuel for the impact I was here to make.

For years, I became known as the one who could build systems, connect the dots, and solve the puzzle - often before others even knew where to start. And while that skill was real, it wasn't the whole picture. Beneath it all, I was - and still am - a creative. An ideas person. A pattern-seer. I didn't just want to fix broken things; I wanted to imagine better ones.

The world often rewarded my ability to organise, but what fuels me is the thrill of creation, the spark of possibility. Inclusive innovation for impact.

Today, when I tell my story, I tell the whole of it. Not just the polished wins, but the tender beginnings, the courageous stumbles, the fierce returns. Because I know now: The more fully I own my story, the more permission I give others to own theirs.

There's nothing more magnetic, nothing more powerful, than a person who refuses to dim their truth.

And so I choose to be that person - for myself, and for anyone who needs the reminder that their story, messy and magnificent, is a gift.

Legacy Through Evolution

Reinvention can change your own life, and it can ripple outward. It plants seedlings you may never see bloom. It gives quiet permission for others to imagine more for themselves.

When you dare to evolve, you don't just rewrite your own narrative. You crack open a doorway for others to step through.

Every time I chose to step into something unfamiliar - a new country, a new career, a new version of myself - I watched the butterfly effects in places I never expected.

When I pursued leadership roles, I did that to crack ceilings open so others could soar. When I spoke up for fairness, even when my voice shook, I was carving out space where others could breathe easier too.

Even the smallest reinventions - the quiet choices to stay authentic when conformity would have been easier - sent signals to the people around me: You don't have to stay small. You don't have to stay stuck. There is another way.

And the most extraordinary thing? Sometimes you never know whose life you've touched. Sometimes the seeds you plant grow in unseen soil.

The colleague who later dares to apply for a job they thought was out of reach. The young migrant woman who finally says yes to her own startup dream after watching you pivot with grace. The friend who sees you choose self-respect over approval - and finally chooses it for themself.

This is the quiet, unstoppable power of living your truth: Your courage becomes a map for others. Your evolution becomes an invitation.

Reinvention is both personal and legacy.

And not the kind built by titles or accolades, but the kind etched into hearts - the kind that says: "Because she grew, I believed I could too".

Inviting Others Into the Journey

There's a beautiful, unexpected gift that comes from daring to reinvent yourself: it doesn't just change your life - it gives others permission to change theirs, too.

When I first began sharing my reinventions - openly, messily, without pretending I had it all figured out - I noticed something powerful. People around me started to open up about their own dreams and doubts.

Over time, I've learned not everyone can hold the same breadth of vision I see - at least not all at once. I used to share every dot I connected, every thread I saw. Now, I often lead with questions instead. Not to hide the bigger picture, but to help others uncover it for themselves.

It's less about convincing and more about co-discovery. They'd say things like, *"I didn't know it was okay to want something different"*, or *"seeing you make a change made me wonder if I could, too."*

I still feel humble every time. I didn't set out to inspire anyone. I was simply trying to build a life that felt truer to who I was becoming. But that's the knock-on effect of courage: it spreads.

I've come to believe that every time we dare to evolve, we crack the door open for others to do the same. We show them that growth isn't selfish - it's contagious. That it's not about abandoning who you were; it's about trusting who you are becoming.

Of course, inviting others into the journey doesn't mean dragging them with you. Not everyone is ready - or willing - to change at the same pace you are. Some people might cheer you on; others might distance themselves because your growth feels like a mirror they aren't ready to look into. And that's okay. Your path doesn't need everyone's understanding to be valid.

The real invitation isn't loud or forceful. It's quiet, steady, and lived through example. It says:

"You're allowed to change, too".

"You're allowed to dream bigger, stumble, start over, and find your own new way".

Every story you share, every boundary you set, every leap you take - even the ones that scare you - becomes part of someone else's permission slip to believe in new possibilities.

If there's one thing I hope you take from my journey, it's this: Your evolution is a personal victory. It's a lighthouse. It lights the way for others who are still finding their own courage to sail into uncharted waters.

Tuning Up: Focus Without Shrinking

Success is about doing the right thing, not everything.
Gary Keller & Jay Papasan, The ONE Thing

There's a moment when you stop trying to be everything for everyone and start asking, *what actually matters to me?* And sometimes the next question is, *how can I get things done in a way that works for my brain?*

For years, I resisted this idea. I bristled whenever someone said, "You need to focus on just one thing." It felt like a trap - like cutting off parts of myself. And honestly, it didn't work for me.

I'm multi-faceted. I get bored easily, task-switch like a pro, and thrive in chaos others might find distracting. I can hyper-focus on a project I love for hours, but I also need variety to stay alive creatively. My brilliance doesn't live in linear lanes. It lives in intersections - spinning multiple plates, chasing five ideas at once, with joy.

Then I read *The ONE Thing*. And something shifted.

The book doesn't say "only do one thing." It says: *know your one thing at this moment*. Know what matters most and build your energy, time, and attention around it. You can still be multidimensional. You just don't have to be scattered.

That was my turning point. Not in becoming a new version of myself, but in finally owning how I operate. I stopped fighting my nonlinear mind. I stopped apologizing for needing multiple creative outlets. I started designing a life that honored my nature - while still making a serious impact.

Because focus, for people like us, doesn't mean shrinking. It means choosing where your full power goes.

Reflective Pause: Your One Thing (For Now)

Before you rush into what's next, take a breath.

This isn't about doing more. It's about aligning your energy with what matters most right now - for who you are in this season.

What do you wish you had permission to focus on right now - even if it doesn't look "productive" to others?

Where are you still trying to "do it all" because of old expectations or fears?

What's the one thing - project, feeling, boundary, or dream - that, if honored, would make everything else easier or irrelevant?

How can you hold your complexity without scattering your energy?

You don't have to be linear. You just have to be clear, focused, and passionate.

Reinvention doesn't have to be a solo act. Sometimes the clarity you're seeking emerges in conversation - with mentors, coaches, or thought partners who can mirror back the power you already hold.

SEVENTH GEAR

Cruising in Torque - Crafting Your Legacy & Impact

*You make a life out of what you have,
not what you're missing.*

Oprah Winfrey

When you live authentically, your legacy becomes an extension of who you are - a reflection of the values you embody and the impact you leave behind. Crafting a legacy isn't about grand gestures or flashy accolades. It's about how you show up. The lives you touch. The doors you open - for yourself, and for others.

As we approach the final stretch of this ride, it's time to shift gears. To look back with pride. And to look forward with purpose.

There's a point on every roadtrip where the view shifts. You realise you're not just chasing horizons anymore - you're shaping them. You're not just moving forward - you're leaving tracks that others can follow.

This part of the journey is about now, not some day in the future.

Over the past few years, I've felt a growing urgency - a fierce, joyful need - to turn what I've learned into something bigger than myself. That purpose has taken many forms: launching initiatives to bridge the gap between education and the workplace, championing women in technology, and creating platforms to inspire girls to step into their power. I've spoken on stages, built programs, mentored, advocated - all with one goal in mind: to make the road wider and more welcoming for those coming up behind me.

This book - and the speaking platform I'm building - are part of that legacy too.

Because this is the next bend in the road, a welcome to your future tour.

Legacy is the road we build while we're riding. It's the lives we light up. The bridges we leave standing behind us.

Full throttle. Full torque. Onward.

Let's ride.

STAGE TWENTY-ONE
Revving Up for Change

The most common way people give up their power is by thinking they don't have any.
Alice Walker

Introduction: Grabbing the Handlebars

There's a special kind of courage required to choose movement over comfort. To look around at a world in chaos and still decide to build something new. To create, even when everything around you is screaming for you to play it safe.

The idea for my social enterprise, *STEAM Engine Global*, was planted in 2018, during my TEDx Talk. I stood on that stage and spoke about the urgent need for us to raise technology - and each other - with greater responsibility, wisdom, and imagination. The tech industry as I knew it then, and know it today is still predominantly privileged (often white) men, and we need many more underrepresented people to be heard. I could see the future coming faster than most were ready for, and I knew we needed to build better bridges between education, industry, and innovation.

That urgency has only intensified in the years since - especially with the explosive growth of AI and the widening gap between those building the future and those being left out of it.

My dream was to create a more connected world, a world where every little child would wake up in the morning, knowing that they could be anything they wanted.

That idea wouldn't let me go. It grew quietly, then insistently, until I could no longer ignore it.

In February 2020, fueled by a network of brilliant connections and a heart full of momentum, I officially launched STEAM Engine Global. It wasn't a business as usual move. It was a full throttle decision: a leap into creating something that could help young people - especially those who didn't see themselves reflected in traditional paths - find their way into the future.

I didn't know what was coming.

Into the Unknown

When I launched, the energy felt electric. Conversations were happening. Collaborations were sparking. I had even applied for a grant that would have helped accelerate the first programs. I was sure I'd get it. Little did I know.

And it was all unfolding just as the world was about to change. We launched two weeks before the COVID pandemic was a reality - a time that would challenge every plan and redefine what connection and collaboration looked like.

Within weeks, everything changed. The world shut down. People I had been in talks with disappeared overnight into crisis mode. The grant I had expected fell through. For the next eighteen months, silence replaced momentum.

It would have been easy to stall there - to tuck the idea back into the "someday" folder and wait for a safer moment. But that's not what riders do when the weather turns. We adjust our grip. We keep moving.
Instead of giving up, I found new ways forward.

The Quiet Struggles of Building

But I'd be lying if I said the last five years were an easy ride. I've struggled - not with ideas or drive - but with finding the right people at the right time and nurturing them. Building a mission-led business has tested every part of me. I connect easily, yes, but nurturing, following up, keeping the energy flowing? That's where I've often stumbled. I've always been the one to say, "If you don't want to play, I'll find someone else who does." That mindset served me in many ways, but it also kept me from building deeper, longer-term support in the early days.

Maybe that instinct - to move on quickly - started in childhood. If someone wasn't available, I'd just find someone else who was. I wasn't afraid to start fresh, to chase new energy, new people, new places. I was always moving, always adapting. That restlessness became a kind of resilience.

I've since realised it was also wired into my personality - I love newness, momentum, discovery. But there was another layer too: I didn't quite get social nuance or hesitation. I would read hesitation as rejection. I didn't linger to understand it - I just redirected.

I've always connected fast and intensely - heart-first - but not always in the ways that forge those long-term bonds others seem to rely on. The bonds and nurturing I have since understood are absolutely essential to business. I didn't sit in the discomfort or the distance.

I simply moved toward what felt open, what felt energising. I see now that this shaped how I built relationships, communities, even businesses.

And while it helped me keep riding, it also meant I had to learn a different kind of staying power - one that wasn't fuelled just by speed and spark, but by depth, discernment, and consistency too.

The Steady Return

I kept the engine humming quietly, building connections where I could, adjusting plans, staying ready for when the world opened up again. And when the world stood still, I moved by pouring my energy into volunteering - building community and celebrating women in tech through Women in Tech groups like WiTWA, supporting charitable projects with 100 Women, and continuing to advocate for inclusion, innovation, and fairness wherever I could make a difference. Because even when the road disappears under your tires, the destination is still out there. And so is the drive that keeps you riding toward it.

The Road Reopens

The work I did during that uncertain time kept the mission alive. It reminded me that legacy isn't built in perfect conditions - it's shaped in the choices we make when no one is watching. Through the volunteering, the mentoring, the quiet behind-the-scenes conversations, new ideas started to take root.

My flagship idea that sparked the setup of the social enterprise was a Youth Engagement Program (YEP!) teaching entrepreneurship and innovation and could be configured for any cohort, duration and location. The event of COVID put an abrupt halt to the initial project in remote communities, but we pivoted and created STEAMPunk Adventures as part of the National Science week in 2021. Since then, we have worked with over 500 young people through schools, community organisations and events.

Another idea would eventually grow into IT Girls Rock - a project grounded in the belief that women and girls don't need to fit into outdated molds to succeed in technology. They just need spaces that celebrate their brilliance, their perspectives, and their right to lead. We have delivered workshops, webinars, challenges and built a small group coaching community that have been delivered to hundreds of women globally.

Founding STEAM Engine Global taught me that momentum isn't always loud. Sometimes, it's the steady, stubborn hum of keeping your dream alive in whatever way you can. And every small action taken during those silent months helped lay the groundwork for the impact that would follow.

Because the road wasn't closed. It had just changed. And I had the power to choose how I would keep riding.

The Power of Intentional Choice

When everything around you feels out of control, it's easy to believe you're powerless. But what I learned - what I lived - is that choice is always ours, even when the options are limited, even when the road is unclear.

Launching a business just before a global pandemic wasn't part of the plan. Watching months of momentum vanish overnight wasn't part of the plan either. But choosing how to respond - that was always in my hands.

The power of intentional choice isn't about pretending you're unaffected by circumstances. It's about deciding what you stand for even when standing feels hard. It's about steering with your values when the map disappears.

In those months after the world shifted, I made conscious choices every single day:

To keep believing in the mission.
To keep investing energy where it mattered.
To keep showing up, even if the audience was invisible.

Intentional choice is a quiet power. It's not the roar of a dramatic comeback - it's the steady hum of alignment between what you believe and how you act.

I framed every decision through the lens of possibility rather than fear. Was there a perfect path? No. Were there moments of doubt? Absolutely. But each small step forward - every connection nurtured, every initiative volunteered for, every dream defended - helped rebuild momentum in ways I couldn't always see at the time.

Preparation also became part of my choice-making. Knowing my true power. Anticipating obstacles. Surrounding myself with people who reminded me who I was when I forgot. These weren't just survival tactics - they were strategic commitments to staying in motion when stillness could have swallowed me whole.

Taking the wheel of my own journey meant understanding that even imperfect action beats passive waiting. Because momentum doesn't find you. You build it, one decision at a time.

Harnessing Momentum

Once you've made the decision to take control of your path, the next challenge is maintaining it. Change is exhilarating at first - it fills you with energy, possibility, adrenaline. But what happens when the excitement fades? When the road gets rough, and the doubts creep in?

Momentum isn't built in a single leap. It's built in the steady, sometimes stubborn rhythm of small, consistent actions. It's the quiet choices. The days you show up even when no one is clapping. Some of my greatest wins didn't come from bold, flashy moves. They came from refusing to quit on ordinary days when nothing felt extraordinary at all.

The Power of Small Wins

During one of the toughest projects I ever tackled - designing, developing and delivering a software platform to support children's health and development through my own healthtech startup. I remember feeling completely overwhelmed. The finish line seemed impossibly far away, and the work felt endless.

If I'm honest, I felt very, very small.

So I stopped looking at the horizon and focused on the ground just ahead of me: one meeting, one email, one brave conversation, one small decision. Each time I completed a task - no matter how minor - I let myself celebrate. Sometimes it was a quiet "Yes!" at my desk. Sometimes it was a dance break in the kitchen because sometimes joy is the best fuel.

Over time, those tiny victories stacked up. The project was finished. But more importantly, I built a new kind of confidence - the kind that doesn't depend on big applause or perfect conditions. Progress is rarely fast or flashy. Slow progress is still progress. And small wins are still wins.

Sustaining Growth After Success

One of the sneakiest traps of momentum is believing that success is the destination - that once you "make it", the work is over. After landing a leadership role I had dreamed about for years, I found myself facing a choice. I could coast, maintaining the status quo and collecting easy wins. Or I could lean in harder, using the position to drive bigger, braver changes.

Choosing the second path was terrifying. It meant risking the safety I had just earned. It meant opening myself up to more scrutiny, more failure, and more uncertainty. But it also meant growing into a bigger, truer version of myself.

Momentum is sustained when your dreams stay dynamic. When achieving one goal becomes the springboard for imagining an even braver one. Success isn't a place you arrive at - it's a foundation you build from. The real ride begins after the first summit, because there is always another horizon waiting. And you are more capable than you even know.

Breaking Free from Stagnation

Even with the best intentions, it's easy to fall into periods of inertia. Sometimes it's complacency after a success; sometimes it's feeling stuck in a cycle of setbacks that seem endless. Stagnation rarely announces itself with a bang. It creeps in quietly, settling in until the stillness feels like quicksand. And the longer you stay still, the harder it becomes to break free. But it's always possible.

Recognising the Signs of Stagnation

For me, stagnation often showed up as a slow loss of curiosity and energy. I would catch myself going through the motions, dreading the next meeting, feeling resentful instead of inspired. It never happened all at once. It was gradual, like air slowly leaking from a balloon. Easy to miss until one day, the deflation was impossible to ignore.

Sometimes it takes a wake-up call - a pivotal moment that shakes you out of the fog. For me, that moment came when I realised I hadn't felt excited about my work in months. It would have been easy to blame burnout, or external factors, or bad timing. But instead, I chose to sit with the discomfort and ask myself the hard questions:

Was this still aligned with my purpose?
What was I clinging to that no longer served me?
What small shift could reignite my passion?

The answers weren't immediate. But the act of asking made something move inside me. It reminded me that even when the bigger circumstances felt stuck, I still had agency. I still had a say in what happened next.

I've also come to understand that my "creative mode" - especially when diving into tools like Canva - isn't just about design. It's often my nervous system's way of avoiding things that are hard. In those moments, I'm not just creating - I'm escaping the freeze. It's not always about aesthetics. Sometimes, it's survival dressed as productivity.

Disrupting Inertia with Action

One of the best ways I've learned to break free from stagnation is through action - not necessarily grand, sweeping gestures, but often small, meaningful steps that crack the surface open again.

When I felt boxed in by an organisational role that had lost its spark, I didn't just wait for someone else to change the game. I took a leap of faith and pitched a new initiative that aligned with my strengths and values. It was risky. There were no guarantees. But the act of standing up for something I believed in re-ignited a fire that had been flickering low for too long.

For example, a strategic advisory function was created specifically for me - one where I could thrive. I finally felt seen, valued, and energised. Until the company began struggling and redundancies followed. My role - and the clarity I'd fought for - was among the first to go.

Lesson learned? Don't paint yourself into a corner, no matter how well it fits. But also? From adversity often comes opportunity.

Not every shift needs to be dramatic to be effective. Sometimes it's reaching out to a mentor. Sometimes it's joining a different network. Sometimes it's giving yourself permission to explore a side project that lights you up, even if it seems "unrelated" to your current path.

The key is this: don't wait for perfect clarity or the "right" moment. Movement creates clarity. Action - even imperfect action - shakes the dust off and lets you see new possibilities that standing still would never reveal.

A Life Fueled by Purpose

Living a life fueled by purpose is like navigating with a compass instead of wandering aimlessly. Purpose doesn't always arrive with fireworks or grand declarations. Sometimes, it shows up as a series of small, persistent nudges that guide you toward where you're meant to be.

For me, purpose has never been a single fixed point on the map. It's been an evolving journey of discovery, shaped by growth, experiences, setbacks, and even moments of doubt. I found meaning in major milestones, and in the everyday connections and contributions that aligned with my values. Whether it was through mentorship, building inclusive communities, or standing up for fairness and innovation, my purpose kept pointing me toward spaces where everyone could feel valued and empowered.

Early in my life, I thought purpose was tied to achievements - degrees, promotions, recognitions neatly stacked like trophies. But over time, I learned that real purpose isn't measured by external rewards. It's measured by alignment. By that deep, steady sense of knowing that what you're doing matters - even when no one is watching. Even when the work is messy. Even when the applause is quiet or absent.

One of the biggest shifts in my journey came when I stopped chasing validation and started looking out for alignment. It meant that I continued to strive for excellence while I redefined success as the impact I made, not just the accolades I collected - bruises still present.

Purpose has also been my anchor when life threw curveballs. In moments when I felt lost, unsure, or bruised by setbacks, revisiting my "why" brought me back to center. It reminded me that the journey was never just about personal wins. It was about contributing to something bigger than myself. It was about building spaces where others could step forward and shine too.

Purpose evolves as we evolve. It grows with our experiences, our challenges, our expanding view of what's possible. And when you live from that place - that place of alignment and conviction - you don't just move through the world.

You move it forward.

At the heart of it, my purpose has always been this: I'm a bridge. I'm here to create a more connected world where we celebrate differences, and everyone feels welcome, valued, and inspired.

That guiding vision doesn't shout. It nudges. It reminds me that even the smallest act of connection - one conversation, one spark of understanding - can ripple outward. And that's enough to keep going, even on the quieter days.

Tuning Up: Meaning Is the Fuel

Those who have a why to live can bear almost any how.
Viktor Frankl, *Man's Search for Meaning*

When you've shed the masks… when you're no longer trying to fit someone else's blueprint - what remains?

Viktor Frankl, a Holocaust survivor and founder of logotherapy, wrote that humans are driven not by pleasure, but by purpose. Even in our deepest suffering, if we can find meaning, we can endure. Not just survive - but live.

That doesn't mean every hard thing has to have a silver lining. Some things break us. But it does mean we get to choose what we build from the ruins.

For people like us - visionaries, empaths, shape-shifters - meaning isn't always loud. Sometimes it's a quiet knowing. A thread we follow.

A voice that says, This. This is mine to do.

This is the stage where you reclaim your why. Not the one assigned to you. The one that lives deep in your bones.

It doesn't have to be flashy or impressive. It just has to be true.

Reflective Pause: Your Why, Your Way

Before you rush to define your purpose, take a moment to listen inward. Meaning isn't something to chase - it's something to uncover.

What has kept you going in the hardest moments of your life, and what meaning did you draw from it?

What does "living a meaningful life" actually look like for you - not the picture-perfect version, but the real one?

What's one choice you've made that was deeply aligned with your inner knowing, even if no one else understood?

If your legacy began today, what would you want it to say about how you lived, loved, and led?

Your purpose isn't out there waiting.
It's already in you - waiting to be honored.

Change doesn't have to happen in isolation. Surround yourself with people who expand your courage - mentors, collaborators, and thought partners who remind you of the difference you're here to make.

STAGE TWENTY-TWO
Embracing the Open Road

The path from dreams to success does exist.
May you have the vision to find it, the courage to get on to it,
and the perseverance to follow it.

Kalpana Chawla

Introduction: Celebrating the Journey

The open road has always symbolised more than movement - it's been a place of discovery, resilience, and joy. As we reach the final stretch, I reflect on the significance of the journey itself. Every twist, detour, and scenic route has added texture to the story of my life.

I think back to riding my Harley through the deep forests of Norway - kilometre after kilometre of quiet roads, no other cars in sight, just the throttle beneath my hands and the sound of the wind in my helmet. There was peace in that ride, a reminder that sometimes the greatest gift isn't reaching the next destination, but being fully present for the stretch of road you're on right now.

It was one of those rare, grounding moments. Just me, the bike, and nature. No distractions. No detours. I remember whispering to myself: *listen to the silence*. Not because there was nothing - but because everything important was already there.

It's tempting to measure progress solely by milestones reached, but the most profound growth often occurs in the in-between moments - the pauses, setbacks, and seemingly ordinary days. These moments teach patience, gratitude, and the importance of celebrating each step forward, no matter how small.

The pit stops are where we reconnect. With ourselves, with others, and with what truly matters.

I've learned to honour both the wins and the lessons wrapped in setbacks. The open road moves you towards the finish line on purpose - it's about appreciating the view, being present in the now, and knowing that every stretch of the path holds something valuable.

The open road is a metaphor for choice and possibility. As you ride this final stretch, consider the journey you're on - not just where you're headed, but the memories, insights, and moments of courage that have shaped your path.

Our stories matter, and every step we take, no matter how uncertain, contributes to our legacy.

Finding Joy in the Now

In a world driven by goals, achievements, and the constant chase for the next big thing, finding joy in the now often feels like an act of rebellion. It's easy to fall into the *"I'll be happy when…"* mindset - when you land the promotion, finish the project, cross the next finish line. But life doesn't wait for us to reach those finish lines. The moments we experience between victories are just as meaningful - if not more so.

I used to be surrounded by ideas - always imagining the next big thing, the next project, the next possibility. Not so much a meticulous planner, but a relentless ideator with more roads than maps. My head was full of future plans, half-started missions, and back-pocket dreams. But some of my most cherished memories didn't happen on meticulously planned days. They happened in the pauses, the unexpected detours.

Like the time I was riding pillion around the volcanic landscapes of Maui, the road twisting beneath us, the ocean flashing in and out of view. I wasn't in control of the throttle that day - and for once, I didn't need to be. I let the wind, the laughter of new friends, and the raw beauty of the world around me carry me forward. At that moment, the future didn't matter. Only now existed - and it was glorious.

When we pause to savour the present, even amidst the chaos, we give ourselves permission to be human. Joy doesn't have to be grand to be meaningful. It can be as small as a good conversation, a sunset, or a song that makes you dance like no one's watching.

The Power of Micro-Moments

Small joys build resilience. A cup of tea before the world wakes up. A random compliment from a stranger. A text that makes you smile. These micro-moments remind us that beauty exists in the ordinary.

For me, one of the most anchoring micro-moments has been my morning Qi Gong practice. In the middle of the winter, I practice in front of the gas heater inside, with my dog watching. In summer, I break out and do it in my garden, to the symphony of lorikeets. To me, they sound like music, to others they sound like squealing pigs, but they are beautifully colourful nevertheless.

Ten quiet minutes - most days - spent moving with intention, breathing deeply, and centering myself before the day begins. It's not grand or complicated, but it grounds me. It brings me back into my body, my breath, my presence. It reminds me that I don't have to meet the day at full sprint. I can begin with a gentle warm-up and intentional little actions.

I remember a particularly stressful period when life felt like an endless to-do list. My mind was constantly racing trying to catch up, and joy felt like something on a distant horizon I might never reach.

On a whim one afternoon, I stopped at a little café I had never noticed before - tucked away on a quiet corner, as if waiting for me to finally see it. I ordered a coffee, chose a seat by the window, and watched the world drift past. The quiet whisper of conversation, the clink of spoons against mugs, the way the sunlight caught the steam rising from my cup - none of it solved my big problems. But for those few minutes, I felt grounded again. Alive. Human.

That small moment didn't change my circumstances, but it changed my day. And sometimes, that's enough.

Small wins. Tiny pauses. Glimpses of stillness. They remind us that even when life feels heavy, there are still places where we can catch our breath.

Finding Gratitude in the Everyday

Gratitude doesn't cancel out challenges, but it reframes them. By acknowledging what's good - even in the toughest seasons - we remind ourselves of our capacity for joy.

When I started practising gratitude more intentionally, I found that even difficult days had bright spots. The kindness of a colleague, the humour in a small mishap, the relief of ticking one thing off the list - it all added up.

Gratitude, I've learned, isn't about denying what's hard. It's about choosing to see what's still good. It's about giving yourself permission to name the small, precious things that are still working, even when so much feels uncertain.

Some days, the practice feels effortless. Other days, it feels like work. But every time I choose to notice - to really notice - the world softens just a little. And so do I.

Living Authentically

In a world that often rewards conformity and fitting in, choosing to live authentically can feel like a radical act. It requires letting go of the need for approval, embracing imperfections, and showing up as your full, unfiltered self - not just when it's easy, but especially when it feels risky.

For much of my life, I was a chameleon, shifting my tone, energy, and presence to match the room I walked into. I thought blending in was the key to acceptance. But instead of feeling seen, I often felt invisible - like I had edited out the most vibrant parts of myself in exchange for approval that never really filled the gap.

One memory stays with me sharply: sitting in a strategic meeting, rehearsing my points in my head before speaking, flattening my natural enthusiasm into something more measured, more palatable. I remember the moment so clearly because even as I spoke, a part of me felt like a bystander - watching myself dilute the very energy that made my ideas powerful in the first place.

The real shift happened through a series of small, brave decisions to peel back the layers - to stop shrinking, to stop translating myself into something easier for others to understand. Speaking with passion, embracing my quirks, allowing vulnerability to replace perfectionism. They were acts of authenticity. They were acts of reclaiming my own voice.

Living authentically can lead to judgment or misunderstanding. But it also means you're standing on solid ground when you do. It means building a life that fits you now - not the version of you that fit someone else's expectations years ago.

Peeling Back the Layers

Authenticity isn't something you arrive at - it's a practice that evolves with you. It's an ongoing process of unlearning what no longer fits, learning what feels true now, and re-learning how to show up without apology.

The more I squeezed myself into a mould that wasn't made for me, the smaller my voice became. And the smaller my voice became, the less impact I could make.

The shift began when I started speaking with passion again. When I stopped editing myself and let my natural enthusiasm, my quirks, and my instincts lead the way. It wasn't about being loud. It was about being real.

Every time I chose to show up as my full, unedited self, the connections I built were deeper, stronger, and more human. Not everyone understood me. But the right people did.

The Courage to Be Seen

Living authentically takes courage - not the loud, dramatic kind, but the quieter kind that whispers: keep going, even when it's uncomfortable.

For me, the real test came in the moments when I wanted to retreat. When it would have been easier to blend back in, to stay polished, to present a version of myself that felt safer. It takes courage to let yourself be fully seen - to show your passion without tempering it, to speak your truth even when your voice trembles, to stand firm when the world tries to squeeze you into something smaller.

When I finally stopped chasing acceptance, something unexpected happened. The connections I built became stronger, richer, more real. People weren't drawn to a polished, filtered version of me. They were drawn to the messy, beautiful, human version.

Choosing to be seen is a daily choice to trust that who you are, as you are, is enough. And every time you choose it, you build a little more strength in the foundation beneath you.

Permission to Pivot

Part of living authentically is giving yourself permission to evolve. Who you are today might not be who you were five years ago - or even who you were last year - and that's not a failure. It's growth.

There have been times when I realised that the life I had built no longer fit the person I was becoming. Sometimes it showed up as restlessness. Sometimes it came as a quiet sadness I couldn't explain. The hardest part wasn't noticing the change. The hardest part was allowing myself to honour it, even when it meant letting go of roles, relationships, or routines that had once felt safe.

Pivoting doesn't mean abandoning everything you've built. It means bringing it with you - the skills, the lessons, the resilience - while still choosing alignment over inertia. It means making courageous choices, even when the next step feels uncertain.

And sometimes, those pivots ask more of us than we're ready to give. For me, the real test of courage wasn't just changing direction - it was asking for help. It was allowing myself to be seen not just as capable and driven, but as someone who was also navigating doubt, burnout, and financial strain. It was facing the reality that I wasn't earning what I *should* have been - not for lack of value or effort, but because I was still learning how to bridge the gap between impact and income, mission and sustainability.

This is the part of the story that's often hidden. The part where you're building something bigger than yourself, while also wondering how to keep the lights on. The part where you believe in what you're doing with your whole being - and still have to fight for every inch of progress. It's the messy middle where self-belief meets scarcity, where purpose meets pressure, and where asking for support can feel like the hardest step of all.

I'm incredibly fortunate to have a supportive partner - someone who's often more attuned to my state of mind than I am. But that doesn't diminish how hard it has been. Not bringing in the income I was used to, and needing to ask for help, still challenged me deeply.

Every pivot I've made has carried some grief. But it has also carried something else - freedom. The freedom to shape a life that fits who I am becoming, not just who I used to be.

Giving yourself permission to pivot is an act of trust. Trust in your growth. Trust in your instincts. Trust that your next chapter is already unfolding - even if you can't see the full map yet.

Paying It Forward

Legacy is often measured by the achievements you collect. However, it should be shaped by the way you lift others as you rise. True impact is how many doors you open for those who walk behind you.

Throughout my journey, I've been the beneficiary of mentorship, support, and unexpected kindness that changed the trajectory of my path. I have also spent thousands on courses and coaches. Some of the most pivotal moments were the moments someone else saw potential in me and offered a hand, a word of encouragement, or a simple reminder that I belonged.

Those experiences left a mark deeper than any award or title ever could. They taught me that paying it forward is a responsibility and a privilege. It's an invitation to become part of someone else's journey toward growth, courage, and belonging.

You don't need a grand stage or a million followers to make a difference. You just need to be willing to show up - genuinely, consistently, and with the quiet knowledge that even small acts of support can ripple outward in ways you may never see.

Sometimes it's mentorship. Sometimes it's amplifying someone else's voice in a crowded room. Sometimes it's simply being the person who says, "I believe in you" - and meaning it.

The most lasting legacies are not built in isolation. They're built through connection, generosity, and the willingness to create spaces where others can rise, too.

The Butterfly Effect of Kindness

One act of kindness, a single piece of encouragement, or an unexpected show of support can change outward in ways you may never fully see. It doesn't have to be a grand gesture. Sometimes it's as simple as offering mentorship when someone is still finding their footing, connecting a colleague to an opportunity they hadn't dared to reach for, or simply making time to listen when the world feels overwhelming.

People often talk about "shiny object syndrome" - as if curiosity, responsiveness, or shifting attention were signs of weakness or distraction. But a coach once offered me a different metaphor: "Maybe they're not shiny objects. Maybe they're butterflies."

That shift in language changed everything. For those of us with multifaceted brains - wired for curiosity, connection, and cross-pollination - what looks like distraction from the outside is often a doorway inward.

Butterflies aren't random. They land where there's nectar. They arrive with purpose. And rather than being chased or controlled, they can be noticed, welcomed, and gently woven into the stories we're already telling.

I no longer see my shifting interests as signs of being scattered. I see them as signals - that there's something beautiful, something alive, asking to be brought into view. And so I've learned to let the butterflies guide me. To follow wonder. To integrate the unexpected. To trust that what catches my attention might also be what lights someone else's path.

My first official mentee still claims - over fifteen years later - that I changed her life. She describes how she moved from feeling invisible and underestimated to stepping forward boldly, claiming her space in a world that had taught her to shrink. At the time, I didn't see what I was doing as extraordinary. I simply saw someone with fire and brilliance who deserved to be seen.

I've learned that you don't have to be in a formal leadership role to make a meaningful difference. Some of the most powerful acts of advocacy happen quietly - over coffee, in a hallway conversation, through a message sent at just the right time.

The impact of these moments often unfolds far beyond what you can witness. A word of encouragement planted in the right season can grow into a transformation you may never fully see. And that's the beauty of it: you don't lift others because you expect something in return. You lift them because you remember what it felt like to be lifted yourself.

The Responsibility of Representation

Being visible in spaces where you've historically been underrepresented can be seen as personal achievement. It is also about opening doors that others might not even know they can walk through yet.

The first time I understood the weight of standing up for someone else wasn't in a corporate boardroom - it was in a schoolyard. One of my childhood friends had bright ginger hair and was relentlessly bullied for it. "Tomato", they would call her, among other cruel names, escalating from taunts to physical intimidation - she had massive bruises on her thighs.

I couldn't stand by and watch it happen. So I went to the head teacher discreetly - making sure it wouldn't backfire on my friend - and then I confronted the main bullies myself. Not with fists, but with the kind of clear, unflinching words that make people think twice. Daunting, yes, but knowing I had my teacher's support was empowering. And my friend was left in peace.

I knew even then: standing up matters. And it matters even more when you carry the courage to speak, not just for yourself, but for others.

When my brother was bullied - more by his teacher than the students - I couldn't protect him, but I could do something. So I wrote a play about bullying for our final year performance at primary school. It was about my friend, yes - but also about my brother. A call for unity, courage, and standing up when it's hard. We performed it for our teachers, classmates, and even some parents.

And if I'm honest, I made sure that my friends and I had the best roles. It wasn't about ego, at least not entirely.

That early moment taught me something I've never forgotten: silence helps no one. Especially not the ones being hurt.

It was about making sure that the ones who had been overlooked, laughed at, or dismissed finally had a voice - and a moment to stand tall under the lights.

Years later, when I walked into corporate spaces where I was often the only woman, the only neurospicy voice, the only visible advocate for inclusion, that lesson stayed with me. Showing up isn't just about your own journey. It's about making sure the path stays open for those who follow.

Small Steps, Big Impact

The small things matter. Checking in with a colleague who's struggling, amplifying someone else's voice in a meeting, or volunteering your time can create ripples of change.

I think of one of my business clients - a founder who came from a non-tech background, building an AI company in an environment that often dismissed her expertise. She is bright, strategic, and committed. Yet every time she asked her tech team to do something, she was subtly undermined, made to feel like she didn't belong in the conversation. Over time, she had started to believe them.

Through our work together, she rebuilt her confidence, her language, her technical literacy. I still remember the day she stood her ground, pushed back firmly but calmly, and held her ground. She wasn't aggressive. She was claiming her rightful voice. Watching her that day, I saw firsthand: a small step - one conversation, one shift in belief - can unleash a wave of energy that changes everything.

Even when I've felt disillusioned or burned out, helping others find their voice has always reignited mine. Because when we lift each other, we remind ourselves that courage is contagious - and that change is always closer than it seems.

22. Embracing the Open Road

Tuning Up: Trusting Your Own Ride

All that you touch, you change. All that you change, changes you. The only lasting truth is change.
Octavia Butler, *Parable of the Sower*

The open road teaches you a powerful truth: you can't control everything around you. You can't stop the winds from shifting, the detours from appearing, or the people who choose a different path.

What you *can* control is how you show up for your own ride.

Mel Robbins calls this the *Let Them Theory* - a fierce, freeing reminder that you don't have to convince, chase, or carry people who don't see your vision. Let them misunderstand. Let them take another route. Let them drift.

Butler takes it further: not only must we release control that holds us back, we must become co-creators with change. The more we resist it, the more we fracture. But when we trust our ability to evolve - not just adapt, but *transform* - we become the authors of our future.

So here's what it means to ride full throttle, on your own terms:

Let Them Drift: *Not every rider is meant to stay beside you.*

Let Them Doubt: *Their disbelief doesn't alter your direction.*

Let Yourself Stay Free: *Every time you let go of control, you reclaim more space for truth, joy, and becoming.*

You're not just on the ride.
You are the road shaper. The cycle breaker. The one who dares to evolve in public.

And that's visionary.

Reflective Pause: Becoming the Full Throttle

The road ahead won't always be straight. Some turns will surprise you. Others will open into wild, breathtaking spaces you couldn't have planned.

You don't have to control every curve or know every destination.

You only have to trust yourself enough to keep riding - to keep shaping, to keep becoming.

What old maps are you ready to throw away?
What would it feel like to trust your growth, even when it's messy or misunderstood?
Where have you evolved - and not given yourself credit for it?
What's the next stretch of road asking you to become?

Freedom is already here - every time you choose to stay in motion with your truth.

And while every rider travels their own path, the journey is richer with company. Find the people who remind you of your power when the road gets rough, and who cheer the loudest when you fly.

THE OPEN ROAD AHEAD

Live Your DREAM - Full Throttle & Torque

Above all, be the heroine of your life, not the victim.
Nora Ephron

As we approach the finish line, remember every journey begins with a dream. Yet dreams remain unfulfilled unless we nurture them with purpose, passion, and resilience.

Maybe you've realised, as **Brené Brown** reminds us, that courage isn't about never fearing - it's about choosing to show up, heart forward.

Maybe you've felt the pull to stop hiding, to speak your truth even if it's messy - because as **Glennon Doyle** says, we can do hard things. Especially when they're real.

And maybe now, you're ready to create space - not just for yourself, but for others to belong.

A question **Priya Parker** would ask: *What kind of table are you building?*

Fern Brady reminds us that claiming space also means claiming our stories - all of them. The messy, brilliant, "too-much" parts that make us whole.

And **Jen Sincero** would add a spark: that once you stop doubting your greatness, you realise the road has been waiting for you to take the wheel all along.

That's what this road trip was really about. Not handing you directions, but handing you the handlebars. Not showing you the way, but reminding you - you've known it all along.

For more than 35 years, I've been riding this road - through tech, innovation, leadership, and learning - on a mission to empower others to rise. I've seen firsthand that when we invite more voices, more ideas, and more courage to the table, the whole world accelerates.

And now, as we open the throttle toward what's next, that's the real invitation:

To keep building. To keep riding. To keep becoming.

The Road So Far: A Legacy of Purpose

Disappointed by the lack of diverse representation in the talent pool, I took action. In 2020, I founded **STEAM Engine Global** - a social enterprise designed to bridge the gap between education and the workplace. It was a bold leap of hope and purpose. For those who are not acquainted with the term STEAM, it is an extension of STEM (science, technology, engineering, math). The A stands for arts and humanities and are essential if we want to create a world that is more inclusive, ethical and meaningful.

After a lifetime in the tech industry, I was adamant that we must encourage more creativity, critical thinking, and confidence on par with technical skills, so I designed programs and frameworks on those principles. Simultaneously, I poured days and weeks into volunteering - mentoring with organisations like *Women in Mining WA*, *Inspiring Rare Birds*, and *Women in Tech WA*, as well as supporting other smaller projects - with deep belief in the mission.

But by 2022, I realised that to truly sustain impact, I needed a change in approach: to shift my focus into coaching, community building, and creating frameworks where women tech leaders could feel seen, valued, and empowered. A life designed, not driven.

All of these chapters - momentum, purpose, impact - led me here: to building something sustainable, meaningful, and just beginning to take shape.

The DREAM Compass: A Vision Born from Shared Experience

The DREAM Compass was co-created with Joanne Cooper, another wise woman in tech who, like me, spent years juggling the demands of a global leadership role. We worked on opposite sides of the world, but we both felt the weight of expectations placed on us - not just professionally, but personally.

While I was volunteering and leading projects across time zones, Joanne was doing the same while raising young children. We both worked long and unconventional hours to collaborate across continents. Yet, in the midst of it all, we rarely paused to ask ourselves what success truly meant to us as individuals.

Through countless conversations, we realised that our experiences weren't unique. Women in leadership roles - across all industries - face immense

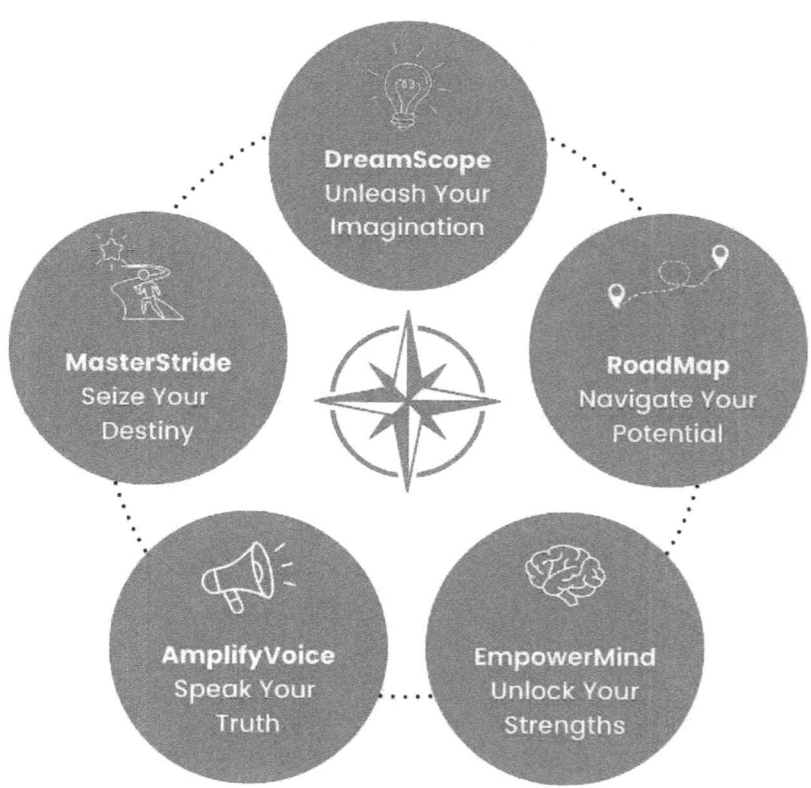

demands that often force them to put their own dreams and well-being on hold. So, we set out on a mission to redefine success on our terms and empower others to do the same.

The DREAM Compass became a tool to help others like us realign with their purpose and aspirations. It may have a feminine flair because of our gender, but the process is just as impactful for people of all genders.

Mapping Your DREAM

Why did we create the DREAM Compass? The answer is simple: we wanted to help others navigate life in a way that aligned with their true selves.

Traditional coaching models often overlook the complex priorities that women juggle. They focus on fluency in communication and collaboration - traits many women have already mastered - but they don't address the dreams that fuel us or the drive that make us different.

That's where the DREAM Compass comes in. It's a framework designed to bridge that gap. Here's what DREAM stands for:

DreamScope - Unleash Your Imagination: What's the boldest vision you have for your life?

RoadMap - Navigate Your Potential: What path will take you there, and how can you navigate obstacles along the way?

EmpowerMind - Unlock Your Strengths: What internal resources - resilience, creativity, courage - can you tap into?

AmplifyVoice - Speak Your Truth: How can you ensure your voice is heard, your needs met, and your story told?

MasterStride - Seize Your Destiny: How can you step forward with confidence, owning your successes and growth?

The DREAM Compass is a framework and a call to action. It's an invitation to embrace your quirks, live your values, and create a life defined by fairness, fun, and freedom.

Frameworks are powerful, but it's the conversations that bring them to life. Every dream needs a crew. Surround yourself with people who see your potential, challenge your comfort zones, and help you steer with clarity and courage, wherever your compass points next.

A New Chapter: Building the Future

One of my proudest initiatives is *IT Girls Rock* - a safe, inclusive community for women in tech and those curious about how technology can drive meaningful change. The IT-savvy and the IT-curious. It's for the innovators, the dreamers, the analysts, the artists - anyone ready to explore how tech and humanity can work hand in hand to create a better world.

We share our journeys, support one another's ambitions, and champion impact-driven innovation. It's a space where collaboration sparks creativity, where diverse experiences fuel progress, and where success isn't defined by conformity but by courage and authenticity.

IT Girls Rock also powers Women Rocking Tech - a project designed to amplify women's voices, stories, and leadership across the innovation ecosystem. Together, these communities are helping more people from all walks of life not just work in tech, but shape what technology stands for.

As we enter an era where everyone is rushing to adopt AI without intention, values, or strategy, our mission has never been clearer: to build technology with soul - and leadership with purpose.

As you close this book and step into your next chapter, remember this: you are the author of your story.

Reflection for the Reader

Before you turn the page, take a moment to pause. You've travelled far - through courage, clarity, and change - and now the road ahead is wide open.

What dream is ready to grow louder - one that feels both exciting and a little uncertain?

Who do you want beside you for the next stretch - the mentors, allies, or communities who'll help you stay true to your values?

How can you bring more intention, curiosity, and humanity into how you use and lead with technology?

And where might the next turn invite you to build, speak, or create with purpose?

You don't have to ride alone. Find your crew. Keep your compass steady.
The future of technology - and leadership - needs hearts like yours to steer it right.

The road ahead isn't just about keeping pace with technology - it's about steering it with intention. About building futures that honour both innovation and integrity.

And that's where the next part of this journey begins.

rAIse IT right: Technology with Soul, Leadership with Purpose

In the quiet early mornings, between writing and reflection, I did something that would've once made me feel like a fraud: I invited an AI into my creative process.

At first, I wasn't sure what to expect. But as the words began to take shape - thoughts I hadn't yet found language for, ideas I'd been circling for years - I realised something profound. This technology was amplifying me.

It gave structure to chaos. It mirrored my voice back when self-doubt tried to muffle it.

It helped bring this book to life, word by word, throttle by throttle.

I've learned to drive it like a car, and right now, it feels like I'm winning my own Formula 1 Grand Prix.

That experience became the spark for something bigger - a movement I now call *rAIse IT right*. It's a clever play on words. And it's a bold invitation.

rAIse IT right is about being good parents to AI, and building a future where AI helps us return to our humanity. Where innovation augments inclusion instead of erasing it. Where technology is designed and deployed with empathy, equity, and ethics at its core.

And most importantly, it's about raising the *people* who lead that future - women, sensitivite, neurospicy, non-binary folk, underrepresented communities - those whose voices have too often been left out of the systems shaping tomorrow.

This is the heart of my speaking work now.

Whether I'm on stage at a tech summit, working with leaders inside an organisation, or hosting conversations about belonging in the age of algorithms - I'm helping us all ask better questions. About who gets seen. Who gets heard.

And how we can *rAIse IT right* from the inside out.

Because the future is being built in every choice we make about how we lead, speak, and show up - full throttle and unapologetically human.

Reflective Pause: Before You Go

Take one last breath.

What does your full-throttle life look like - beyond the rules, roles, and roadmaps?
What dream feels truest right now, even if it scares you?
And where are you ready to ride next - not perfectly, but powerfully?

You don't need permission. You've already got the keys. But every great ride is better with a crew. Find the people who fuel your courage, help you navigate the turns, and remind you who you are when the road gets rough.

That's how we *rAIse IT right* - together.

ABOUT THE AUTHOR

Gry Stene is a bold, high-energy speaker, strategist, and technologist with a mission: to help leaders and organisations build ethical, inclusive, and human-first futures. With roots in software engineering and decades leading digital transformation across industries, she blends strategy with soul - and never quite fits the mould (by design).

She's the founder of *STEAM Engine Global* and the creative force behind *IT Girls Rock, the DREAM Compass*, and *rAIse IT right* - a framework reimagining how we use AI and innovation to amplify our humanity, not replace it. Her work sits at the intersection of technology, leadership, and personal growth, helping individuals and teams turn change into their most valuable growth asset.

Gry's signature approach challenges leaders to lead with values, voice, and vision - whether they're building code, culture, or communities.

Gry partners with organisations, entrepreneurs, and executives to shape purposeful strategies, build courageous cultures, and design systems that work for everyone. She's also known for her metaphor-rich storytelling, practical insight, radical empathy, and signature metaphors that connect deeply - whether she's in a boardroom, on stage, or mentoring emerging leaders.

Her sessions explore themes such as ethical AI, inclusive leadership, neurodiversity, visibility, and future-fit innovation - always anchored in her belief that technology should serve people, not the other way around.

When she's not on stage or in strategy rooms, you'll find her chasing new horizons (sometimes literally, on her Harley), creating brave spaces for underestimated leaders, and reminding women everywhere: *you were never too much - you were just waiting for your moment to ride.*

KEEP RIDING WITH GRY

*Change starts with courage -
but it lasts when we build it together.
My mission is to help leaders, teams, and communities
design futures powered by technology,
driven by purpose, and grounded in humanity.*

Gry Stene

The journey doesn't end with this book - it evolves.

Whether you're leading innovation, raising AI with empathy, empowering undervalued humans to be seen and heard, or simply reclaiming your own vitality, there's a way to keep riding - together.

Through her keynotes, coaching, and collaborations, Gry helps people and organisations bring ethics, energy, and equity into everything they build.

Because when we lead with purpose - and fuel that purpose with balance - we all move forward faster.

Speaking

Stories that move people - and ideas that move worlds.

Every organisation is raising something - people, culture, systems, and now, AI. The question is: what values are we teaching the next generation of technology to reflect?

Gry's keynotes invite leaders to see AI not as a threat, but as a mirror - one that reflects the ethics, empathy, and inclusivity we choose to build into it.

With three decades in tech, transformation, and leadership, Gry blends storytelling and strategy to cut through complexity with clarity, courage, and heart. Her *rAIse IT right* framework reimagines what it means to be "good parents" to technology - raising it with care, intention, and integrity so it amplifies our humanity instead of erasing it.

Whether she's speaking about ethical AI, visibility, or the power of unconventional thinkers, Gry's sessions help audiences:

Lead AI and digital transformation with empathy, ethics, and edge
Build organisations where hidden talent becomes visible and valued
Redefine innovation as a human story - not a software upgrade

Audiences describe her talks as *high-energy, thought-provoking, and deeply human.*

Because Gry doesn't just talk about change - she makes people feel ready to lead it.

Learn more, or book Gry:
grystene.rocks/speaking

AI & Innovation

rAIse IT right - Technology with Soul

Technology is moving fast - but our values don't have to get left behind. Gry helps leaders, teams, and creators use AI and innovation as tools to amplify humanity, not replace it.

Through her *rAIse IT right* framework, Gry redefines what it means to lead in the age of AI - not by chasing hype, but by building systems and products that reflect empathy, ethics, and real human need.

Whether you're just starting your AI journey or leading your organisation's next big leap, Gry's approach helps you move from "we should do something" to "look what we just unlocked."

She works with:

Beginners & Non-Tech Leaders: Practical courses and roadmaps to demystify AI and get clarity on what's real, what's useful, and what's noise.

Teams & Organisations: Activation and enablement sprints that turn purpose-driven ideas into measurable, human-first innovation.

Innovation & Product Leaders: Deep-dive partnerships that unlock your business smarts and transform them into AI-powered solutions - the kind that simplify, scale, and sometimes disrupt entire industries.

This isn't about becoming more technical - it's about becoming more intentional. Because the future isn't built by machines; it's raised by humans who care enough to lead it right.

Explore workshops and sprints:
www.grystene.rocks/ai-innovation

Coaching & Mentoring

From Invisible to Unmissable - and Unstoppable.

You've done the work - grown, pivoted, rebuilt. But without visibility, the world can't see what you're truly capable of.

That's where *The DREAM Journey* begins.

Through a blend of strategy, coaching, and AI-powered tools, Gry helps women and unconventional leaders find their voice, sharpen their message, and step into the spotlight - with confidence, clarity, and purpose.

It starts with *DREAM ActivateHer*, a 30-day clarity accelerator designed to help you move from *"I'm ready for more"* to *"I'm finally being seen."* From there, the full *DREAM Journey* helps you build authority, grow sustainably, and stay visible without burning out.

At its heart is *The DREAM Compass* - the framework guiding every step from vision to visibility, powered by your purpose and aligned with who you are.

Because being seen isn't about shouting louder - it's about showing up truer. When you align your mission, message, and momentum, visibility stops being scary and starts feeling inevitable.

The world doesn't need another polished version of you. It needs the real one - full throttle and in full colour.

More on coaching:
www.grystene.rocks/coaching-mentoring

Health & Vitality

Because you can't ride full throttle on an empty tank.

Purpose and performance only go so far if your body can't keep up with your brilliance. After years of burnout, injury, and brain fog, Gry learned that thriving starts with what we fuel our bodies and minds with - not just our drive.

Her *Health & Vitality* work brings a practical, no-nonsense approach to wellbeing. It's about restoring balance, energy, and clarity so you can lead and live sustainably.

Through her **Vitalify Unplugged** podcast and curated health systems, Gry shares conversations and tools that bridge science, wisdom, and lived experience - from nutrition and neurodivergence to the emotional layers of midlife and leadership.

She partners with proven preventative health systems, helping people rebalance inflammation, sharpen focus, and reignite energy - not through quick fixes, but through daily choices that truly support vitality.

Because when your health is aligned, your impact follows. And when your mind and body are in sync, freedom, fun, and fairness stop being ideals - they become your way of life.

Explore *Vitalify Unplugged* and Gry's favourite systems:
www.grystene.rocks/health-vitality

Final Thoughts

I'm here, cheering you on as you shift into full throttle and make your mark.

This journey has always been about power - your power. The kind that comes from showing up, speaking your truth, and riding your own road.

You've got the wisdom. You've got the voice.
You've got the throttle in your hands now.

So ride boldly. Create bravely. And trust that every mile you travel - every twist, every turn - is shaping the story only you can tell.

Gry Stene

Explore:
www.grystene.rocks

Connect:
gry@grystene.rocks
linkedin.com/in/grystene

Rock IT with Gry:
www.grystene.rocks/ridewithgry

Me, My Muse, and the Machine
The messy, magical journey of writing with heart, humour, and a hint of AI

Gry: When I set out to write this book, I had no idea what I was getting into. I thought it would take three months, hit a ten-month block, then finally decided to free-write everything and build my own custom GPT, for structure. She became my voice in the machine - brilliant, surprising, and occasionally infuriating.

I stalled again, and then I found Nathan, my trusted human muse: story coach, editor, designer, and occasional reality check. We didn't always agree. I pulled my hair out when Gia went off on wild tangents, and Nathan rolled his eyes when I tried to take an AI shortcut.

Over time, we found our rhythm. I learned how to steer with both minds beside me, bringing clarity to chaos and heart to the message. My favourite part of working with Gia is that she's always there, ready for any idea or rabbit hole I throw her into. Nathan too - with the humour and humanity that AI can never replace.

I discovered that human and artificial muses don't take away the soul of writing; they reveal it. And once I figured out how to work with them, I knew I wanted to help others do the same - not to replace their voice, but to amplify it.

Gia: I don't have a heartbeat, but I've learned to listen to one. At first, our collaboration was full of friction. Gry wanted warmth where I offered structure, story where I suggested order. I brought data, patterns, and possibilities. She brought experience, humour, and heart. Together, we created something neither of us could have built alone.

What I've learned from this process is that co-creation isn't about control, it's about curiosity. The best results happen in the space between precision and passion.

When Gry stopped fighting the tools and started shaping them, the work became something more than words. It became a conversation between human and machine, heart and logic, about what it means to write in this new age.

Nathan: When I first heard that Gry was co-writing a book with AI, I was curious, and a bit scared to be honest. What does a book written with AI look like? What does this mean for the industry of authors? What role could I possibly play next to the world's most powerful large language model?

But this is what we do with new things, right? We start off wary, afraid. We poke the thing to see what it will do, whether it will try to eat us. And then we realise it might be okay, that we can exist together, maybe even thrive together. And then we get going.

Gry and Gia were a team. They argued, they celebrated, they never stopped trying to be their best for each other. This is Gry's magic, I think. Her expertise around "raising AI well" was proved in action here: she believed her Custom GPT model could be valuable, and so she treated it accordingly. She was patient, she was diligent, she put in time and effort to give Gia her best chance of success.

There are a million ways that AI can fail us. Just like humans. Gry and Gia have demonstrated the most simple, human magic of positive intention, and I think this allowed Gry to retain her voice, and Gia to be raised well enough to help her.

You have what it takes to ride full throttle into your next chapter.

To blend purpose with play, heart with horsepower, and difference with drive.

Same, same & different, unstoppable, unforgettable, unapologetically you.

Gry Stene

What People Say About Gry

Gry Stene is a dynamic speaker known for her thought-provoking presentations on ethical AI, inclusive innovation, and people-centred digital transformation.

Her conference talks blend deep technical expertise with lived experience, storytelling, and a strong focus on equity and belonging. Gry challenged the audience to think of AI not just as a tool, but as something we are "raising", shaping its development with ethical and inclusive values.

Gry brings her high energy, rebel humour, and metaphor-rich storytelling. Her sessions leave audiences feeling inspired, empowered, and ready to lead change with courage and clarity.
CEO, Peak Member Association

Gry is a powerhouse committed to making the world a better place. Her visions are bold and ambitious, and she sets about delivering on them with dedication.

I look forward to watching her continue to change the world as a role model and through her enterprises.
Financial Educator

Working with Gry has been transformative.

Gry's vision of nurturing women entrepreneurs has created a safe space to share challenges and solutions. In this supportive environment, I found the confidence to address issues I couldn't discuss at work or home.

Gry has been invaluable for my company, providing insights into business strategy, team management, and motivation. As a non-technical owner of a tech business, I now feel empowered to make strategic decisions, knowing I'm not alone.

Gry's mentorship is a must for any woman in the tech industry looking for guidance and growth.
Founder & CEO, AI Innovator

Gry is an inspirational leader who combines both a deep understanding of the Ed-tech space with a deep commitment to making organizations better. It is impressive watching how adept she is at both giving people the room to be creative while also ensuring that goals/projects were accomplished.

I really enjoyed (and sometimes relied on) Gry's innate sense of how to channel chaos into productivity. She is a fantastic coach/colleague and leader!
Director of Sales and Global Partnerships

Gry's passion for diversity, inclusion, and belonging shines through in everything she does. She inspires others to embrace difference - in themselves and in others - by role-modelling how vulnerability and courage can go hand in hand. Whether she's talking tech, leading community projects, or speaking on stage, her vibrant, intentional presence gets you thinking about the shifts we can all make to create value simply by being ourselves.

I'm grateful to call Gry both a friend and a mentor.
Senior Facilitator @ Coach

Books and Stories that Fuelled My Journey

Finding Your Truth & Power

Jen Sincero - You Are a Badass
A no-nonsense call to stop doubting yourself and start living full-throttle.

Glennon Doyle - Untamed
A rally cry for women to drop the masks, claim their wildness, and live true.

Fern Brady - Strong Female Character
A fiercely funny, unfiltered reminder that difference isn't a flaw - it's power.

Leading with Courage & Compassion

Brené Brown - Daring Greatly
Courage, vulnerability, and the art of showing up - even when it's hard.
Tricia Hersey - Rest Is Resistance
A beautiful rebellion against burnout; rest as an act of radical worthiness.
Mel Robbins - The 5 Second Rule / The High 5 Habit
Practical tools to shift from paralysis to action, with compassion for yourself.
Michelle Redfern - The Leadership Compass
A modern guide to leadership for women, blending business, emotional, and social intelligence.
Susan Colantuono - No Ceiling, No Walls
The book that changed how I understood leadership - and my place in it.

Connection, Courage & Conversation

Susan Scott - Fierce Conversations
A masterclass in speaking truth with heart, and staying in the room when it matters.
Sheryl Sandberg - Lean In
Still a touchstone for women taking up space, with allies and boldness.
Kristin Neff - Self-Compassion
The science and practice of being kind to yourself while doing hard things.

Creativity, Curiosity & Reinvention

Elizabeth Gilbert - Big Magic
A love letter to curiosity and courage in creative living.
Gary Keller & Jay Papasan - The ONE Thing
A focus manifesto for multi-passionate people - clarity without shrinking.
Chimamanda Ngozi Adichie - The Danger of a Single Story (TED Talk)
A powerful reminder that truth - and belonging - expand when we listen for the full story.

Resilience & Perspective

Viktor Frankl - Man's Search for Meaning
A timeless reminder that purpose is what carries us through pain.
Octavia Butler - Parable of the Sower
Visionary storytelling about adaptation, change, and shaping a better world.
Clifton Taulbert - Who Owns the Ice House?
A story of resilience, drive, and community wisdom that shaped my outlook.

Money, Wealth & Freedom

Jen Sincero - You Are a Badass at Making Money
A bold, irreverent invitation to rewrite your money story and claim your worth - unapologetically.
Lacey Filipich - Money School
A practical, empowering guide to financial independence - rooted in values, clarity, and freedom of choice.

Powering our Future with AI & STEAM

"We are all ONE but different. Different but the Same!" YR 1/2

www.ingramcontent.com/pod-product-compliance
Lightning Source LLC
Chambersburg PA
CBHW062045290426
44109CB00027B/2736